WHY NOT ME?

Why Not Me?

FINESSING LIFE'S
SLINGS AND ARROWS

Rev. Donald H. Wheat

ISBN 978-0-578-75061-3
ISBN 978-1-7338485-9-6 (ebook)

Cover photo of Lake Michigan by Nicholas Wheat
Author and mural photos by David Boulanger
Book design by Amber Morena

For Ann Wheat, who spearheaded the first efforts to compile this book.

Contents

Part Three | Bear Others' Burdens

Part Four | Enjoy Life

Part Five | Humanism

Foreword

Good preaching has always been important to me. When I was a child growing up in First Unitarian Church of Pittsburgh, I noticed on those occasions I attended the "adult service" that my parents were riveted on the preacher, Irving Murray. "Isn't Mr. Murray wise?" my mother would often observe on the drive home from church. My father, a law professor at the University of Pittsburgh who rarely seemed in intellectual awe of anyone, also listened absorbedly to what Irving had to say and even occasionally shed a tear, which was truly astonishing to me. As an only child who grew up in a world of adults, the idea that there was a profession in which you were *paid* to talk at people for twenty minutes and they were "required" to listen, would later come to seem enormously attractive!

After I determined on the ministry as a profession in my teen years, I would go to a different church in Pittsburgh—Presbyterian, Congregational, Disciples of Christ, Baptist, Methodist— every Sunday for about two years just to compare preaching styles. I used to make up sermon titles for sermons I imagined I would one day preach and, indeed, I preached my first sermon when I was nineteen. (It was awful.)

Perhaps it is therefore not surprising that, when I arrived in Hyde Park in Chicago in 1975 to attend Meadville Lombard Theological School, the Unitarian Universalist (UU) seminary there, I set out to survey all the UU preachers in the city to see which one warranted my fidelity. First of course I went right across the street from the seminary to First Unitarian Church of Chicago where the renowned minister, Jack Mendelson, presided. Jack was not only a fine preacher but tall, handsome, wrapped in his crimson red Harvard robe and occupying a high pulpit, he cut a mighty impressive figure—especially in the neo-Gothic confines of that church building. I listened to quite a few of his sermons at First Church.

Then I decided to branch out. First I would try Third Unitarian Church in the west side neighborhood of Austin, followed by Second Church, All Souls

First Universalist, Evanston, Hinsdale, and so on. The fact is though that I never got beyond Third Church. I kept going back there Sunday after Sunday even though it was a thirty-minute drive from Hyde Park

Partly it was that quirky congregation that is described so well in the Editor's Note. Eventually it would come to be my friendship with Ann and Don Wheat, including their irrepressible, if unsuccessful, efforts to hook me up with prospective life partners. But mostly and always it was Don's preaching.

If I had been asked before I read the sermons contained in the book you are now reading what it was about that preaching that so drew me, I would have said it was Don's passion, his authenticity, his humor, and his ear for the telling anecdote, insight, quote or quip. His passion—not just for justice but for life itself—was immediately self-evident. His authenticity? Well, it was not that Don talked about his own life very much (though I will never forget a sermon he preached after Ann had at the time been incorrectly thought to have cancer in which he said that the only appropriate response to such news was just to say "Shit!"). It was that each topic he addressed really *mattered* to him, had really claimed his energy and imagination. And Don was funny. He was funnier out of the pulpit than in it but many of his sermons contained an ironic insight that captured the absurdity of a situation and made you laugh in order not to cry. And those quotes and quips and stories! I came away from almost every sermon with the Order of Service covered with notes of telling insights or inspiring images, many of which I later "stole" for my own sermons.

All that I just described is here in these sermons in abundance but now, having read this collection, I have noticed other things. How he integrated glorious Biblical passages into his unflinchingly humanist sermons. His Christian roots provided him a well of beautiful language and powerful imagery upon which to call to deliver a decidedly non-Christian message. How he refused to sugarcoat existence. Unlike some humanist preachers, Don never preached see-the-flowers-how-they-grow-tra-la-la-la-la sermons. I once saw a cartoon of two churches on a street corner, their wayside pulpits each announcing the minister's Easter topic. The Episcopal rector was preaching on the topic, "The Power and Promise of the Risen Christ." Across the street the Unitarian Universalist minister's sermon title was "Upsy-daisy." Don never preached upsy-daisy sermons. Whether he was an existentialist or not, he preached like one and, as an existentialist myself, I loved that. I still do.

This is not to say that there are no flaws in these sermons. Some of them were first preached more than forty years ago by a white male preacher and they both bear that mark and reflect the tenor of their times. There are references here to people and events that only the most studied of younger people will understand. I've taught preaching for the past twelve years and we would not today use non-degenderized language; we would center the words of women and people of color more consistently; and we would address white privilege in a more comprehensive way. (We would also refer to Unitarian *Universalism*, not just Unitarianism, but of course the bulk of these sermons were addressed to Third *Unitarian* Church.)

But whatever their failings, the vast majority of these sermons remain giddily alive and inspiring. As Don says in one of them, "What moves me is the spiritual power that some people marshal . . . to conquer adversity" and you could look to few better places than here to find out how to do that. Don was determined to instill a sense of possibility in each of us—a conviction of our own agency and a faith that a better world was truly within reach. For me at least he succeeded—and succeeds—admirably.

I hope you enjoy reading these sermons as much as I enjoyed recalling the sweet strong man, still going at age 86, who preached them. And, if you do, as Don would say, "Bless your heart!"

William F. Schulz, February, 2020

BILL SCHULZ served as President of the Unitarian Universalist Association (1985–1993), Executive Director of Amnesty international USA (1994–2006) and President of the Unitarian Universalist Service Committee (2010–2016). He is now retired and lives with his wife, the Rev. Beth Graham, on Cape Ann, MA.

Editor's Note

n the summer of 2018 I rummaged through moldering boxes in a Michigan shed to fish out essays that my father wrote after leaving the Christian Church to become a Unitarian minister in 1969. Digging through reams of clippings and papers, we unearthed more than 500 of them written between 1969 and 2010. Here is a collection of 40 of them.

Don Wheat was the minister of Third Unitarian Church of Chicago for a quarter century from 1969 until his 1996 retirement (with brief stints as minster of First Unitarian in Albany, NY and heading a community center outside Chicago). Throughout that period—and into his retirement—he worked the circuit as a guest speaker throughout the Midwest. Still, he addressed most of these essays to the eclectic, maddening, oddball, and wonderful congregation of Third Unitarian—located in Austin, a hard-luck African American neighborhood on Chicago's Westside.

A fifth of its members were Jews and there was a small—but significant—minority of black members. It was the sort of place where Commies, PhDs, nudists, feminists and plain kooks shared a pew. Members were outspoken against the Vietnam War, the draft, segregation, redlining, and nuclear bombs. The Chicago Police's Red Squad smoke bombed the church in 1969 during the screening of a documentary film about the 1968 Democratic Convention.[1] Don addressed his flock as a chosen people—from whom much is expected. His most painful moment came in 1979, when about half of his members formed a splinter congregation in the suburban safety of nearby Oak Park: Beacon Unitarian Church.[2]

Many of the essays collected here tackle the immediate issues of the day or timeless existential questions in remarkably simple, direct language. They

---

1. "75 Viewing Riot Film Hit by a Smoke Bomb," *Chicago Tribune*, June 7, 1969.

2. Beacon Unitarian merged with Oak Park's Unity Temple Unitarian Universalist in 1994.

are the product of a curious mind burrowing into religion, philosophy, psychology, politics, war, history, the arts, overpopulation, race, humor, euthanasia, and ecology. Taken together, they offer guidance on how to live a moral, fulfilled, meaningful and sometimes happy life in an indifferent universe. In the "Broken Hearts" essay included here, Don says that his writing addresses three main themes:

- Life's absurdity and unfairness;
- The obligation to live with joy and zest; and
- The need to bear the burdens of others.

We resurrected those themes as chapter headings and added two others. One is on humanism. Because humanists view people as products of evolution rather than supernatural creation, they believe that humans are solely responsible for creating meaning and justice in this world. A fifth chapter is dedicated to a few of Don's saints (each of the five chapters are illustrated by one of the murals depicting "liberal saints" that the late Chicago artist Andrene Kauffman created for Third Church).

These essays were written on deadline, on a manual Royal typewriter for oral delivery. Approximate punctuation and spellings sufficed. On the rare occasion when Don revised a first draft—he did the cutting and pasting with scissors and tape. Hardly texts writ in stone, we tidied up the original spelling, punctuation and quotes. We also trimmed some words and switched around some sentences or paragraphs for readability (all errors are mine). Nonetheless, those who first heard these words live will recognize Don Wheat's distinct ideas and voice here.

We used crowdsourcing to complete this book in the author's lifetime—cajoling family and friends to read stacks of essays. Those first readers helped flag "A+" manuscripts that:

- Are excellent throughout, possessing good flow as they deliver on their themes;
- Are timeless, timely, or peg an important bygone era (e.g. McCarthy's witch hunts or the hippies); and
- Expound aspects of Don's worldview.

This book would not exist without its first readers: Dave Boulanger, Julia Bower, Sharon Bower, Larry Christmas, Bill Dring, Joan Engel, Ann Masur, and Tim Staley. After two tours of reader duty, Ann Masur also solved an editing challenge involving repetitious Holocaust sermons.

Gary Wood is the only Third Churcher who lived parts of his life as a Catholic, a Protestant and a Jew. His priests, ministers and rabbis vehemently differ over which of those faiths taught him not to horde fancy office equipment unto himself. Gary scanned more than 100 essays to electronically distribute to those far-flung first readers and to convert hard copies of the best essays into the text of this book. When many of those messy originals scanned poorly, Frank Olderr retyped them at a furious pace (Frank previously produced a book of Don's short meditations titled *In Pursuit of Joy*). Told that he was the only person qualified to do so, Don's friend Bill Schulz modestly agreed to write the foreword.

In an early objection to the idea of compiling this book, the author protested that too many of his essays narrowly addressed his former congregation. While the most personalized of those essays don't appear here, many of these essays do mention those people. To distinguish them from the many other folks cited in these essays, we italicize the names of Third Church members below. One of them, *Tinker Hammack*, was known to goad Don to get to the point of his oratories. At *Tinker's* urging, let's do just that . . .

Andrew Wheat
February 2020
Austin, Texas

Donald Wheat

The Author

Donald H. Wheat was born in Dayton, Ohio to William and Frances Wheat on Halloween 1933. In 1955 he graduated from Hiram College and married Ann Warren Wheat in Leipsic, Ohio. He graduated from the University of Chicago Divinity School in 1958. After serving Christian Churches in Rensselaer, Indiana and Oak Park, Illinois, Don found his philosophical home at Third Unitarian Church of Chicago, where he served from 1969 to 1996 (apart from brief stints at First Unitarian of Albany, New York, and heading a Chicago-area community center). He retired to South Haven, Michigan, where Ann Wheat died in 2015. Third Church's annual Wheat Lecture is named for its minister emeritus.

WHY NOT ME?

The American was astonished. He stood up shakily, spitting blood. He'd had two teeth knocked out. He had meant no harm by what he'd said, evidently, had no idea that the guard would hear and understand.

"Why me?" he asked the guard.

The guard shoved him back into ranks. "Vy you? Vy anybody?" he said.

—KURT VONNEGUT, *SLAUGHTERHOUSE-FIVE*

"Why *me*?" said Harry. . . . People were always asking that as they were loaded into ambulances after accidents of various kinds, or arrested for disorderly conduct, or burglarized, or socked in the nose and so on: "*Why me?*"

—KURT VONNEGUT, *BREAKFAST OF CHAMPIONS*

"Why me?"

"That is a very *Earthling* question to ask, Mr. Pilgrim. Why *you*? Why *us* for that matter? Why *anything*? Because this moment simply *is*. Have you ever seen bugs trapped in amber?"

"Yes."

"Well, here we are, Mr. Pilgrim, trapped in the amber of this moment. There is no *why*."

—KURT VONNEGUT, *SLAUGHTERHOUSE-FIVE*

Part One

Life's Unfair

I grew up like a neglected weed—
ignorant of liberty, having
no experience of it.

HARRIET TUBMAN

Play Your Own Hand

hope at the end of this talk you will say, "You aren't telling me anything that I do not know." The U.S. Constitution says, "We hold these truths to be self-evident. . . ." What I'm saying should be self-evident to any thinking person. My defense for not being more original is that we need periodic reminders of the important things that we already know. Our reading this morning dealt with a teenager who doesn't want to go to church where they always tell him what he already knows. When he cites examples of what he already knows, however, it is an impressive list!

The *New York Times* recently reviewed a book titled *Origins*. It's about how the nine fetal months before birth shape the rest of our lives. Author Annie Murphy Paul quotes a British physician who found that poor nutrition puts babies at risk for heart disease decades later. Pregnant women in low-income areas tend to be more exposed to anxiety, depression, and to toxins from car exhaust and pesticides. They are more likely to drink or smoke and less likely to take vitamins, eat healthy food, and get prenatal care. Fetuses in gestation in the Middle East at the time of the 1967 Six-Day War were more likely to develop schizophrenia as young adults. We know crack, alcohol and tobacco take a toll on a fetus but external events also effect the fetal child. Swedes who were fetuses during the 1986 Chernobyl nuclear accident had slight physical effects from radiation exposure yet their cognitive abilities were somehow affected, making them one-third more likely to fail middle school. Children in utero during the Great Flu Epidemic of 1918 were 15 percent less likely to graduate from high school and 20 percent more likely to have heart disease in old age.

Though those findings may be surprising, this sermon addresses the obvious truth that we are not born equal. Even before birth, factors are shaping our future. The moment in history that we are born, the nation we are born to, the neighborhood and schools we attend, the education and maturity of our parents—all are determining factors. We all have different mixes of advantages and disadvantages. We are not born equal.

I'm going to use a playing-card analogy. Some people are dealt a good hand; others are not so lucky. Yet we have no choice but to play the hand that we're dealt. It is not about how the cards are dealt but about how we play the hand we get. Sometimes we complain, "She got all the good cards!" But that isn't entirely true. She had skill and may have played better than others with the same hand. If you were raised Baptist and are uncomfortable with card games, then think of Jesus's parable. One man received five talents, and another two and a third man received just one talent. In the Old Testament we're told, "The race is not to the swift nor the battle to the strong, nor bread to the wise, nor riches to the intelligent, nor favor to men of skill, but time and chance happen to us all." So each person must invest, develop, and embellish whatever he or she is given.

Kids understand this better than most adults. They often say, "That's the way the cookie crumbles," or, "That's the way the ball bounces." Some find it comforting to think of God "as the dealer," suggesting that there is a reason why we are given certain cards to play. Hindus believe in karma—that we are reincarnated according to how we played our cards in a previous life. I think that each religion and each person tries to understand the distribution of cards or talents. A blind man passed by, and the disciples asked Jesus, "Was it because of the sins of his parents that he was born blind? Jesus replied 'No,' it was not that this man or his parents had sinned. Jesus spoke to card distribution when he said, "God makes his sun rise on the evil and on the good and sends rain on the just and unjust." One thing that drove me from the Christian ministry was being asked, "Why me?" when bad things happened—and only then! I wanted to scream, "Why you? Why anyone?" But that didn't seem very understanding or compassionate.

Take such a simple thing as temperament or disposition. Children vary within the same family. Some are born sunny-side up. Early on, some children seem to have a sense of rhythm or a sense of humor. Some are selfish. Some enjoy giving grandma a kiss—others you have to bribe with a Hershey bar. We know life is unfair—but it starts so young. Research shows that even parents give more attention and supervision to "pretty ducklings" than to "ugly ducklings." Pretty ducklings frequently grow up to be knock-outs in high school—and often are graceful, athletic, and sexy. Warren Beatty says in his autobiography that he slept with 12,775 women. In a working lifetime, the typical above-average-looking man will earn $250,000 more than the least-attractive men. Maureen Dowd wrote in *The New York Times* about Debrahlee

Lorenzana, who filed suit against Citigroup, claiming that she was fired for looking too sexy. "Plaintiff was advised that as a result of the shape of her figure," the lawsuit reads, "her clothes were purportedly too distracting for her male colleagues and supervisors to bear." She told the court, "You are discriminating against me because of my body type. This is genetic. What am I supposed to do?" Dowd elaborates, "Attractive professors get better evaluations from their students. Good-looking and tall people get a 'beauty premium'— and earn an extra five percent an hour."

Isn't it interesting, a columnist, wrote that "there is no visible gray hair on the heads of any of the 16 female U.S. senators age 46 to 74?" San Francisco's Human Rights Commission passed a law 11 years ago to prevent "discrimination on the basis of appearance." In one case before the Commission, a plaintiff said, "Being fat carries as much stigma as AIDS, drug addiction and criminal behavior." Thank God that I live in Michigan—the only state that has a law against appearance discrimination (remarkably just 30 complaints are filed annually).

Is anyone surprised that the five-foot, five-inch French President Nicolas Sarkozy had a custom-built podium flown to the U.S. to make him look taller during a speech at Columbia University? Labor Secretary Robert Reich is 4'10". The first man in space—Yuri Gagarin—was 5'1". Actor Danny DeVito is 5'2". Napoleon, Caesar, Hitler, Mussolini, Stalin and Franco were of short stature. A recent study of 4,000 high school and college students with acne found that they were twice as likely to have mental problems. One fourth of the acne sufferers had contemplated suicide. Acne comes at a crucial time, when self-image and self-confidence are being established. Teens with bad skin are more likely to be aloof with friends and to do poorly in school. Not only do fat children suffer more bullying in school but people believe that having a fat child reflects poorly on parenting. A Cornell University professor of human development writes in a book called *The Body Project* that "Having a fat daughter is a failure."

All of this about our height, weight, sex appeal, charm or athletic prowess may seem superficial. What about those who were dealt really bad hands? Helen Keller was born deaf, blind and dumb. Jimmy Durante was born with a nose almost as big a Cyrano's. Stephen Hawking has a brilliant mind and ALS. FDR (where is he when we need him?) also was confined to a wheelchair.

Many people derive satisfaction from playing the bad hands that they were dealt. They like to take risks as if they are trying to "shoot the moon" in the card game "hearts." People go to horse races and casinos, they play the stock market and play lottery tickets. All of life is a bet. You choose this college or that spouse, take that job and move to a particular neighborhood. You join a particular religious group or choose a circle of friends. Playing the cards we're dealt is not enough. We seek out risks. Hardly a day goes by that I don't read an article about a blind man climbing Mount Kilimanjaro or legless Iraqi vets forming a basketball team. Listen to this Associated Press story. "A Frenchman whose arms and legs were amputated swam across the English Channel this weekend using leg prostheses that have flippers attached. Philippe Croizon, 42, had expected the tough crossing to take up to 24 hours—and instead, he finished in only 13 and a half . . . The swimmer lost his arms and legs after suffering an electric shock in 1994 as he stood on a ladder, adjusting his TV antenna, that touched a power line."

Perhaps you have heard my friend Al Gini, "the resident philosopher" on WBEZ FM. Al is a Loyola University professor who wrote six philosophy books. As a radio philosopher, Al has to keep things simple. He says, for example, that "the goal of life is to escape doing wrong and to live well with others." What we call "ethics" are simply choices, he says, the unavoidable fact that we continually have to choose what to do in one situation after another. I once asked him, "If you could recommend only one philosophy book, what would it be?" He replied, *Man's Search for Meaning* by Viktor Frankl (my choice, too).

Frankl was an Austrian Jew sent to the work camps with his parents, his brother and his new bride. Dr. Frankl had completed his medical studies and was working on a psychiatry specialization when he suddenly became prisoner No. 119,104. He was forced to dig ditches 12 hours a day on less than 1,000 calories. That was the hand that he was dealt. If he did not play it extremely well he would die. Those who despaired and lost the will to go on were transferred from the work camp to a death camp. Observing his fellow prisoners, Frankl concluded that we are stronger than we think and can endure more than we realize. We have the ability to transcend our surroundings. No matter what our predicament, we have the ability to make choices. Everything can be taken from us—except for this one thing. The last human freedom is to choose one's attitude in any given situation. The sort of person that each person became in the camps was the result of an inner decision. Some prisoners acted like saints and some like swine. The saints proved that apathy can be overcome and irritability suppressed. Every day, every hour, decisions had to be made. They determined whether or not you would submit to the powers that threatened to rob you of your inner freedom and dignity. They determined whether you would be molded into a "typical prisoner." As such, becoming a saint or a swine did not hinge upon outward circumstances—the cards the Nazis dealt. Instead, it turned on the inner decisions made by each Jew.

It did no good in the camps to ask about the meaning of life in general. Each person had to decide, "What is the meaning of my life in this day stretching before me?" The meaning of life differed from man to man, from day to day, and hour by hour. The only way to endure the atrocities was to have a goal, a dream to believe in, some task to accomplish. "I will survive to see my wife again." "I will be of some help to this prisoner who needs me." "I will dig this ditch to the best of my ability and return to the barracks tonight for soup and sleep." In Frankl's words, "Man is ultimately self-determining. He does not 'simply exist' but always decides what his existence will be, what he will become in the next moment, hour, day." After surviving three years of slave labor, Frankl later used this same approach with clinical patients who suffered from physical pain, poverty, boredom, emptiness, or depression.

Our ability to choose is both a curse and a gift. Even if we are dealt horrible cards, the gift we retain is the freedom to decide how to play our hand. We are all imprisoned in some way—limited by certain conditions. In the reading earlier this morning, an imprisoned friend of mine reminded us that we can choose to look up at the stars. This may sound corny coming from a dude from Chicago's Westside 'hood.

Now everyone knows that there are just two kinds of people in this world—and in this room. Those who play the cards they have been dealt as best they can, and those who complain about their hand. I hope that you play as much cards at your house as I do with my grandsons. It's easy when they are winning. But it's also fun to watch them learn to lose. Our most famous Unitarian poet, e e cummings, wrote, "We do not believe in ourselves until someone reveals that deep inside us something is valuable, worth listening to, worthy of our trust, sacred to our touch. Once we believe in ourselves we can risk curiosity, wonder, spontaneous delight or any experience that reveals the human spirit." Let us be that someone to children with hands too small to hold their cards—or to the elderly with hands too frail to hold theirs. Let us be the one to say, "That hand is not all that bad. I believe that you will play it well."

Delivered November 7, 2010, Berrien Unitarian, St. Joseph, Michigan.

Broken Hearts

Columnist William Raspberry recently wrote that a friend asked him how many columns he has written. Raspberry pretended to do the math, multiplying three columns a week over 29 years, and then answered, "Three." I don't know how many sermons I have written since June 1958, but I would give the same answer. My sermons have been variations on three themes: Acknowledging the absurdity of life; The need for zest and joy in living; and The obligation to bear the burdens of others.

This summer I read a book of sermons by Chicago's most popular minister. As Unitarians we are probably closest to the Congregationalists and he is minister of this city's largest church of that denomination. Most of his sermons promote Hollywood endings. There is a huge market for such a message. But in religion, as in theater, there is a need for great Broadway shows and also for small, intimate "off Broadway" theaters that explore unconventional points of view. It would be ridiculous for all playwrights—or ministers—to write for the mass audience.

I titled this sermon "Broken Hearts," for this is a congregation that understands that we will not get out of this world without having our hearts broken. There was a great deal of talk in seminaries a few years back that the church should not say anything that would not be understandable to a mother in the Third World who just lost a child to hunger. That certainly would eliminate a lot of fluff and undoubtedly would reduce the length of sermons. But I simply am not equipped to speak to the Third World. So I have limited myself to an "off Broadway" congregation that knows about broken hearts.

Anton Chekhov wrote, "There are a great many opinions in this world and a good half of them are professed by people who have never been in trouble." It is interesting to me that the great dramatists have spoken to people who understand trouble—Brecht, Ibsen, Shaw, *McCarrell*, Chekhov, Sartre, Albee, Pirandello, Strindberg, Shakespeare, Ionesco, Lillian Hellman, John Osborne, Tennessee Williams, Arthur Miller. Serious theater, art, poetry, novels, and religion all have the same function: To give us what we can't get on TV or in the newspaper. William Carlos Williams wrote:

> It is difficult
> to get the news from poems
> yet men die miserably every day
> for lack of what is found there.

It is the purpose of off-Broadway theaters and churches to deal with that which men and women are miserably dying from the lack thereof.

After I gave one broken-heart sermon a woman asked me, "Did you have to rub our noses in it?" That's a crude but accurate retort to an "off-Broadway minister"—or to a drill sergeant getting his troops ready for battle, or the 1950s mother who goes over the facts of life before her teenage daughter goes to prom with the captain of the football team.

In shopping for a church (I encourage people to do so), find one that understands your plight and provides answers that make sense. Different religions provide different answers. My friend Joanne Murphy went to a liberal church in Park Ridge but left after several months of hearing the minister tell his congregation how wonderful they all were. This was a turn off because Joanne Murphy was a woman who knew herself to be "one mean son-of-a-bitch!" So if I don't address your broken heart, find another "off-Broadway church."

Broken hearts have nothing to do with whether you are rich or poor, black or white, educated or uneducated, married or single, gay or straight, old or young, male or female. Religion means literally to "bind us together." It must attempt to speak to what is fundamental, enduring and essential. We are all broken. We all carry burdens. We all suffer the "slings and arrows of outrageous fortune." What's unique about that? Life is tragic. Begin with that and go on from there. Harold Clurman, the *Nation* magazine drama critic, writes, "The nature and source of the burden may differ, the suffering caused is the same. In this sense, all people are equally burdened, no matter how different and special their burden may make them feel."

I am 61. I spent the first 36 years of my life as a Christian. I was driven from the Christian Church because I could not bear to hear people wrestle with the question, "Why me?" Millions of people have lived and died without obsessing over this question. We have to get on with it and accept the fact that the universe is indifferent to us as individuals. It is benign indifference at best.

Lewis Mumford describes the tragic dimension as well as anyone:

> Man's destiny is a great one because the essence of it is tragic. All that he builds crumbles; all that he embodies turns to dust; all that he loves most, he must one day leave behind him. That which alone endures on earth, is the spirit in which he understands and meets his fate. This he passes on to his children and his comrades; only a breath indeed, but the breath of life. Death comes to all; but death comes best to those who are ready to die.

I inherited the cross and the cup of hemlock depicted on the murals above this pulpit. More important than anything anyone says from this pulpit is your need to come to an understanding with the mysteries of life surrounding these symbols.

Listen to these words and tell me who said them:

> When we consider the immensity of the universe, we must confess that mankind is insignificant. The world began, as it were, yesterday; it may end tomorrow. Life has existed in the universe but a brief second, and certainly human life can hardly be considered the goal of the universe. Its margin of existence is always precarious. Study of the geologic periods shows that. So does the battle against disease. When one has seen whole populations annihilated by sleeping sickness, as I have, one ceases to imagine that human life is nature's goal. In fact, the Creative Force does not concern itself about preserving life. It simultaneously creates and destroys.

That was Albert Schweitzer, known for his "Reverence of Life." He wouldn't hurt a flea—yet he accepts the world for what it is. We must come to terms with the world as it is—not as we want it to be.

The Psalmist tells us that, "He prepareth a table before the presence of our enemies." He tells us that we will "walk through the valley of the shadow of death." The prophet Amos warns us what life is like. "It is as if a man fled from a lion, and a bear met him! Or went into the house and leaned with his hand against the wall, and a serpent bit him." St. Paul told us—years before Freud— that, "We will what is right but we cannot do it. I do not understand my own

REV. DONALD H. WHEAT   11

actions. For I do not do what I want but I do the very thing I hate." Shakespeare rubs our noses in it, "As flies to wanton boys are we to the gods; They kill us for their sport."

Most of us were born into theistic homes and later became post-Christian. Our mothers taught us that we could depend on the everlasting arms, that His eye was on the sparrow, that the hairs on our head were numbered. The severest shock that we can withstand is that the universe is indifferent to us, that it is not moral, that life is unfair. Mother Nature is worse than any mother on crack. She doesn't care about us. She doesn't hear our cries, doesn't comfort us, is not concerned with our dreams.

Of course our hearts are broken! We hoped and longed for something better. We are like children trying to understand why pain intrudes upon our lives. Yet pain is no intruder. It is an essential part of life. The one thing that you can be sure of. Saying "Yes" to life is saying "Yes" to pain. Saying "Yes" to love is saying "Yes" to the inevitability of separation. Saying "Yes" to parenthood is also saying "Yes" to the suffering and pain that will afflict your children. I wonder how differently our outlooks would be if we grew up in Athens at the time of Sophocles, Euripides and Aeschylus. Only 33 out of perhaps 1,000 plays performed in Athens around the fifth century B.C. survive. These plays did not portray pain as an intrusion on life. They did not wrestle with the question, "Why me?"

The happy Hollywood ending came much later in films, sitcoms, soaps, and mysteries. Contrast what Americans got out of the Super Bowl last Sunday compared to what the Athenians took away from the Greek tragedies. That was a time in history when men and women got from the theater what "we die miserably every day for lack of." If only the Christian gospels could have ended with Jesus on the cross crying out, "My God, my God, why hast thou forsaken me?" Instead, they added the Hollywood ending of the resurrection. I believe that Jesus triumphed in his defeat the same way that others do. The parent who loses an only child and volunteers at the Children's Hospital. The old man whose leg was paralyzed by a stroke who carries that leg with the same acceptance as Sisyphus pushes his stone uphill. Or Anna in *The King and I*, encouraging young lovers in Siam to escape, "For I've had a love of my own." Lewis Mumford wrote, "That which alone endures on earth is the spirit in which we understand and master our fate."

The American theater was born in 1920 with the production of Eugene

O'Neill's "Beyond the Horizon." O'Neill's mother was a drug addict and his brother was an alcoholic. He endured an unhappy marriage and a long, final struggle with Parkinson's disease. This broken-hearted dramatist wrote:

> The tragedy of man is perhaps the only significant thing about him. What I am after is to get an audience leaving the theater with an exultant feeling from seeing somebody on the stage facing life, fighting against eternal odds, not conquering, but perhaps inevitably being conquered. The individual life is made significant by the struggle!

My goal in preaching is the same as O'Neill's. We should leave here on a Sunday morning exultant—not that life has a happy ending, but that the struggle of life has been worthwhile. Sartre was convinced that "human life begins on the other side of despair." Camus tells us that we must imagine Sisyphus happy as he pushes the boulder up the mountain. Our salvation and our satisfaction is to be found in the struggle. It is as though we are shipwrecked. But to be shipwrecked is not to be confused with drowning. It is within our power to keep our arms moving and to remain afloat. Others can help us some, but don't forget that their hearts are broken, too. They are also bearing burdens. And we must believe in ourselves as capable of keeping afloat. When King Lear has lost everything, he says, "We must endure our going hence, even as our coming hither." There comes an awareness to our condition—a brave acceptance, a yea-saying fortitude. The world is going to break our hearts, but some will be stronger at that broken place.

It has been beyond my wildest imagination. No playwright, no novelist, no poet prepared me for what I would find in this church. Over and over I have been cautioned, "Don't put *that* in the newsletter" or in a sermon. It would be so much easier on you if I preached Hollywood endings. Yet many of you have inspired me with your resilient, courageous struggles. The African Americans I have known here who have endured hate but lived their lives with dignity. Those who have suffered for their political beliefs or for their sexual orientation. Those who raised small children as widows or widowers. Those who suffered blindness, deafness or unrequited love. Those who watched loved ones stricken with multiple sclerosis, Alzheimer's, and cancer. Those who emerged on the other side of addictions or mental illness. Those who raised mentally or physically handicapped children. Those who care for aged parents. Those left behind by suicide. Those who have lost a son or daughter. Those raised in homes that were impoverished or that lacked intellectual or aesthetic stimulation but moved far beyond their origins.

Our resident writer, *Stuart McCarrell*, described many here when he said that our scars are badges of victory! Tennessee Williams wrote, "After all, high station in life is earned by the gallantry with which appalling experiences are survived with grace." St. Paul wrote, "We are afflicted in every way but not crushed, perplexed but not driven to despair, persecuted but not forsaken, struck down, but not destroyed." Mumford said, "That which alone endures on earth is the spirit in which we understand and meet our fate."

Nikos Kazantzakis says that as a boy he came home one day to find that the spring rains—that fall on the just and unjust—had washed away the whole year's grape crop.

> I was anxious to see how my father had reacted—would he be weeping, would he be cursing or crying out? I found him standing motionless on the threshold biting his mustache. "Father!" I cried. "Our grapes are gone." "We're not gone," he answered. "Shut up!" I never forgot that moment. I believe that it served as a great lesson in the crises of *my* life. I have always remembered my father standing calmly, motionlessly on the threshold, neither cursing, entreating, nor weeping. Motionless he stood, watching the disaster, and alone among the neighbors, preserved his human dignity.

His father was not angry, bitter, surprised or cynical. He seemed to feel a kinship with all who have lost but who have known the satisfaction of losing a game well played—against difficult odds.

Delivered February 5, 1995, Third Unitarian Church of Chicago.

Eugene O'Neill Centennial

was never more serious about a topic than I am about Eugene O'Neill. There is that which is temporal and that which is permanent in life. We are dealing this morning with what's permanent. In O'Neill's play "The Great God Brown," Dion says, "This is daddy's bedtime secret for today: Man is born broken. He lives by mending. The grace of God is glue." In his autobiographical play *Long Day's Journey into the Night*, O'Neill's mother said: "None of us can help the things life has done to us. They're done before you realize it, and once they're done, they make you do other things until at last everything comes between you and what you'd like to be, and you've lost your true self forever."

O'Neill left the Catholic Church as a boy and he never returned to organized religion. Yet almost all of his plays center on religious questions. He wanted the theater to give us what the church gave medieval man—a reason for living and hope in the face of death (as classic Greek theater did). He sought to translate religious concepts into a secular language. He wrote for an audience like himself, who had experienced the death of God and the failure of science and materialism to give their lives meaning. Aesthetics replaces formal religion for O'Neill, making life livable. He sought a theater "returned to its highest and sole significant function as a Temple where the religion of poetical interpretation and symbolical celebration of life is communicated to human beings, starved in spirit by their soul-stifling struggle to exist as masks among the masks of living!"

A reporter once asked O'Neill what one of his plays meant. He replied,

If the human race is so stupid that in 2,000 years it hasn't had brains enough to appreciate that the secret of happiness is contained in one simple sentence (you'd think any school kid could learn and apply) then it is time that we dumped it down the nearest drain and let the ants have a chance. That simple sentence is: "What shall it profit a man if he gain the whole world and lose his own soul?"

American theater remains divided between the platitudes and trivialities that came before O'Neill and what came after (Tennessee Williams, Arthur Miller, and Edward Albee). The only American playwright to win the Nobel Prize in literature, O'Neill won four Pulitzer Prizes. In this, his centennial year, some of us watched his "Strange Interlude" on television last month.

His father was a celebrated American actor. O'Neill's father didn't sing in the bath tub, he recited Shakespeare. O'Neill himself was born in a hotel as the family moved about the country. He was the third son. The first son died in infancy and his older brother died an alcoholic. Either following childbirth or after a mastectomy, his mother became so addicted to morphine that his father kept her in the stage wings, glancing out periodically to make sure she was there. Eugene was sent to boarding school at an early age. Because of the father's travels, the family was only together in the summers in a big old home in New London, Connecticut. O'Neill wrote of those summers in his only happy play: *Ah, Wilderness.*

The future dramatist learned tragedy early. His brother, Jamie, was expelled from Notre Dame for drinking and Eugene was expelled from Princeton for skipping classes. Jamie was gay, witty and charming. He used women as he used drink—to release tension. He seemed determined that his younger brother's life would be no more successful than his own.

Eugene O'Neill was a precocious student at boarding school and prep school. Early on he was influenced by Ibsen, Marx, Engels, Shaw, Schopenhauer, Jack London, Conrad, Nietzsche, and Sandburg. He discovered his mother's morphine addiction as a teenager. "God, it made everything in life seem rotten." He hated math and science and his required courses at Princeton. He escaped to New York City to roam used bookstores. He saw Ibsen's *Hedda Gabler*, returning for 10 consecutive nights. At the age of 21, he consented to marry Kathleen Quinlan, who was pregnant with his son. The boy was named Eugene Gladstone O'Neill. The father didn't see his son until he was 10, instead going off to sea immediately after his marriage. The symbolism of the sea—especially experiencing life in a fog—cropped up in many of his plays. His life sank to the depths during this period. He contemplated armed robbery and eventually took an overdose of drugs in an attempted suicide.

Returning home, he was diagnosed with tuberculosis and experienced a second birth in the sanitarium. He discovered that his life had a purpose; that he was destined to be a writer. He is now 26 and his father gives him a year at Harvard, a small class of 13 with a professor who was the midwife to American theater. He gets involved with a theatrical colony in Provincetown, Massachusetts, where he falls in love with Louise Bryant, the wife of his best friend, John Reed (as depicted in his play *Strange Interlude*). O'Neill's second wife, Agnes Boulton, bore a son, Shane, and a daughter, Oona, who later married Charlie Chaplin. His first son, Eugene, Jr. committed suicide and his second son became addicted and institutionalized. O'Neill eventually married Carlotta Monterey. In *Strange Interlude*, Nina reveals the need for three men in her life: Sam, her husband; Ned, her lover, by whom she has a son; and Gordon, who represents the father image in her life. No one person can meet all of our needs. O'Neill sensed the ambiguities of marriage as he sensed the tradeoffs in everything. Marriage conquers loneliness and the sterility of egotistical isolation, but in it, each robs the other of freedom. One of his characters says, "Love, the insult we swallow as the price of life."

O'Neill's early play *Beyond the Horizon* won the Pulitzer Prize in 1920. He would dominate the American theater from then until his death in 1953. Many would say he continues to today. If the Greek dramatists portrayed man fighting fate, the gods, or the furies, O'Neill portrayed a raging within. You struggle to overcome your heredity and environment and to try to save your soul and yourself. The dying sailor in his first play, *Bound East for Cardiff*, longs for a farmhouse of his own. The character of O'Neill's father in his last play contrasts the material success that he is with the actor he might have been. O'Neill wrote, "It was a mistake, my being born a man. I would have been much more successful as a sea gull or a fish. As it is, I will always be a stranger who never feels at home, who does not really want and is not really wanted, who can never belong, who must always be a little in love with death."

Self-realization is life's most difficult task. As the battle wages within, one aspect of our being wants this and another aspect wants that. Who has not known the experience of feeling like two people pulling in two directions? There is continual conflict, and it can be enough to tear us in two. In some of his plays, characters will wear masks to express these divided selves. In stage interludes, the character will express one thought and then, as an aside, will express what he or she is really thinking.

The conflict raging inside of you also is being waged inside the people around you. One of his characters says, "One's outer life passes in a solitude haunted by the masks of others; one's inner life passes in a solitude hounded by the masks of oneself." He wrote as Freudian psychoanalysis was becoming more widely established in the United States. He portrayed on stage what some in the audience discovered on the analyst's couch. Our conscious intellect is at war with our unconscious drives—and the desperate search for our real self among the many masks that we wear.

The enlightened—or saved—are those who recognize these tragic tensions and accept the fact that life is an endless struggle between opposite images of the self. One of his critics wrote, "The goal of life, then, is the recognition that all men's dreams and romantic imagining, are indeed illusions. When man accepts the fact that he can never find 'the secret hidden over there' and reconciles himself to the impossibility of finding it, he may realize perfect peace." What we want is unattainable and that is tragic. But if we accept the fact that it is unattainable and that we will be disappointed—that is to transcend tragedy.

I would have found all this unacceptable 10 years ago but I now feel that it is the most important message that I can share with you. Man is born broken, there is a crack in everything that God made, there is a blind spot, there is an Achilles' heel. We live by mending and patching. None of us can help the things that life has done to us (heredity and environment). They're done before you realize it and, once they're done, they make you do other things—until at last everything comes between you and what you'd like to be. Because man struggles against things that are greater than he is, there is an inevitability of defeat. Man's condition precludes forever the full realization of his ideals. French diplomat Jean Monnet said, "Incompleteness is a part of nature and it needs great art and great wisdom to know when to lay down the brush." The dream and the reality will never coincide. Life is going to be incomplete, imperfect. We will our own defeat when we pursue the unattainable. But the struggle is our success. To recognize that we have sought the unattainable is not reason for despair. It is exhilarating.

After winning his first Pulitzer Prize in 1924, O'Neill tried to explain his approach to an audience that had been fed so many trivialities and platitudes that it expected no more of the theater than it expected of Hollywood or television. "What I am after is to get an audience to leave the theater with an exultant feeling from seeing somebody on the stage facing life, fighting against the eternal odds, not conquering but perhaps inevitably being conquered." Do you recall James Dean in *East of Eden*? Remember that scene when Rock Hudson refuses to leave a Texas restaurant that won't serve his Mexican daughter-in-law? He pursued the unattainable in taking on that whole restaurant, but seeing him lying there in his own blood conveyed an exultant feeling.

You misunderstand me if you conclude that O'Neill was pessimistic, or cynical. The goal of his plays was to make the audience feel an urge toward life, and ever more life. He wanted them to leave the theater exhilarated. There is dignity and nobility in the struggle which Rock Hudson pursued, even though it ended in his defeat. It is hard to understand O'Neill because the enemy and the struggle are within. We struggle against the tyranny of our own contradictory emotions. O'Neill dedicated his life to celebrating the "dreadful journey." His heroes are doomed to assert their humanity by a struggle with ghosts in the dark night of the soul. The opponent is the most vicious and evasive of all enemies—the self.

O'Neill died in 1953 after suffering 10 years from Parkinson's disease. He had never been able to write by dictation—only in long hand. Parkinson's robbed him of writing in his final years. His autobiographical *Long Day's Journey into Night* was not to have been produced until 25 years after his death. Since Eugene O'Neill, Jr. had committed suicide, the playwright's widow, Carlotto, felt that she did not have to withhold the play. It was published just two years after his death. It unfolds during a single day in the life of the O'Neill family: Eugene, his brother, James, and his parents. The sons accuse their father of being cheap and failing to spend what was needed to prevent their mother's illness. The mother confesses her loss of faith in the Church and admits that, in her addiction, she has lied to them all and to herself. The mother blames the father for the death of her infant son, saying it wouldn't have happened if they hadn't been tramping all over the country. The older brother says that because his younger brother was mama's baby and papa's pet, he sought his revenge by deliberately leading Eugene astray. It seems that there is nothing that has been left unsaid. And it might seem that when the curtain falls that nothing has happened. Yet a family has come to some new understanding about themselves.

It is as if they have tried every other route but truth. They find that they are capable of loving and hating at the same time. After confessing that he tried to corrupt his young brother, Jamie then tells him that he loves him. O'Neill says to his father: "I know you a lot better now." Confession, understanding, new knowledge of one's self and one's family. These are the kind of values that O'Neill tried to project on the American stage. He believed that the really important truths that we need can only be conveyed symbolically and grasped emotionally. This is why O'Neill and his message cannot be understood easily. He focused his life on the question, "What difference does anything really make unless you come to know and understand the conflicting drives and emotions within yourself?" While these conflicts cannot be reconciled, self-understanding is the pearl of great price.

What shall it profit you if you gain the whole world and lose—or never discover—your true self?

Delivered April 17, 1988, Third Unitarian Church of Chicago.

One Day at a Time

hope that this sermon will have value to all of you at some time in your life. It grows out of an experience in my own life when my oldest son called on November 16 at 8:30 a.m. to tell us that he had cancer. Life has not been the same—nor will it be.

Impatient with hearing from anyone who not faced the "void," I have gone back to read the works of Viktor Frankl. He was a student of Alfred Adler and a successful psychiatrist at the time of Hitler. He was arrested in 1942 and survived four concentration camps, including the notorious Auschwitz. His mother and wife died there. Frankl suffered from typhoid fever among other things; he weighed 80 pounds when rescued at the end of the war.

He returned to the University of Vienna and added a doctorate in philosophy to his previous degree in psychiatry. Frankl fathered "Logotherapy." It differs from his mentor, Alfred Adler, who believed that we are driven by the urge to power, and from Freud's belief that we are driven by the urge for pleasure. Frankl believed that the primary motivational force in life is to find and make meaning. He does not object if one *can* find a *comprehensive* meaning to life. But he believes that we are more likely to find meaning for a particular time, a particular day. In other words, the motivation for living in the concentration camp might be simply to get out. He previously had believed that we cannot exist without sleep for more than a stated number of hours. Yet he observed prisoners who contradicted this. People wore the same clothing for half a year. They were unable to wash, they had no toothbrushes, and they observed cannibalism. Yet some of them survived.

What kept them going? It varied. The desire to finish a book, to tell the story of what the Nazis had done, to see a wife, child or friend. A hospitalized person similarly may hold on until a son arrives home from the service. Or a person may decide against suicide because the cats need to be fed, the plants need watered, or the person in the next bed depends on him to ring for the nurse. The smallest of reasons for living can keep one going. In the camps he observed that that person who could not create some kind of meaning for himself or herself—that person would die. Frankl compares life to a chess game. A chess player, in any one move, is limited by his ability and by the skills of his opponent. The conditions are always limited. But you must make your move, projecting yourself into the future.

Dr. Frankl's patients sit up in a chair, with both the patient and the doctor speaking. He often directs sessions with questions like, "What is your next move? What can you do when you leave this session?" Dr. Frankl prods the patients, often saying things that are unpleasant to hear. But it takes place within a warm and reassuring atmosphere. Carl Rogers says that the *nature* of an encounter is more important than any precise set of techniques. Personality change is initiated by attitudes which exist in the therapist. Patients sense that Frankl has faced the void and gone through hell himself. Frankl is fond of quoting Nietzsche, "Who has a why to live for, can bear almost any how." He directs a patient to make a commitment to something that he or she finds worthy of doing.

In the concentration camps, Frankl observed differences in how prisoners endured and survived the same experiences. He left the camps convinced that we all have the chance for self-determination. Our existence does not depend upon the objective conditions in which we find ourselves but, rather, upon our personal decisions about how to respond to those conditions.

Freud had said, "Subject a number of very strongly differentiated human beings to the same amount of starvation. With an increase in the imperative need for food, all individual differences will be blotted out, and in their place we shall see the uniform expression of one unsatisfied instinct." Frankl countered that, "In the concentration camps we witnessed to the contrary, we saw how, faced with the identical situation, one man became a swine while another attained almost saintly status."

Robert J. Lifton's studies of American prisoners in North Korea came to the same conclusion. "There were examples among them both of altruistic behavior as well as the most primitive forms of struggle for survival." In other words, there is no one, predictable human response to a serious illness, a debilitating handicap, poverty, the Depression, being blacklisted, the loss of a loved one, or life in a nursing home. We are not simply the products of our inheritance and our environment. We ultimately decide for ourselves what our attitude will be to any set of circumstances.

So far, the main thrust of medicine has been in treating the disease. The job of assisting the patient in shaping his or her attitude to that challenge is not given the importance that it deserves. Frankl observed that,

> The experiences of camp life show that man does have a choice of action. There were enough examples, often of a heroic nature, which proved that apathy could be overcome, irritability suppressed. Man can preserve a vestige of spiritual freedom of independence of mind, even in such terrible conditions of psychic and physical stress. . . . And there were always choices to make. Every day, every hour, offered the opportunity to make a decision, a decision which determined whether you would or would not submit to those powers which threatened to rob you of your very self, your inner freedom; which determined whether or not you would become the plaything of circumstance, renouncing freedom and dignity to become molded into the form of the typical inmate.

Man is not fully conditioned by his circumstances or by his past. Instead, we must each determine whether we will give in to those conditions or stand up to them. The *New York Times* had a recent article about a woman who had been in a mental hospital for 15 years following a series of unhappy foster homes and an attempted suicide. She went on to earn her Master's degree and works with those who face similar challenges. Her simple explanation is that, "I decided to fight back."

I just read a review of a book titled *We the Victors*. It is the story of 31 cancer survivors. The author summarizes common survivor characteristics. One is a sense of self-determination, some reason to go on living. The author quotes a teenage athlete who lost his hair, threw up in the car, and had a leg amputated. "I believe that we the victors should help others coming after us. We should turn about and take three steps backward and pick up at least two people on their way out of the cancer concentration camps." The last freedom that is offered to us is the freedom to determine our attitude in any given set of circumstances.

I have observed older people for whom there are no chances left to accomplish anything else in life who look upon aging and death as a challenge. It represents the last chance for a sense of victory, of accomplishment, of doing a task well. Frankl writes, "When a man finds that it is his destiny to suffer, he will have to accept his suffering as his task, his unique opportunity lies in the way in which he bears his burden." We all have known those who have looked upon those last days in a nursing home, or surviving the loss of a loved one, or dealing with a child that is severely handicapped, as a task that they are going to do well, a test of their strength, a proof of who they are. There is something in them that looks upon it with dignity and even pride.

Norman Cousins's book *The Healing Hearts* asks if physicians can communicate negative information in a way that patients embrace as a challenge. The last chapter in that book is written by Cousins's physician, who says,

> If I had to single out any one idea from the book that needs to be widely accepted, it is his belief that serious illness should be regarded as a challenge and not as a pronouncement of doom, a challenge that calls for the best that the patient has in himself or herself.

Carl Sandburg has a poem in which he depicts death as life's last great challenge.

Animals respond to situations instinctively. Even early man or individuals in more structured societies have strong traditions that tell them how to respond in particular situations. But we must decide what our own attitudinal response will be when we are faced with a fate that cannot be changed, when there is no free choice in the situation other than to determine the manner and mode in which we will meet our fate.

Dr. Frankl has an optimistic view of the potential strength that each of us possess. He believes that it is our nature to deliberately impose demands on ourselves. He doesn't believe that we thrive when our lives are void of tensions.

> Mental health is based on a certain degree of tension, the tension between what we have already achieved and what one still ought to accomplish, or the gap between what one is and what one should become. This tension is inherent in the human being and therefore is indispensable to mental well-being.

We don't need equilibrium. When we have it, we'll go run a race, enter a contest or go see a movie with traumatic conditions.

Dr. Frankl tells the story of a man in one of the camps who said he could not go on, there was nothing more that he could expect from life. Frankl turned the question around, asking, "Is it possible though that life can still expect something from you?" The message that Frankl chooses to take from the concentration camps is that when life is not good to some people, they still remain good to life.

This is not the depraved worldview that envisioned the Holocaust. Frankl says, "I am absolutely convinced that the gas chambers of Auschwitz and Treblinka were ultimately prepared not in some office or other in Berlin, but rather at the desks and in the lecture halls of nihilistic scientists and philosophers." Frankl witnessed prisoners in the camps who rose above such nihilism, proving that each of us are uniquely capable of doing much more than even we ourselves can imagine.

This year I was struck by the sheer *audacity* of the first Thanksgiving. That is the only word that I can think of to describe it. The Mayflower carried 102 passengers. During the first winter, 51 of their number died of under nourishment, exposure, and disease. At one time there were only seven adults still able to nurse the sick and hunt for food. Our Thanksgiving observance grows out of that experience, when the 51 survivors gathered to express praise and gratitude. Can you think of a more audacious response to a more devastating experience? Shouldn't they have had a therapy session to complain about all the injustices? Wouldn't it have helped to blame their parents for bringing them there—or the man who organized the trip? Couldn't they have put on a sackcloth and groveled in self-pity? Of the dozens of options open to them, they chose to have a day of Thanksgiving!

The conditions of life are unfair and unjust. Yet there is no intelligent or healthy choice but to seek to be just and fair ourselves. Frankl tells the story of leaving the camps and coming near a field of newly sown crops. He immediately moved to go around the crops but his friend tried to drag him straight through it. The friend justified his actions on the fact that so much had been taken from him when his wife and child were gassed to death. Frankl wrote later, "Only slowly could these men be guided back to the commonplace truth—that no one has the right to do wrong, not even if wrong has been done to them."

I can testify that tear ducts have their limits. It is possible to cry until you can cry no more. I have been thinking these past two weeks of the attitude that my son must take—without realizing that I have asked for a response from him that I have been incapable of performing myself. It may be that we shall not—any of us in our family—cope with this task with the kind of strength and maturity that it demands. Only those who themselves have faced "the void" are capable of judging us. And they are the least judgmental people of all.

Delivered December 2, 1984, Third Unitarian Church of Chicago.

In Defense of the Elder Brother

To celebrate April Fools' Day a few years ago, I spoke in defense of the Bethlehem innkeeper who told Mary and Joseph that there was no room in the inn but that they could sleep in the stable. The poor innkeeper has been castigated for 2,000 years. It seemed to me that if the Pope can forgive the Jews—and even is contemplating forgiving Galileo—then surely we should forgive the poor innkeeper. The story always seemed simple enough to me. All the rooms were taken. The inn was full. It was as simple as that. Rather than demean him, we should credit his humanistic response to offer them hospitality in the stable.

Well there's another Biblical character who has had bad press lo these many years. I'd like to say a good word this morning on behalf of the elder brother. As you may recall from hours spent in the musty basements of Methodist or Baptist churches, the story begins with these words, "There was a man who had two sons." I identify with the story, for I have two sons. In this case, the younger son took all of his inheritance and squandered it in loose living. It got so bad that he gladly would have eaten the scraps tossed to swine. He decided that he would be better off at home as one of his father's hired servants. His father, however, met him at a great distance as he was coming down the road. He put his own robe and ring on his son and ordered the servant to kill the fatted calf for a great feast. About this time, the elder brother—who had been working hard for his father these many years—comes on the scene and asks his father why there has never been a party for him (not to mention a new robe or ring). I can still remember the picture in the Bible storybook, which depicted the elder brother like a villain.

My problem with the story, as both a parent and a son, is that it was not fair. Had I been the scriptwriter, the younger brother's return would have been cause for rejoicing—but the party would have been given in both of their honors. Why not a ring for the young son and a watch for the elder one? Why not make this a time to reward the elder brother for his faithfulness? Why not deed him a few acres or turn over a few head of livestock? The elder brother was justified in his feelings because his father was unfair. I have had a hang up on fairness the first 40 years of my life. And it is only during this last decade that I realized that life is not fair.

As a child, I wanted all the athletes to be ugly. And I wanted these who were dumb to be handsome or pretty. I wanted those in the honor society to have obnoxious personalities. I wanted all the rich to be unhappy and for the lives of the poor to be filled with laughter. In other words, I wanted all the goodies to be evenly distributed. If a person had been slighted in one area, then I wanted him or her to be gifted in another.

At my first church, in Rensselaer, Indiana, they had what were called "pay backs." If you received an invitation to someone's "pay back," that was when they paid back all those who invited them to dinner during the past year. It was understood in that community that the brunt of entertaining was not to be borne by any one person. If you accepted an invitation, you were expected to reciprocate. I found it to be a very just system! I have made a habit of picking up hitchhikers through the years. I grew up in a family that never owned a car and I always managed to get back and forth from college because of the kindness of strangers. It is no accident that I am a big supporter of my church's scholarship fund, since I received a scholarship from my church. I think I have made my point and to continue would do no one any good.

I'm sure that some of you regret the day that I lost my innocence and realized that life is not fair, the universe is not moral, that we do not reap the evil or the good that we sow, that the innocent suffer and the wicked prosper and justice does not triumph over wrong. Jesus said that the sun rises on the evil and the good and gentle spring rains fall on the just and the unjust. The Harvard philosopher William James wrote that the question "whether this world is at bottom a moral or immoral universe is the most radical question in life." Sometimes I feel that I am some kind of humanist Billy Graham. Rather than asking if you are saved, I demand to know, "Do you think this is a fair or moral universe? Do we reap what we sow? Do the innocent suffer and the wicked prosper?"

John Dietrich was the first minister in America to preach "humanism"— at our Unitarian church in Minneapolis. He said,

> To be tumbled out of the enfolding arms of a cosmic purpose into a
> world where evil and wrong must be faced as real and actual, where
> there is no foreordained triumph for man as the darling of the universe,

where all of man's values must take their chance in a complexity which gives them no final validity or eternal guarantee is naturally disconcerting to an idealistic person. The sense of loss ls overwhelming.

My sense of urgency is because we must make this decision about life before the slings and arrows of outrageous fortune have done their utmost to us. Before then is the time to make up our minds as to whether this universe is fair and just or not. It's bad enough to have to deal with tragedy—the mental breakdown of a 16 year old daughter, a 40-year-old wife dying of cancer, a parent's unfair favoritism, or crippling arthritis. But it's far worse if you simultaneously wrestle with the added dimension of "Why did this happen to me?" "Is it something that I did or didn't do that caused me to lose favor with the gods?"

The author of Ecclesiastes understood that life is unfair. "The race is not to the swift, nor the battle to the strong, nor riches to the intelligent, nor favor to men of skill, but time and chance happen to them all!" We live in a universe of time and chance where the deck is not stacked, the dice are not loaded, and no guarantees reward good and punish evil. Leo Durocher translated Ecclesiastes into the vernacular, saying, "Nice guys finish last." The good die young. Isaac Singer said that he would like to picket the almighty with a sign that reads, "Unfair to life." Bertrand Russell described the real world when he said, "brief and powerless is man's life; on him and his race, the slow sure doom falls pitiless and dark. Blind to good and evil, reckless of destruction; omnipotent matter rolls on its relentless way." Put another way, the assassin's bullet hit Martin Luther King—but missed Adolph Hitler.

Copernicus told us in the 16th century that man is not the center of the universe. Darwin told us in the 19th that we were not created but evolved. Man is a natural phenomenon, the same as animals and plants. The universe is neutral toward us. We are not its darlings. The answer to the question, "Why do the innocent suffer?" is "Why not?" Those who understand the neutrality of the universe do not even ask the question! Pity the poor existentialists, wallowing in their anguish, bemoaning the fact that this is an absurd universe. The earth is what it is. It is audacious to say that life is "absurd" because it does not meet our expectations for fairness and justice.

I found this quote of a man describing his grandmother who was widowed at 35 and who had a difficult life raising several children. "As I recall, she did not feel deprived. She kept her head high, her values seemingly unchanged, her expectations—by our contemporary standards—small. The fact of being alone was hard, but then she had not learned any other lesson than that life was hard." I have had such a hang up that the world was somehow made for me and the rest of the human species. This unscientific view still predominates my mind, producing expectations for meaning, justice and reciprocity.

My favorite preacher, Dr. Duncan Littlefair in Grand Rapids, told his congregation,

> There is no need for things to work out, no need for things to be all right. No reason at all why justice should prevail. No assurance whatever that it will. You've got to learn to live with insecurity and with being a trivial occasion to the massive forms of life.

We will not take the nuclear arms race seriously. Like the Jews in Germany, we do not believe that God will permit such a thing happen to us. I believe this is the greatest obstacle to stopping the potential destruction of our civilization—the belief that someone's got the whole world in his hands.

I have told you many times that we are like survivors on a life raft. No shore is in sight and no rescue ship is coming. We are orphans in the universe—a trivial occasion—and there is no one to save us but ourselves. It's Albert Camus's image of modern man rolling a stone up the hill, only to have it roll back down. The process continues until death. Such a process is not fair. Yet it is the human condition and we gladly accept it over the alternative (death!).

I have been speaking to the point that life is unfair. But consider what your own life would be like if it were fair. What would your fair share of the earth's resources be—of its food, medicine, education? If the heavenly father divided up the earth's bounty equally among all of his children, what would your closet look like? Your home? Your pantry? You who are in the upper 2 percent of the world's annual income. If we want to talk about justice and fairness, we at the wide end of the cornucopia had better speak softly.

John Dewey did not believe in the heavenly father but he did believe in grace. Listen to his words.

> The things in civilization that we prize the most are not of ourselves. They exist by the grace of the doings and sufferings of the continuous human community, in which we are a link. Ours is the responsibility

of conserving, transmitting, rectifying, and expanding the heritage we have received for those who come after us.

He is saying that what we have received or inherited is not fair or just but it is grace. All these things that we do not deserve.

Joshua speaking for the Lord in the Old Testament says,

For I have given you land for which you did not labor, and cities which you did not build, and yet you dwell in them. And all the yards and vineyards which you did not plant and yet you eat of them.

In other words, from the beginning, when the universe conspired to create human life, you have been receiving more than you deserve. Human life itself is a gift that comes to us unearned, unasked and unsought. Your health, the genes that you inherited, how can you say you deserve them or that you earned them? The same with your intelligence, your talents. Isn't it interesting how we say your "gifts?" What a revealing and appropriate word. Any love that we have received in life, any friendship, is a gift. If it could have been marketed, American capitalism would have done it—and most of us would have been eager to purchase it.

Chicago, with its lakefront, parks, zoos, museums and symphonies—you were simply born here or moved here. You and I dwell in a city which we did not build. I inherited a culture, a language, a liberal religious tradition, universities and libraries built up by the labors of others through generations. The family that you were born into, what you received from the day that you were born were more than you deserved, earned or could even ask for. It was a gift. It was grace. It was more than fair!

I'll wind this up. John Dewey said that the things that we prize the most are not of ourselves. We are not comfortable with the idea that we have received more than we deserve, reaped more than we have sown. Lo the day that we begin to acknowledge all that we have received freely. That is the day that we begin to say, "What shall I render unto the Lord for his benefits?" And that is a day that we must postpone as long as we can! Abraham Maslow says that a common response of those who live life fully is, "I don't deserve this. A feeling of gratitude grows out of an all-embracing love for everybody and everything, leading to an impulse to do something good for the world, an eagerness to repay, even a sense of obligation."

And so, life is less than fair—and it is more than fair. Even the elder brother knows it. The picture in my Bible storybook caught him on one of those days when he experienced life as unfair. But certainly there were other days when he felt obligated, as he looked out over the city that he did not build, and as he sat under the trees that he did not plant. The pleasures of life go to those who understand that we cannot look in isolation at any one experience, or at any one day or year in our lives. Instead, we must see life in its totality, and we must experience it as it is, always has been, and always will be. Be it less than fair or more than fair, life is unfair.

Delivered March 6, 1983, Unitarian Universalist Church of Indianapolis.

No Rhyme or Reason

No isle can shelter you from final grief,
No tide can bear you from the coming season;
The hieroglyphics on a winter leaf
Must reconcile you to the great unreason."
LENORE MARSHALL

Easter always reminds me of an attorney who belongs to the Unitarian Church in Hobart, Indiana. He and his wife are Unitarians every other Sunday of the year. But on Easter she "puts on the hat and the white gloves" and they drive in to Chicago's Fourth Presbyterian Church on Michigan Avenue. That one Sunday each year they seem to need the reassuring Easter message that good will triumph over evil. Most of us here believe in an open universe that offers no assurance that good triumphs over evil. The dice are not loaded. There is no cosmic guarantee for the good, beautiful, and truthful.

The text for this morning's sermon comes from the Sermon on the Mount, where Jesus says, "The sun rises on the evil and on the good; the rains fall on the just and the unjust." The world operates, then, without rhyme or reason. There is no way that we can make sense out of history. There is no pattern to be discerned. There is no evidence that good will win out nor that there will be a "final triumph of righteousness," as the Apostles' Creed affirms.

I hope that every other minister and priest will join me this morning in admitting to scriptural gerrymandering. In my case, I could have chosen the contradictory text, "But even the hairs of your head are numbered." This conveys the reassuring idea that a power in the universe takes a personal interest in guiding and looking out for you. I have no problem with those who believe this. But Jesus better described my life experience when he observed that the sun and rain equally affect the good, evil, just and unjust.

I wish that the sun would rise some morning exclusively for the just. Part of me longs for an orderly and just world. I would like people—other than myself—to get what they deserve. We have a saying, "He had it coming." That's what we say when the boss who fired us loses his job or when the woman who leaves her husband for another man gets dumped, too. We like to believe that it is a universe where people reap what they sow. A woman in my previous congregation had her house broken into while she was at church preparing a Thanksgiving dinner. People were not so much shocked that her house was robbed—but rather that it could happen while she was out "doing good."

We do not like this universe to operate on blind chance, the fall of cards. Good often goes unrewarded and evil unpunished. Wicked people enjoy riches, acclaim and healthy children. We treasure honesty, service, and truth. Yet nature does not care about these values—much less guarantee that they prevail. We live in a world where the assassin's bullet missed Hitler but killed Martin Luther King. What is preached in church on Sunday rarely reflects what happens on the nightly news.

My son got to experience the real world recently, thanks to a traffic ticket. In waiting and observing the court for three hours before his turn came up, he correctly concluded that justice is a form of Russian roulette. There was no apparent rhyme or reason separating those who were convicted from those who walked out "scot-free."

Jean Paul Sartre's story "The Wall" depicts prisoners captured in the Spanish Civil War. The enemy tortures them to learn where their comrades are hiding. Choosing death over ratting out others, the men decide to have the last laugh by sending their captors on a wild goose chase. They tell them that their leader, Ramon Gris, is hiding out in a vault in the cemetery and imagine them futilely lifting up stones and opening the vault doors. The next day, another inmate tells them that, not wanting to endanger others, Ramon Gris hid in the cemetery, where he had been found that morning in the gravedigger's hut. "Everything went round in my head," one of the prisoners says. "I was laughing so much my eyes were full of tears."

Sartre's story captures the way that the universe operates. Absurdity is born at just this point—where what we desire and long for collides with what the world offers. We have to find some interpretation of life that makes sense out of it. I want religion to "work" for the individual. I have no problem with people who believe that "the very hairs on their head are numbered" by God. I have no desire to convert them to my perspective. All I am saying is that absurdity is the concept that makes the most sense of my life.

Some find it meaningful and helpful to believe that retribution is postponed to the next world. "Sure the wicked prosper and the righteous suffer.

But there will come a time when God settles the score." Others say, "But can't we believe in God in spite of life?" Princeton philosopher Walter Kaufmann writes, "The only theism worthy of our respect believes in God not because of the way the world is made, but in spite of that." This was the approach of Job and Jeremiah. "Even though he slay me, yet will I love him."

In Albert Camus's novel *The Plague*, a priest preaches that the plague has swept the town as punishment for the townspeople's sins. The character Rieux confronts the priest with the death of an innocent child. Noting that this "passes our understanding," the priest says, "perhaps we should love what we cannot understand." Rieux replies, "No, Father, I've a different idea of love, and until my dying day I shall refuse to love a scheme of things in which children are put to torture." For Camus, even recompense in another life does not justify the innocent suffering, or children killed by a plague. Beyond being intellectually incomprehensible, Camus refuses to believe this on moral grounds.

A person of the caliber of Dale Evans could write a book about her Down's Syndrome child titled "Angel Unaware." It gave meaning to her to believe that God had given her "something special" to care for. Someone else who had a special-needs child disagreed, writing that God chastens those whom he loves with such a "burden." Being chastened more than others, she felt more loved by God.

Legions of explanations seek to make sense of a universe where the sun rises on the good and evil alike. Here I'll make the case for the absurdity explanation:

1. It has been a relief for me as a Unitarian minister to not have to deal with the "Why?" question. Even the disciples invoked this absurd question when they asked Jesus if blindness was caused by the sins of the blind man— or by the sins of his parents? When we accept the absurdity of life we no longer have to wrestle with the question of why tragedy strikes us or the ones we love.

2. The absurdity of life eliminates arrogance and judgment. Those who believe that goodness is rewarded may attribute their success to their virtues. The head of the Pennsylvania Railroad, for example, said that God—in his infinite wisdom—had given him his millions. On the other hand, our society has too often treated sin as the cause of poverty. Acceptance of absurdity undercuts such arrogance and judgment.

3. Recognizing absurdity also undercuts disillusionment at life and resentment of God. An alcoholic told me 20 years ago, "Do not raise your children to expect life to be just." Otherwise, when the day of unjust reckoning comes, they may drink to blot out the realities of life. How many people who

are breaking down and turning to drugs and alcohol simply were not prepared to cope with the facts of existence? Acceptance of absurdity enables one to see life with open eyes, reducing the resentment and disillusionment that can accompany belief in a just universe.

4. Those who accept life's absurdity actually may find more happiness. Camus biographer Thomas Hanna writes, "In his most despairing moments Camus never loses sight of the great task of man, which is to learn to be happy, and he clearly thinks that the absurd man, who has become conscious of the nonsense of everything, is better disposed than anyone else to live intensely, and know happiness."

Therapist Viktor Frankel writes, "When you can no longer find meaning in the larger picture, you look for meaning in the events around you." In Archibald MacLeish's play about Job, Job realizes that life is irrational and uncanny. As the play ends, he says to his wife, Sarah:

> If the lights go out all over the world
> and if even the candles of the churches
> are dimmed and eliminated
> Blow on the coal of the heart, my dear.
> Blow on the coal of the heart,
> And we will have a light to see
> and we will have a fire that will warm us.

Some scientists believe that the sun will burn out, the earth will grow cold, and such life as there is in the universe will run slowly down. We must find individual meaning to our lives, even if there is no ultimate meaning to life. What is important is each moment of life—accepting them and living them to their utmost. Camus updated the ancient myth of Sisyphus, depicting the plight of a day laborer who rolls a massive stone uphill, again and again. One might think that Camus painted life at its worst. But his Sisyphus suffers no illusions. In the last lines of the book, Camus writes, "I leave Sisyphus at the bottom of the mountain. His burden is always there. The struggle itself toward the summit is enough to fill the heart of man. We must imagine Sisyphus as happy."

We must find a philosophy of life that explains our experiences of it. The notion that life is absurd is repulsive to some. Even I would prefer the world of the orthodox Christian. I would like to believe that men reap what they sow, that innocent men do not suffer, that wicked men do not prosper, and that history will end with the final triumph of righteousness. Like Edna St. Vincent Millay, I am not reconciled to the world as it is:

Down, down, down in the darkness of the grave
Gently they go, the beautiful, the tender, the kind.
Quietly they go, the intelligent, the witty, the brave,
I know. But I do not approve. And I am not resigned!

I am jealous of the worldview that enables people to celebrate Easter with a belief that the universe's deepest meaning buttresses human hopes and ideals. John Dietrich, America's first humanist minister, wrote,

To be tumbled out of the enfolding arms of a kindly cosmic purpose—into a world where evil and wrong must be faced as real and actual, where there is no foreordained triumph for man as the "darling of the universe," where all of man's values must "take their chances" in a complexity which gives them no final validity or eternal guarantee is naturally disconcerting to an idealistic person. The sense of loss is overwhelming.

But then come the resounding words of Camus,

Nothing is given to men, and the little they can conquer is paid for with unjust deaths. But man's greatness lies elsewhere. It lies in his decision to be stronger than his condition. And if this condition is unjust, he has only one way of overcoming it, which is to be just himself.

We must not spend our time asking, "Why?" Nor must we squander time in resentment, disillusionment, arrogance, or judgment. Instead, we must find happiness amidst the absurdities of life. The goal of this congregation is to build a community that is more just and more loving than the known powers of the universe. If no one is looking after us, then we must look after each other. We have resolved to be more just and more loving than what has been given to us. This is man's greatness. And it is enough.

Delivered March 26, 1978, Third Unitarian Church of Chicago.

Paul Powell

There was a crooked man, and he walked a crooked mile,
He found a crooked sixpence against a crooked stile;
He bought a crooked cat which caught a crooked mouse,
And they all lived together in a little crooked house.
MOTHER GOOSE

This Thursday marks the second anniversary of the death of Illinois Secretary of State Paul Powell. It is fitting that we constituents pause to remember him. He was born in the Southern Illinois town of Vienna (pronounced Vi-Enna) on January 21, 1902. His parents named him for St. Paul. After graduating from Vienna High School, Powell went to work in his father's drug store. The editor of the *Vienna Times* reminisces that Powell also operated a small restaurant during the 1930s. During those hard times, "He just added some more water to the soup to make it go further."

When Powell was 26, the citizens of Vienna elected him to the local school board—the start of 42 years in public service. Soon they promoted him to mayor. But Vienna was too small for Paul Powell. In 1934 he was elected to the state legislature, the august assembly in which he would serve for 30 years. One of the opponents whom he defeated was a Vienna minister who travelled to Springfield to give the legislature's invocation. The reverend was so impressed with the legislative lifestyle—the drinks and the steaks—that he tried to unseat Powell the following year.

State veterans groups named Powell Man of the Year; he would have received the AMVETS Silver Helmet Award for Americanism had he lived until April. He was a member of the Eagles, the Elks, and the Moose. The week before he died he learned that he was to be raised to a 33rd degree Mason. Powell's peers in Springfield chose him as Democratic minority leader on three occasions. Reporters in the Illinois Correspondents Association twice selected him as outstanding legislator of the year. Powell was widely acknowledged as the man most responsible for delivering Illinois for Harry Truman in 1948 and JFK in 1960. President Kennedy thanked him with a dinner at the White House (we can only imagine what John, Paul and Jackie discussed that evening).

In 1964 Powell was elected to the first of two terms as Illinois Secretary of State. Second only to governor, that office is the elected position that "most directly affects the citizens." He was keeper of the great seal of the state of Illinois, controlled 4,000 patronage jobs, granted corporate charters, and registered cars and trucks. He was so folksy that his office directed motorists renewing their vehicle registrations to make the checks payable simply to "Paul Powell." In a measure of his clout, 10 days before he died 6,000 people paid $25 each to attend the "Garden Party" cocktail event that raised $100,000 for Powell's "flower fund." It didn't hurt ticket sales that the boss required his employees to buy set numbers of tickets proportional to their salaries.

Paul Powell was a no-nonsense American, believing that we should love it or leave it. He repeatedly condemned "Hippies, Yippies, Dippies and all other long-haired animals." The editor of the *Vienna Times* recalled,

> I saw him the last time at the National Popcorn Farmer's Day. As usual, he rehearsed for me a speech he planned to make—this one in Carbondale. He had decided in the heart of the arena—disrupted by the militants—to speak loud and strong for law and order and for respect for the flag of the United States, which he loved!

He spent $5,000 of his own money to buy gold lapel flags for his employees. He said, "The flag does something for me every time it waves."

The only scintilla of doubt to touch this upstanding American during his lifetime was quickly cleared up. A grand jury investigated the stock that Powell purchased in a horseracing company. After championing legislation for the company, he was able to buy its stock at just 10 cents a share. But Powell was exonerated and, when he was, he gushed to the press, "I wound up with the grand jury wanting to know from me where they could buy racetrack stock!"

In October 1970 Secretary Powell visited Rochester Minnesota's famous Mayo Clinic for a checkup. His faithful red-headed secretary, Marge Hensey, accompanied him for the trip (no 9-to-5er was she!). While Powell's name for Hensey was "Little Bit," we do not know what term of endearment she may have used for him. Nor do we know what strain, what stress, what excitement caused Powell's sudden, severe heart attack in the $125-a-night Rochester hotel suite that they shared that evening. We do know that the faithful Little Bit was at his side. Fearing that people back home in Vienna might get the wrong idea, Little Bit delayed reporting the death for more than 24 hours. This allowed for Powell's wife and his aide, Nicholas Ciaccio, to fly to Rochester from Springfield. It also allowed Powell's staff to visit his office at 3 a.m. to clear out his personal effects and any documents that could be misconstrued. It was only after Powell was buried that a friend entered the Springfield hotel room that Powell occupied during legislative sessions, discovering close to $800,000 in cash stuffed into briefcases, suitcases and shoeboxes.

Powell's friends knew he had been frugal. Yet here was a public servant whose annual salary peaked at $30,000 who nonetheless reported a 1969 taxable income of $200,000 and managed to accumulate a $3 million fortune—including $169,000 in racing stock alone! He left part of his estate to the local historical society to preserve his humble family home as a museum—open to the pilgrimages of Boy Scouts, civics classes and 4-H Clubs. A Powell friend told *Time Magazine*, "He was just a big, old country boy—he could shake you down and make you like him." Powell himself once said, "There's only one thing worse than a defeated politician, and that is a broke one."

Between the time that Powell's death became public and his stash of cash was discovered the entire state went into mourning. His body was draped in black and laid to rest in the Capitol rotunda on the same catafalque where President Lincoln's body had lain. His pallbearers included Presidents Truman and LBJ, Governor Richard Ogilvie, Lieutenant Governor Paul Simon, Attorney General William Scott, Public Education Superintendent Ray Page, Treasurer Adlai Stevenson III, and Chicago Mayor Richard J. Daley.

Addressing the memorial service in the rotunda, Governor Ogilvie called Powell,

> a man of his word. No handshake was necessary; only his plain statement of intentions. And he could be counted on always to honor the commitments he made. He was above all a man who demanded of himself a sense of honor that stood the test of service spanning four turbulent decades.

Future U.S. Senator Adlai Stevenson added, "His death leaves an emptiness in Illinois politics that will never be filled."

Unwilling to let the Republican governor down in Springfield dominate the moment, Chicago Mayor Daley introduced a resolution recognizing that Powell "had been in the forefront of nearly every battle that brought help to the helpless and gave hope to the young and old."

At another service at Vienna High School, Powell's bronze casket was flanked by a horseshoe-shaped floral arrangement from his friends in the horseracing industry. Father Paul Hoban's eulogy praised Powell's soulful, unfailing, unqualified and unyielding service to others. Father Hoban urged Governor Ogilvie and Mayor Daley to erect a Powell memorial "to give young people an understanding of the duty of serving one's neighbor and an understanding of America, as Powell defined it." Powell "will especially be remembered by the poor, the handicapped, the veteran, the little fellow!" added the editor of the *Vienna Times*. "Paul Powell has left this life but he has left behind a life that speaks of deeds untold." In one such example, Powell's friends at Sportsman Park and Washington Park established a $2,000 annual scholarship for the racetrack worker's child who wrote the best essay on "Paul Powell and Americanism." When all the ceremonies were finally over, Powell was laid to rest in the family cemetery in Vienna under a tombstone simply inscribed, "Here lies a life-long Democrat." (Columnist Mike Royko later urged the Democratic Party to sue for libel!)

While the newspapers, statisticians and morticians all say that Paul Powell is dead—don't believe it. You won't find him in that low, green mound in the Vienna cemetery. Paul Powell lives today in the Democratic Party—and all the political parties in the United States, the USSR, Sweden, and Spain. His spirit lives in white-collar executives and union leaders. It is alive in the policeman in your neighborhood precinct, the tax evader next door, and the welfare cheater down the block. It flows in every restaurant where the proprietor adds water to stretch the soup. It lives wherever people speak of "law and order" as the solution to our nation's problems—or where wearing lapel flags passes as a viable substitute to laboring for justice and equality for all. Paul Powell lives wherever bribes tempt politicians, building inspectors or driving-test administrators. He inspired Cook County Clerk Edward J. Barrett, who has been indicted on charges of taking $180,000 in bribes from a voting-machine company. His spirit surely was present when Governor Otto Kerner, formerly known as "Mr. Clean," was accused of taking a bribe from a racetrack official—who dutifully reported it as an IRS business expense.

The spirit of Paul Powell is most alive wherever men thank God that they are not like him. He lives wherever we fail to ask ourselves, "What does it profit a man to gain the whole world and lose his soul?"

Dear friends, Paul Powell lives today in you and me!

Delivered October 15, 1972, Third Unitarian Church of Chicago.

Editor's note: Chicago folksinger Steve Goodman immortalized Paul Powell on an album released six months after this sermon:

> Paul Powell got laid to rest in a casket lined with gold,
> But his ghost lives on in other thieves, or so I've been told.
> And there's crooks in every walk of life, and that I know is true.
> But the biggest bums are some of the ones we give our power to.

TIME

THE WEEKLY NEWSMAGAZINE

Oct. 23, 1972   Vol. 100, No. 17

Remembering Paul

When Illinois Secretary of State Paul Powell died in 1970, he left behind an unexplained fortune of $2,000,-000, including $800,000 in cash stashed away in shoeboxes in a Springfield hotel. To celebrate the second anniversary of Powell's demise, the Rev. Donald Wheat, pastor of the Third Unitarian Church of Chicago, held a memorial service last week. "If we hold services for Gandhi, Washington, Lincoln and other greats," explained the pastor, "then maybe people like Powell should be remembered by their constituents too."

Powell was given a service with all the trimmings. After reading the parable of the rich fool, Wheat followed up with a nursery rhyme, *The Crooked Man.* Wheat reviewed Powell's career: twice voted the state's outstanding legislator, named Man of the Year by veterans' groups. He recalled how Powell's secretary, affectionately known as "Little Bit," accompanied the old pol on his last trip and tried, unsuccessfully, to spirit away the shoeboxes before authorities discovered them. Wheat wound up with a favorite Powell quote: "There's only one thing worse than a defeated politician and that is a broke one"—a condition Powell steadfastly avoided. The church collection was taken up in shoeboxes.

Time Magazine's *coverage of the Paul Powell sermon.*

Part Two

The Saints

If a man has not discovered
something that he will die for,
he isn't fit to live.

MARTIN LUTHER KING JR.

Giving Thanks for Homer Plessy

observe anniversaries. At the start of this year, I went to the library to see what was happening in 1896, 1796, or 1696. This year, we could celebrate the 100th anniversary of Tootsie Rolls, Cracker Jacks, "When Those Saints Go Marching In," "Stars and Stripes Forever," *La bohème*, and composer Anton Bruckner's birth. Good Unitarians would celebrate the centennial of our own *Fannie Farmer's Cookbook*. Leaving those celebrations to my colleagues, I am focusing on Homer Plessy. Unknown to most of us, he prompted a Supreme Court decision that shaped this nation for 60 years.

The male counterpart of Rosa Parks, Homer Plessy staged his sit-in 100 years ago. Significantly, he was a loser and history rarely names schools or streets for losers. I have a $100 bill for anyone who can find me Homer Plessy's photo. For some reason I imagine him as small, meticulous, and shy. In any case, this 34-year-old mulatto boarded a train in New Orleans bound for Covington, Louisiana. He settled into a coach designated for whites, refused to leave, and was arrested for his crime.

Imagine the response of the white passengers on that railcar 100 years ago when Homer Plessy entered. Did he have a razor hidden on his person? Would he rape their daughters or rob their wives before the train left the station? Perhaps for these very reasons, Louisiana had passed its 1890 railcar-segregation law euphemistically titled "An Act to Promote the Comfort of Passengers." Plessy's fine for violating that law was $25, a substantial amount a century ago. He appealed to the Supreme Court of Louisiana, which unanimously upheld the "Act to Promote the Comfort of Passengers." Friends helped Homer Plessy appeal to the U.S. Supreme Court. With one justice not participating, a seven-justice majority upheld Louisiana's law. The lone dissent came from the sole Southerner on the bench, former slaveholder John Marshall Harlan of Kentucky.

Let us celebrate Dr. King's birthday by reflecting on civil-rights pioneers Homer Plessy and John Marshall Harlan. Plessy died unknown and unrecognized, and Justice Harlan remained on the bench for 34 years, one of the longest high-court terms in history. The majority decision in *Plessy* helped to establish the legal right to designate racially segregated facilities until the court finally overturned "separate but equal" in *Brown v. Board of Education* in 1954.

Those of you watching the PBS series on the Civil War appreciate how decisively the North won the war. Sherman's march to the sea had all the makings of beating a dead dog. Afterwards, the Confederate States sought ways to preserve the Southern Way of Life, including the Jim Crow laws mandating racial segregation. It is one thing to segregate by practice or custom and quite another to segregate by statute—with the consent of the highest court in the land. That is the significance of Homer Plessy.

A Brit traveling in the U.S. five years before the Plessy case wrote:

> On most railways, Negroes were expected and told, to take a particular
> coach in each train, and they usually did so; but the rule did not seem
> to be strictly enforced. Well-dressed Negroes sometimes traveled in the
> same car with first class white people, ladies and gentlemen, and there
> were usually some white people, poor whites, working folk, in the Ne-
> gro car.

George Campbell, a member of British Parliament, found in touring the seaboard south in 1879 "that the humblest black rides with the proudest white in terms of perfect equality and without the slightest symptom of malice or dislike on either side." Thomas Wentworth Higginson, a Unitarian minister who backed abolitionist John Brown and led an all-black Civil-War regiment, found that white southerners in Virginia, South Carolina, and Florida accepted the presence of Negroes to a degree comparable to that of his native New England. He himself rode in first-class cars with black passengers in those Southern states.

After the Civil War, from 1870 to 1896, Americans elected 40 blacks to the U.S. Congress. Southern whites retaliated by devising ways to disenfranchise black voters through poll taxes, grandfather clauses, property requirements, intimidation, and terror. By 1901, there was just one black legislator left in Washington. The South did not elect another black to Congress until 1972— the gifted and eloquent Barbara Jordan.

After a first wave of relative "acceptance" after the war, racial separation became even more pronounced. Tennessee passed the first formal state Jim

Crow law in 1881. Many more states passed a slew of such laws from 1907 to 1922, as a new generation of free blacks grew up without their parents' deference to whites. Whites claimed that segregation in no way implied black inferiority—and blacks who interpreted it that way must be paranoid! Nor were black leaders all opposed to separate but equal. Addressing a New England Women's Club in 1890, Booker T. Washington said, "The Negro is forced to ride in railroad coaches that are inferior in every way to those given the whites and they are made to pay the same fares that the whites pay." Washington appears to be complaining not about racial separation but the inferiority of black accommodations. In 1871 a black legislator in the Virginia House of Delegates proposed that separate rail cars be provided for Negroes so that they would not be relegated to the smoking cars. Robert Smalls, a black Congressman from South Carolina, said in 1884 that separate cars were acceptable—so long as they were of the same character as those provided to whites.

Immediately after the Civil War, Congress outlawed segregated public transportation in the nation's capital but permitted segregated schools. In *Roberts v. the City of Boston*, the Massachusetts Supreme Court decided that all persons—without distinction of age, sex, birth, color, or origin—are equal before the law. Yet this did not prohibit Boston's school board from using race to "classify students." The Supreme Courts of six other states upheld school segregation: Ohio, Missouri, California, New York, Indiana, and Kentucky. As late as 1908, the U.S. Supreme Court ruled against Berea College to uphold a Kentucky law that barred schools from serving both white and black pupils. Justice John Marshall Harlan again filed the lone dissent, 16 years after the *Plessy* case. He wrote,

> Have we become so inoculated with prejudice of race that an American government, professedly based on the principles of freedom, and charged with the protection of all citizens alike, can make distinctions between such citizens in the matter of their voluntarily meeting for innocent purposes simply because of their respective races?

Jim and Jane Crow laws may have become easier to implement once Frederick Douglass died in 1895 and Booker T. Washington became *the* spokesman for black Americans. Booker T. Washington's historic Atlanta address months after Douglass's funeral was a sweeping concession to the white South's desire for segregation. It was unheard of for a black man to speak on a platform with southern whites; Washington told them what they wanted to hear. "In all things that are purely social we can be as separate as the fingers, yet one as the hand in all things essential to mutual progress." Washington continued,

> The wisest among my race understand that the agitation of questions of social equality is the extremist folly, and the progress in the enjoyment of all privileges that will come to us must be the result of severe and constant struggle rather than of artificial forcing.

It is against this background of accommodation that 34-year-old Homer Plessy boarded a "whites only" coach in New Orleans and refused to budge. As Plessy and his attorneys took their appeal to the U.S. Supreme Court, I would love to know which justices they looked to for support. It is hard to believe that it was John Marshall Harlan. The court's sole Southerner had inherited 12 slaves from his father and had been a member of the Know-Nothing Party, which despised blacks, Jews, Roman Catholics, Orientals, and immigrants in general. Granted, Harlan fought with the Union Army but that was because he believed in preserving the union—*not* to free the slaves. Once the Thirteenth and Fourteenth Amendments passed, however, Harlan called himself a "repentant slave holder" and opposed the Ku Klux Klan. Harlan lost Kentucky gubernatorial campaigns in 1871 and 1876.

After Justice Harlan sent his son east to college, he wrote him this letter,

> If you find any boy in your class who is continually and deliberately piling indignities upon others, he is a mean and cowardly fellow, who will turn pale and cower when confronted by a brave, self-respecting, justice-loving comrade who has the courage to resist a personal insult.

If there was such a thing as a "southern gentleman," and I believe there was, Justice Harlan was one. He believed that anyone worthy of calling himself a man did not brutalize others regardless of their rank. Any American who loved justice had a duty to fight those who abuse power. Justice Harlan had a motto worthy of our consideration, "I would rather be right than consistent." When President Rutherford Hayes appointed Harlan to the Supreme Court, the stage was set for the confrontation between two views of America. Thirty states now had "separate but equal" laws that were held to be consistent with the Constitution. The courts ruled that the Thirteenth and Fourteenth Amendments were never intended to abolish race-based distinctions. It fell to a "repentant slaveholder" to write in an eloquent dissent that "the Constitution of the United States is colorblind."

Justice Oliver Wendell Holmes called Harlan the "last of the tobacco-spitting judges." Covering the *Plessy* decision, the *New York Tribune* reported,

> Harlan pounded the desk, shook his finger under the nose of the chief justice and turned more than once, almost angrily upon his colleagues of the majority, and expressed dissent from their conclusions in a tone and language more appropriate to a stump speech at a Populist barbecue, than to an opinion on a question of law before the Supreme Court of the United States.

He ridiculed the majority opinion in *Plessy*. How eloquent he was!

> There is in this country no superior, dominant, ruling class of citizens. There is no caste here. Our Constitution is colorblind, and neither knows nor tolerates classes among its citizens. In respect of civil rights, all citizens are equal before the law. The humblest is the peer of the most powerful.

The *Plessy* decision, he wrote,

> will, in time, prove to be quite as pernicious as the decision made by this tribunal in the Dred Scott case. The destinies of the two races, in this country, are indissolubly linked together, and the interests of both require that the common government of all shall not permit the seeds of race hate to be planted under the sanction of law.

Had not Homer Plessy's attorney pleaded in that same vein?

> Why may the state not require all red-headed people to ride in a separate car? Why not require all colored people to walk on one side of the street and the whites on the other? Why may it not require every white man's house to be painted white and every colored man's black?

Justice Harlan stood alone. And segregated railcars, schools, libraries, restaurants, parks, public housing, and blood banks became the law of the land. Segregation pursued black citizens even into prisons, wash houses, coal mines, telephone booths, and the armed services. In Florida, school textbooks that had been used by one race were to be stored separately from those used by another! Only the Third Reich was more ingenious in its racial classifications.

When *Brown v. Board of Education* declared segregated schools unconstitutional 58 years after *Plessy* in 1954, the *New York Times* editorialized that not one word of Chief Justice Earl Warren's opinion was inconsistent with Justice Harlan's 1896 dissent! Yet the *Times* was as late to the parade as most of America. The day after the *Plessy* decision, the *Times* reported three other minor court decisions on its front page, relegating its *Plessy* coverage to a page-three story under the header "Railway News"! Three out of every four editorials supported the majority decision against Homer Plessy. It would be fascinating to do a study of what important stories make the first page of our daily papers versus those that are buried inside. If I thought that what was on the front page of the newspaper is what is really important, I could never be a minister. Dr. King wrote "I believe that unarmed truth and unconditional love will have the final word in reality. That is why right temporarily defeated is stronger than evil triumphant."

Like all the rest, this sermon is about you and me. We can be Homer Plessys or John Marshall Harlans, guided to dissent by our own internal compasses—or we can stick with the majority. Is there any greater lesson to take from the life of Dr. King? President Truman said of him, "Martin Luther King is a rabble rouser who has hurt the Negro's cause, a damn fool." Congressman Adam Clayton Powell mocked him as "Martin Loser King." Yet whose birthday are we celebrating tomorrow? Does anyone here know—or care—which day Truman or Powell were born? Future history books will note with an asterisk that Jim Folsom was governor when Rosa Parks staged her sit down, just as Herod is remembered as king only because he ruled the year that Jesus was born in a stable, to a carpenter and his betrothed.

Dr. King said that, "The hope of the world is still in dedicated minorities. The trailblazers in human, academic, scientific, and religious freedom have always been in the minority." We must choose. "Will we continue to march to the drumbeat of conformity and respectability, or will we, listening to the beat of a more distant drum, move to its echoing sounds? Will we march only to the music of our time, or will we, risking criticism and abuse, march to the soul-saving music of eternity?" "The salvation of the world lies in the hands of the creatively maladjusted."

W. E. B. Du Bois stated that, "The problem of the twentieth century is the problem of the color line." And when we gather here four years from now to celebrate the new millennium, we will admit that it is the problem of the 21st century, as well. But we agree with James Baldwin who, when asked, "What do you see as the main task facing black writers today?" replied, "To make the question of color obsolete." Cornel West asked what could be more absurd than "that we view something as irrational and capricious and arbitrary as skin pigmentation as a benchmark of one's humanity, as the mark of whether one is inside or outside or on the margins of the human family?"

I'd give $100 to know how this congregation responded to the *Plessy* case in 1896. What shall happen to our species, our little planet, unless each of us seeks to live by our own conscience, as did Homer Plessy, John Marshall Harlan, Rosa Parks, and Martin Luther King? Oh, keep your eyes on the prize! Keep your hands on the plow! Don't be discouraged that truth is temporarily defeated. Our task is to "feed the future," as the lives of Homer Plessy and John Marshall Harlan feed our spirits today. We plant the seed—or water the seed that others planted. Leave the rest to history!

Delivered December 1, 1996, Third Unitarian Church of Chicago.

The Trial of the Century

His mother's name was Jane but she renamed herself Speranza after the muse who brought hope to a people whose glories and sorrows had not yet found a tongue. She was a large woman, the Gertrude Stein type, who wrote poetry and entertained the great names of Dublin and London. Artists, critics, bohemians, and revolutionaries came to her salon. Conviviality and brilliant conversation was the order of the day. His father—a knighted physician—was a tireless womanizer. George Bernard Shaw said that Sir William Wilde left a family in every farm house he visited. At least one of Dr. Wilde's patients sued, alleging that the doctor had taken liberties while she was under the influence of chloroform.

After having a son, Willie, Sir William and Lady Speranza Wilde expected their second child to be a daughter. When Oscar was born on October 16, 1856, his mother treated him accordingly. "She dressed the little one in girl's clothes, let his hair grow long and in all ways treated him as she would have the delicate girl baby she had dreamed of through the months of her pregnancy. People who came to her house saw something very wrong in the spectacle of the little boy in ribbons and laces hung all over with jewels until he looked, as someone remarked, like a tiny Hindu idol."

They sent Oscar to boarding school at age nine, followed by Trinity College in Dublin, and on to Oxford University, where he carried off honor after honor. He was a six-foot, handsome man who dressed uniquely and wore his hair long. He abhorred sports. He decorated his room with peacock feathers, burned incense and wore either lilies or sunflowers in his lapel. He created a persona at Oxford. He later said, "There is only one thing in the world worse than being talked about—and that is not being talked about."

At Oxford, Wilde came under the influence of James Abbott Whistler's "art for art's sake" movement. John Ruskin stirred his conscience and Walter Pater his senses. Pater's philosophy was to live for the moment with passion.

No one was surprised when, upon graduation, Oxford invited Wilde to join the faculty as professor of aesthetics.

Wilde published a book of poetry titled *Poems*. He was not well known outside of Oxford but Gilbert and Sullivan were; their *Pinafore* played at 18 New York City theaters at the same time. In their show *Patience*, Gilbert and Sullivan had a young, dandy poet named Bunthorne. When word got around that he was modelled after Oscar Wilde, Wilde was invited on a U.S. lecture tour. He arrived in knee britches, a green overcoat with fur collar and cuffs, and a sunflower in his lapel. Upon disembarking, a customs official asked if he had anything to declare. With all modesty, Wilde replied, "nothing but my genius."

For nine months in 1882 he toured U.S. cities. Most people attended to see Wilde—not for his aesthetics lectures. The highlight of his tour was an afternoon with Walt Whitman, who was every bit the individual as Wilde. As the tour progressed, he found himself as a lecturer, unleashing his wit. It was Wilde who said that it is absurd to divide people into the good and bad, since they were either tedious or charming. The charming Wilde was effervescent and overflowed with merriment. I do not know anyone on our national scene who compares. He combined Abbie Hoffman's wit and passion for living with Gore Vidal's sophistication, intelligence, and culture. Wilde's only novel, *The Picture of Dorian Gray*, taught that beautiful thoughts make a beautiful soul and that a beautiful soul makes a beautiful face. His plays *Lady Windermere's Fan* and *The Importance of Being Earnest* will provide catharsis through laughter as long as there are theatergoers in the world.

At age 28 in 1894, Oscar Wilde married Constance Floyd. He designed her wedding dress and to that union, two sons were born. His biographer describes their new home in London, "The house was to be no mere dwelling but the habitation of poetry and beauty; the showplace of aestheticism. It had to be at once original and impeccable, chaste yet subtly luxurious."

Reading about Wilde, I kept thinking that I cannot do him justice. His goal in life was to be himself, to realize his own perfection, and he resolved that he would do nothing in moderation. He said, "I am one of those made for exceptions, not for laws." He wrote, "Evolution is the law of life, and there is no evolution except towards individualism. Where this tendency is not expressed it is a case of artificially arrested growth, or disease, or of death." He said "Give me the luxuries of life, anyone can have the necessities." His heroes were Jesus

Christ and Napoleon Bonaparte—two men who lived life to the hilt, who attempted the impossible. Wilde could not tolerate the mediocre; he wanted to wring life dry, go for broke, shoot the moon.

No one in history had his appetite for living. His biographer writes, "He had avoided the shadow, indeed, he had lived life as if all had been sunshine. It has always been springtime in his heart, and the joyousness that was in him communicated itself to everyone about him, calling forth like the light and warmth of the sun." All who entered his radiant presence became better than their best. The tongue-tied found words that made them marvel at themselves, the dull shone with unaccustomed light. For Wilde, the great sin is imitation. No artist should want to paint like another, nor any poet to write like any other. Looking at an Oxford friend, he commented, "His left leg is a poem."

I loved his essay "The Soul of Man under Socialism." Wilde was apolitical, though he had written that, "A map of the world that does not include Utopia is not worth even glancing at." His only interest in socialism was that no one would have to be obsessed with money. He had said, "There is only one class in the community that thinks more about money than the rich, and that is the poor." Freed of that obsession, we would no longer center our lives on what we have. "The true perfection of man lies not in what he has but in what he is. Nobody will waste his life in accumulating things. One will live. To live is the rarest thing in the world, most people simply exist." "A red rose is not selfish because it wants to be a red rose. It would be horribly selfish if it wanted other flowers in the garden to be both red and roses."

When Oscar Wilde is 37 in 1891, a young, aspiring poet comes to meet him at his London home. From this day, events transpire that culminate in the trial of the century. Oscar Wilde could not live, he would have suffocated, were he not living in the presence of youth, joy, beauty, and vigor. He had once said: "I choose my friends for their good looks." And the young Lord Alfred Douglas who showed up at his door was too beautiful to be man. He would write Wilde a sonnet that closed with the words, "I am the love that dare not speak its name." Wilde had said, "In this world there are only two tragedies. One is not getting what one wants, and the other is getting it." Oscar Wilde and Lord Alfred Douglas now had what they always wanted.

While Lord Alfred Douglas loved Oscar Wilde, he hated his father even more. His father was the Marquess of Queensberry, who devised the rules for boxing. The Marquess was a notorious womanizer whom his wife divorced. The Marquess sought to get back at his wife through their son. Wilde had said,

"A man cannot be too careful in the choice of his enemies." The Marquess of Queensberry was a ruthless one. Lord Alfred Douglas wanted to destroy his father and was quite willing to use Oscar Wilde to do so. Wilde was dragged into the family squabble like a lamb to slaughter. His biographer writes, "The horror grew as Wilde found himself bandied between the father and son, the helpless pretext of their expressed enmity."

Oscar Wilde who had always walked on the sunny side was about to experience man's inhumanity to man. He was arrested and refused bail. His books were removed from stores; the theaters performing his plays closed their runs. While he was awaiting trial, all that he owned on Tite Street was put up for sale to satisfy his creditors. The mob trampled his home during the auction, pillaging, forcing doors and drawers for valuables. The press loathed Wilde; not a single article came to his defense. Wilde had said that "Modern journalism, by giving us the opinions of the uneducated, keeps us in touch with the ignorance of the community." There were 900 sermons preached against Wilde between 1895 and 1900. Even his tailor refused to make him a suit for the trial. Had he killed Lord Alfred Douglas rather than loved him, the public would have been less cruel.

Wilde's biographer writes that had he been a sparrow, his case never would have gone to trial but Wilde was an eagle. He refused to leave the country and was determined to stand trial. It opened on April 26, 1895. He confronted charges of 25 counts of "gross indecency." The jury's verdict appeared on the marquees where his plays had previously been performed: "Oscar Guilty! Sentence Two Years of Hard Labour!"

He served in the Reading Jail (or "Gaol"), where he was refused writing materials or books. His wife visited once but the sight of him in those conditions was too much; she never came back. Lord Alfred Douglas did not attend the trial nor visit Wilde in prison. Wilde's children were legally taken away from him. He came to the conclusion that there was no alternative but to accept the inevitable. His biographer wrote, "From then on, he bore up against adversity, facing each sorrow with a fortitude he had never known, as he strove to convert every blow that fell to spiritual experience."

In the past, his friends came to him to learn the pleasures of life and art. Now he would teach them the meaning of sorrow and pity. The only good thing left was the Paris opening of his play *Salome*. Sarah Bernhardt played the lead and the program had a lithograph of Wilde on the cover by Toulouse-Lautrec. Based on his prison experience he wrote *The Ballad of Reading Gaol*, perhaps the most moving ballad in Western literature. "He had attained the peak of his poetic achievement. Higher he could not go; there was no greater elevation."

Even after serving his time, there was no place for him in Victorian England. "The cruelty of a prison sentence starts when you come out," he said. He changed his name to Sebastian Melmoth and moved to France for the last three years of his life. He lived off the generosity of his friends but one by one they fell away. Every day was like another and all were full of nothingness. He seldom rose before mid-afternoon. Why hasten a day that no longer held anything for him? He had become a bloated caricature of his old handsome self. He was re-united with Lord Alfred Douglas for one night in Rouen, where they made plans to spend three months in Naples. But their love was spent; they never saw each other again.

His comforters were like Job's. Frank Harris wrote a two-volume Wilde biography and financially supported him until his death. He comforted Wilde by saying that his defense was pathological and not criminal. Wilde replied, "It is all ignorant prejudice, Frank; the world is slowly growing more tolerant and one day men will be ashamed of their barbarous treatment of me, as they are now ashamed of the torturing of the Middle Ages." His biographer wrote, "Had he changed his manner of life, reneged or equivocated, it would have meant his admission that such love was ignoble, whereas he maintained that it was not only noble, but more exalted than all other forms."

On his death bed, he was baptized into the Roman Catholic Church and received a Catholic burial. Long before, Wilde had said that Catholicism is the only religion to die in. He was buried in a small cemetery in France. Lord Alfred Douglas joined the small group that gathered there. His remains were later transferred to the famous Père Lachaise Cemetery in Paris. Five years ago we visited there, where Oscar enjoys the company of Isadora Duncan, Sarah Bernhardt, Gioachino Rossini, Victor Hugo, Balzac, Proust, Modigliani, and Jim Morrison. Visitors pay tribute to their favorite heroes and heroines but the most decorated tomb was that of Oscar Wilde.

This past February 14th, a stained glass window was dedicated to Wilde in the poets' corner of Westminster Abbey—finally admitting Wilde to the pantheon of English literature. The present Marquess of Queensberry joined in that Valentine's Day celebration that—100 years after the fact—accepted "the love that dare not speak its name." The room was so full and the passions so intense that it was difficult to separate the living from the dead. There was a U.S. Congressional delegation headed by Barney Frank, Gerry Studds and Steve Gunderson. Present were James Baldwin, Langston Hughes, Bayard Rustin, Tennessee Williams, Edward Albee, Gore Vidal, Gertrude Stein, May Sarton, Anne Sexton, Virginia Woolf, Cole Porter, Willa Cather, Allen Ginsberg, Lord Byron, Michelangelo, Walt Whitman and, of course, Lord Alfred Douglas. In their lapels they all wore sunflowers and a small pin. It read, "Be Thyself."

Delivered March 5, 1995, Third Unitarian Church of Chicago.

The Damnedest Radical

ast week you refused to respond to what I felt like was some good humor. So I was determined that we would enjoy ourselves today. Within 24 hours I saw two reviews of the same book and I took it as a sign from heaven. *The Damnedest Radical* is about "Chicago's celebrated social reformer, hobo king and whorehouse physician!" There is no question in my mind that Ben Reitman should have been a member of Third Church. I hope that he will inspire us to find his contemporaries and bring them into the fold.

Reitman was the most ardent champion of Chicago's underclass. He was Chicago's infamous clap doctor, who toiled as Al Capone's whorehouse physician. He befriended prostitutes, dope fiends, bohemians, con men, thieves and outcasts of all stripes. Let me titillate you by quoting just one paragraph from Roger Bruns's biography.

> As Reitman trekked through the bohemian and vice districts of Chicago, every policeman, panhandler and streetwalker called the old anarchist "doc." Like a mustachioed Mexican general reviewing his troops, Ben patrolled the streets, joking with the ladies, interrupting for a few minutes of conversation the booze-induced sleep of men bundled in newspaper on park benches, giving to almost everyone advice on sex, marriage, health and politics. Sporting the usual slouch hat, wild-colored necktie and large walking stick, Reitman radiated a kind of infectious enthusiasm that seemed somehow out of place among these people. He could make them laugh as no one else could.

Ben Reitman was born in St. Paul in 1879 to immigrant Russian Jews. His father was a peddler and left the family before Ben and his brother started school. They moved with their mother to Chicago when he was four, living in South Clark Street's red-light district. The young Ben ran errands for Carrie Watson, a well-known madam. Reitman claimed that he found more life, warmth and human compassion among the ladies of the joy houses than in any other segment of society. Later he wrote, "It did not appear to me that these girls were vicious or immoral. They were kind, sympathetic, generous—human." I remind the self-righteous among us what Jesus told the people of his day, "Truly, I say to you, that the tax collectors and the harlots go into the kingdom of God before you."

To help his mother, young Ben Reitman sold newspapers and shined shoes. As the only Jewish boy in an Irish neighborhood, he grew up with the nickname "Sheeny Ben." At the age of 11 he had his first encounter with the law. His biographer said that something about it "unleashed a great current" that filled him with a lifelong "interest in and identification with the outcasts." As a boy he chanced into a Presbyterian Church at State and 14th Streets, triggering a life-long association with Protestantism. He often carried a Bible and would teach Sunday school wherever invited to do so. He admitted that his unorthodox prayers included, "God, give me luck, and I will beat that fellow out of $200." Some had trouble reconciling his religion with his vulgarity, licentiousness, bohemianism, radicalism and anarchism. "My religious life may be a mystery to others, but to me it is perfectly clear," Reitman said. "They are mystified because—to them—religion is a piety, morality and inhibition. To me, religion is love and service."

Reitman's life changed at age 18, when he met two tramps at the railroad tracks near Clark and 18th Streets. Just as young Brits such as Winston Churchill ran off to sea, American boys like Jack London and Eugene O'Neill "took to the rails," seeking freedom and adventure. His life took another turn at age 21 in 1900. While working in a lab researching syphilis, a pathologist encouraged him to try medical school. He paid his way by selling stray dogs for medical dissections.

He was engaged twice while in medical school. He met the first girl while teaching Sunday School at Bethany Baptist Church. Tellingly, 20 minutes before that service, Reitman found himself "beaming into the jet-black eyes and fondling the soft hands of the minister's sister, a flirtatious beauty who was unaware that she was sitting with the imminent groom." In front of his mother, brother and fiancée's family, "Ben got as far as 'Do you Ben L. Reitman take . . . ,' then he went berserk. 'First I let out a wild yell that I [had] heard in an Indian Reservation in Arizona. This was followed by a correct imitation of drunken Buffalo Fat when he was trying to lick three men with one hand behind his back. Then I gave a sincere but perfect imitation of an elephant calling his mate . . .'" It all ended when "The bride knelt down and gave thanks to God that He had saved her from marrying a lunatic."

Soon after, Ben went through the full marriage ceremony with a maiden from the Immanuel Baptist Church, where he also taught Sunday school. The girl's family financed a honeymoon to Europe, where Reitman lost track of his bride. He never saw her again, although that union produced a daughter. Returning to Chicago, he graduated from the College of Physicians and Surgeons in May of 1905. He set up shop at 39th and Cottage Grove, across from Scotty's Gambling Parlor. His patients were prostitutes, pimps, dope addicts, and sexual perverts. His working hours were punctuated by frequent visits to Scotty's craps tables and much boozing and carousing. Still, he found time to teach a few classes at local medical colleges.

When even this life became too confining he would take to the rails or hop a cattle boat to Europe. He worked for a while with Buffalo Bill's Wild West Show in Paris, treating the circus boys who contracted venereal diseases. "About the only ones who didn't get the clap," he said, "were those who already had it." Reitman had a knack for timing. He was on a boat that docked in San Francisco the day the earthquake struck, with Reitman volunteering to provide medical relief. He then signed on as a doctor with the Southern Pacific Railroad, travelling to Mexico.

Dr. Reitman met one man and one woman who radically changed his life. In 1907 Reitman read a St. Louis newspaper ad inviting hobos to a meeting. The 300 who responded were invited to speak. Reitman said, "Friends, we ought to do something to stop the police and sheriffs from picking men up and sending them to jail for vagrancy." This impressed the meeting's host—Rev. James Eads How.

Rev. How was a Unitarian minister who graduated from our own Meadville Seminary in 1895 and then from the College of Physicians and Surgeons in 1908, followed by stints at Harvard and Oxford Universities. Rev. How founded the International Brotherhood Welfare Association to assist tramps, hobos and vagrants. He himself was born into wealth. His father was a vice president of the Wabash Railroad and his grandfather was the engineer who designed the Eads bridge—the first steel structure spanning the Mississippi River. The young How began revealing eccentricities in seminary. He lived in a barren room and sold his expensive clothes to give money to the poor. One Sunday he bought out all the newspapers from the newsboys so that they could attend Sunday school. When his father died, he gave his estate to the mayor of St. Louis to distribute to those who earned it—the poor. When his mother died and left a larger inheritance, he proceeded to give it away. He apparently had a lifelong income from tolls paid on the Eads Bridge. He used it to underwrite the International Brotherhood Welfare Association, earning the moniker "The Millionaire Hobo."

To serve itinerant and migrant workers he established "hobo colleges" in major American cities. Veterans of the tracks would gather in skid-row locations to hear lectures on philosophy, industrial law, politics and health. Although How was a socialist, his colleges were not so much political as cultural meeting centers where hobos could enjoy security and fellowship. How impressed Reitman, who said, "If America produced a Christ figure, it was he." Reitman left St. Louis to establish a hobo college in Chicago.

As a Sunday school teacher, Reitman must have known the banquet parable. Jesus said that when you give a banquet you shouldn't invite your friends, relatives or neighbors—lest they repay you. Instead, he preached, invite the poor, the maimed, the lame, and the blind and you will be blessed because they cannot repay you. To launch his Chicago hobo college in 1907, Reitman held a banquet at the Windsor-Clifton Hotel at Monroe and Wabash. Heeding his call were panhandlers, tramps and the lost, including Lazy Luke, Traveling Pete, Dirty Joe, and Peg Leg Wilson. The *New York Times* headline read, "Dining in State." The menu included Manhattan cocktails, boiled halibut, pommes parisienne, prime rib of beef au jus, brie, coffee and cigars. The Women's Christian Temperance Union criticized Reitman for serving hobos liquor. Ben's speech that night, titled "Kindness and No Red Tape," lambasted social agencies that made assistance contingent on conversion or some other insult. The host knew his guests. Reitman had been arrested 40 times for vagrancy, had stowed away at sea and knew the rejection of the respectable.

Reitman opened his college on Harrison Street. At least 500 wanderers arrived in the city each day, 75 percent of them men under the age of 21. Those who found their way to the college were reminded that they were human. The college sought to feed their intellect and prepare them for a hostile society. Ben arranged for speakers on philosophy, literature, art, religion, vagrancy laws and venereal diseases. The opera singer Mary Garden performed there. The Hobo College debated another south-side school—the University of Chicago. Pity the members of the University of Chicago debate team who had to face off against such masters of elocution, deduction, evasion and quick wit as Boxcar Bernie and Larry the Loud!

Soon, Reitman again gave into wanderlust—and lust. The next person to transform his life was Emma Goldman, who came to Chicago on a 1908 speaking tour. She, too, was born of Russian, Jewish parents. She had distinguished herself in the New York sweatshops as a woman who could voice the hurts and aspirations of the working class. She lectured across the United States and edited the anarchist magazine *Mother Earth*. She spoke against the need for laws and government, while endorsing free speech, women's rights and birth control. The editor of the St. Louis paper said, "She is a woman 8,000 years ahead of her time: vibrant, a font of ideas on arts . . . free from truculence and coarseness and swagger; holding out the vision of a noble humanity rescued from cant and tyranny and free from the restraints of convention, ceremony, gods, rulers and stifling institutions."

The Reitman-Goldman love affair could consume an entire sermon on this day after Valentine's Day. She was the Queen of Anarchy. She was 5'5" and weighed 140 pounds. She was a woman with a past; her many lovers included the revolutionary Alexander Berkman. Reitman heard her speak and left with her on the next train, becoming her manager and lover for the next 10 years. Goldman wrote Reitman what every straight man dreams of hearing from a woman,

> You have opened up the prison gates of my womanhood. And all the passion that was fettered and unsatisfied in me for so many years leaped into a wild reckless storm, boundless as the sea. I am famished, you hear, the woman in me is famished, what else is there for me to do? Where to hide? But to follow "the call" of the wild, the savage, the master lover.

Ron Dorman writes in his *Chicago Magazine* book review that Reitman introduced Goldman to the "wonders of cunnilingus and fellatio, apparently making her orgasmic for the first time." Although they crisscrossed the country for a decade, her home base was Greenwich Village, where their circle of intimates included Mabel Dodge, John Reed, Theodore Dreiser, Big Bill Haywood, Elizabeth Gurley Flynn and Walter Lippmann.

As World War I approached, it was increasingly difficult for Goldman to speak. President William H. Taft wrote his attorney general that she was headed for California with anarchists and other undesirables to set up a new government or no government at all. It wasn't simply her words and ideas. Emma Goldman embodied defiance and resistance. She was a:

symbol of resistance to hoary barriers, the archetype of modern womanhood! From open attacks on traditional family structure to her advocacy
of free love, from openly puffing on cigarettes with men in barrooms or
talking about contraceptives, Emma was the consummate rebel, personally taking on established customs at great risk. "Harlot," "devil,"
"alien," "traitor," the biting epithets from much of society followed, but
she brought new spirit to many who were tired of institutions that, like
the insufferable steel corsets, had for too long crushed American women.

In the end, Goldman proved to be too much for America. In the notorious
Palmer Raids, she and 247 other immigrants were deported to Russia in 1919.

Before Emma's deportation, Ben's wanderlust trumped his lust and he
hopped the rails back to Chicago. In 1917 he opened an office at Chicago Ave.
and Clark near Newberry Library. The following year a woman named Nina
Martindale bore his son Brutus. Ben and Nina remained together until her
death 12 years later. Ben spent his remaining 23 years in Chicago among his
people. Journalist Walter Lippmann said that the underworld "lives by performing the services which convention may condemn and the law prohibits
but which, nevertheless, human appetites crave." Dr. Reitman ministered to
many of the whorehouses owned by Al Capone. His patients ranged from Bed-
Bug Row to the opulence of the Everleigh Sisters, who ran a high-end whorehouse on South Dearborn. He led marches on behalf of the poor with Lucy
Parsons and Mother Jones. He held an Anti-Billy Sunday Rally, arguing that
the poor didn't need to hear about hell—since they already lived it.

Reitman believed that birth control was essential to the battle against poverty. It was not until 1936 that doctors were exempted from laws that prohib-
ited dissemination of birth-control information. It wasn't until 1965 that the
U.S. Supreme Court ruled that individuals have a privacy right to birth control. Reitman opened Chicago's first venereal disease clinic in 1917—20 years
before President Roosevelt authorized his surgeon general to launch a national
attack on syphilis. Reitman was fired as head of the Chicago Syphilis Project
for proposing that the government provide free condoms to all sexually active people (Walgreen's was raided as late as 1938 for illegally selling condoms).

Reitman was a stalwart of the Dill Pickle and Bug House Square. When I
came to the University of Chicago in 1955, Bug House was still operating near
the Newberry Library. Every night in good weather poets, evangelists, philosophers, politicians and plain nuts gathered to promote their ideas. The Dill

Pickle was founded by Jack Jones, the former spouse of Rebel Girl Elizabeth Gurley Flynn. Jones wanted all ideas, no matter how bizarre, to receive a respectable hearing. The Pickle was a melting pot for every fragment of Chicago society: tycoons, pickpockets, artists, hobos, professors, politicians, whores, labor organizers, and social workers. The clientele included Carl Sandburg, Sherwood Anderson, Edgar Lee Masters, Vachel Lindsay, Theodore Dreiser, Ring Lardner, Clarence Darrow, Harriet Monroe, Big Bill Haywood, and even Mae West. More than 700 people would sometimes jam the lecture hall. In the midst of it all, with a flowing cape, a walking cane, a fedora and Windsor tie was the irrepressible Dr. Reitman. Where in Chicago today can the editor meet the labor leader, the criminal meet the sociologist, and the minster meet the prostitute?

On a cold day in 1932, Reitman met Medina Oliver on the steps of the Art Institute, inviting her to warm her hands in his pockets. They married and had five daughters. One was born after his 1939 stroke and the last after his death at the age of 63 in 1942. He was buried at the Forest Park cemetery where Emma Goldman and the Haymarket Square martyrs lie. The 700 people attending his funeral ranged from hobos to academics. In keeping with his wishes, Chicago's hobos were treated to a free dinner afterwards. "Always a crusader," the *Christian Century* eulogized, "he made serious efforts to bring health to his footloose friends. He represented the type of philosopher that gives the sweet, intoxicating drink of hope to the weary, thirsty, starving pedestrian plodding down the dusty road of life."

Christianity preaches that we must leave the 99 who are safe in the fold to look for the one lost sheep. Judaism reminds us that we must remember when we ourselves were strangers in the land of Egypt. I never lose sight that our mission here is to the lost, to the stranger and to the least of our brethren. We have much to gain for ourselves if we make this a home to the misfit, the eccentric, the iconoclast and those on the fringes of society. Yes, we are a church. But we are also something of a British pub, a Dill Pickle, a Bohemian tea room in the Village, like Mabel Dodge's Salon. One reason we exist is to attract— and keep—the Ben Reitmans of Chicago.

Delivered February 15, 1987, Third Unitarian Church of Chicago.

The World According to Vonnegut

His paternal grandfather was a religious sceptic and Indiana's first licensed architect. His parents were married by Rev. Frank Wicks at the Unitarian Church in Indianapolis. He writes, "My ancestors, who came to the United States a little before the Civil War, were atheists. So I'm not rebelling against organized religion. I never had any. I learned my outrageous opinions about organized religion at my mother's knee." Also an Indianapolis architect, his father's life was deeply affected by two tragic events—serving in World War I and the Depression. "Part of the trick for people my age is to crawl out of the envying, life-hating mood of the Great Depression," he writes, "After I'm gone, I don't want my children to have to say about me what I have to say about my father: 'He made wonderful jokes but he was such an unhappy man.'"

Kurt Vonnegut Jr. was born in Indianapolis on November 11, 1922. The depression forced his parents to pull him out of private school. He says that his public school education made him who he is. "I was taught in the sixth grade to be proud that we had a standing army of just over a hundred thousand men and that the generals had nothing to say about what was done in Washington. I was taught to . . . pity Europe for having more than a million men under arms and spending all their money on airplanes and tanks. I simply never unlearned junior civics. I still believe it." Because of what he learned in Public School No. 43, he describes himself as a pacifist, an anarchist, and a planetary citizen.

He graduated from Shortridge High School, where he wrote for the school paper. He studied chemistry at Cornell University until he went off to World War II. When the war ended, he and his wife, Jane, moved with their first child to Chicago, where Vonnegut studied anthropology at the University of Chicago. There, he wrote short stories for *Collier's* and the *Saturday Evening Post*. He left without a degree but the University of Chicago later accepted his fifth novel, *Cat's Cradle*, as his dissertation.

Vonnegut did a stint in public relations for General Electric in Schenectady. That job shaped his skepticism toward scientists and technology—a prominent theme in his writing. A character in his first novel, *Player Piano*, says, "If only it weren't for the people, the goddamned people, always getting tangled up in machinery, if it weren't for them, earth would be an engineer's paradise." Another character says, "Anything a scientist worked on was sure to wind up as a weapon, one way or another." An admirer of George Orwell's *1984*, Vonnegut is similarly disillusioned about our scientific and technological future.

In contrast, Vonnegut's writings long for the Midwest of the 1920s and 1930s. "I have seen the past and it works!" this Hoosier wrote. Almost everything he wrote featured at least one character from Indianapolis. "Vonnegut writes as though the Midwest is the center of the earth," noted literary critic Alfred Kazin. I share Vonnegut's Midwestern bias.

Still, I admit that I have difficulty reading Vonnegut. My three children are much more comfortable with his novels then I am. He writes for a pop audience and, to me, his novels read like modern art looks or modern music sounds. But his two essay books, *Palm Sunday* and *Wampeters, Foma and Granfalloons*, took me inside the man and his philosophy.

The central event in this pacifist's life was his experience as a German prisoner during the Allied bombing of Dresden in World War II. He survived that saturation bombing by taking cover with others in a slaughterhouse. When they surfaced after the bombing, Dresden looked like the surface of the moon. From that day on he wrestled with how to describe to others a reality that exceeds human imagination—the reality of a Guernica, Hiroshima or Auschwitz. He feels a duty to try to describe the unimaginable so that we can comprehend the horrors of life in the 20th Century. "My wife begged me to bring you light, but there is no light," he told Bennington College's 1970 graduating class. "Everything is going to become unimaginably worse, and never get better again. If I lied to you about that, you would sense I'd lied to you, and that would be another cause for gloom. We have enough causes for gloom."

Because Dresden was a city of civilians with no tactical value, it was considered a "safe city." For this reason, its population had doubled through an influx of refugees and prisoners of war. On the night of February 13, 1944, however, 800 British RAF bombers attacked, leaving behind flames that could be seen for 200 miles. The next day, American B-17 Fortresses carried out a second raid, followed by P-51 Mustangs, pushing the estimated collective death toll to 200,000. The Allies didn't just burn Dresden; they melted it.

In Dresden, Vonnegut lost his innocence and confronted the absurdity of life. His novel *Slaughterhouse Five* tells about a schoolteacher who salvages a teapot from the bombing and is arrested for plundering. A society that condoned mass destruction executed a man for salvaging a pot from that destructive wreckage. "Being present at the destruction of Dresden affected my character far more than the death of my mother or the break-up of my marriage," Vonnegut writes.

Like Socrates, Vonnegut has been accused of poisoning the minds of youth. Oh, that he would poison more of them! "We don't need more information," he told Bennington graduates. "We don't need bigger brains. All that is required is that we become less selfish than we are . . . I suggest that you work for a Socialist form of government. Free enterprise is much too hard on the old and the sick and the shy and the poor and the stupid, and on people nobody likes. They just can't cut the mustard under Free Enterprise . . . So let's divide up the wealth more fairly than we have divided it up so far." Vonnegut is open about his political motivations. In a *Playboy* interview he agrees with Stalin and Hitler that the writer should serve his society. Vonnegut believes that he serves his, by being an agent of change—increasing the number of people who think of themselves as planetary citizens. "We will become influential," he told a writers' conference in Stockholm, "when those who have listened to our myths have become influential."

Vonnegut is sympathetic to those who cannot stand up to life and impatient with those who think that it is easy for people to get out of trouble. It goes against the American storytelling grain, he says, "to have someone in a situation he can't get out of, but I think this is very usual in life . . . It strikes me as gruesome and comical that in our culture we have an expectation that a man can always solve his problems."

Loneliness is another Vonnegut concern. "Any time I see a person fleeing from reason and into religion, I think to myself, 'There goes a person who simply cannot stand being so goddamned lonely anymore.'" Governments also capitalize on loneliness. "We're being kept apart from our neighbors. Why? Because the rich people can go on taking our money away if we don't hang together. They can go on taking our power away. They want us lonesome; they want us huddled in our houses with just our wives and kids, watching television, because they can manipulate us then . . . How did Americans beat the Great Depression? We banded together . . . Members of the unions called each other 'brother' and 'sister' . . . We're going to bring that spirit back!"

Vonnegut urged George McGovern to adopt the presidential campaign slogan, "Lonesome no more." He directed the president to issue everyone a new middle name through the Social Security system so that there will be 20,000 people who share each middle name. Each "family" of 20,000 will have its own directory and family magazine. Everyone will have relatives in shouting distance, helping them overcome hardships and loneliness so that we can share wealth and work more fairly.

Unitarians should take pride that "one of their own" is an internationally renowned writer. Vonnegut learned at his mother's knee that organized religion is anti-Christian. Like H. L. Mencken, he does not hate religious people— he simply finds them comical. He believes that the most ridiculous religious superstition is that humanity is at the center of the universe, that we fulfill or frustrate the grandest dreams of God Almighty. Vonnegut argues that we can accept our place in a universe without meaning or purpose, in a cosmos whose workings remain inscrutable, where "the ways of God are too mysterious" to discern. "Anyone with any sense knows that the whole solar system will go up like a celluloid collar by and by," he writes.

"I am, of course, a sceptic about the divinity of Christ and a scorner of the notion that there is a God who cares how we are or what we do," he says. In a world of change and chance, we all should embrace the words of his character, who says, "I was a victim of a series of accidents, as are we all." One of his novels introduces the "Church of God the Utterly Indifferent." Centered on an uncaring God, its motto is, "Take care of the people, and God Almighty will take care of himself."

"Death itself is a bad enough joke on us, but human schemes to get around it are worse," Vonnegut argues. He wishes that more of us were prepared early on for the trauma of confronting reality. "Why doesn't someone write to Creative Playthings to educate children not to expect peace and order but to learn that this is the kind of world where individuals are executed for stealing teapots by governments which have just burned alive 200,000 civilians?" When *Slaughterhouse Five's* Billy Pilgrim is struck for no reason by a German guard, he asks, "Why me?" The guard replies, "Vy you? Vy anybody?" This is the short answer to those who question the slings and arrows of outrageous fortune.

He suggests that we drop the word "religion" altogether since it has many bad connotations. An alternative could be a "heartfelt moral code" that teaches that anything that wounds the planet is evil and anything that heals or preserves it is good. "I do moralize," he says in an interview. "I tell young people not to take more than they need, not to be greedy. I tell them not to kill, even in self-defense. I tell them not to pollute water or the atmosphere. I tell them not to raid the public treasury. I tell them not to work for people who do these things . . . and to avoid getting involved in war crimes . . . and to be kind."

"Comedians and jazz musicians have been more comforting to me than the preachers or politicians or poets or painters or novelists of my time," Vonnegut writes. "Historians in the future, in my opinion, will congratulate us on very little other than our clowning and our jazz." He dedicates the novel *Slapstick* to Laurel and Hardy. Slapstick comedy recognizes that our limited agility and intelligence bungle the expectation that we will do our best. For Vonnegut, humor or laughter is the lubricant that keeps the machinery of society moving.

Naval regulations refer to the minor offense of "skylarking" as "an intolerable lack of seriousness." Vonnegut wishes that the Navy had dishonorably discharged him for recidivist skylarking! He skylarks about everything. He writes about: A woman who avoids prison by proving that everything she did was her parents' fault; A man who knowingly purchases a Cadillac that literally costs "an arm and a leg;" A woman happy that her broken washing machine gives her something to do; and a program that doles out a bathroom scale or table lamp to incentivize abortions. He writes of a new religion that foists handicaps on people to ensure that everyone is equal and nobody exploits others. Those with physical advantages are forced to carry weights. Others wear distorting glasses to curb superior vision. A man of extraordinary sex appeal is paired with a wife nauseated by sex.

In a book on Vonnegut, University of Minnesota professor Peter Reed writes: "The essential Vonnegut pattern is of an unheroic man who is a wanderer and prisoner in an absurd universe, a perpetual child dominated by forces he scarcely understands, shocked and stunned by incomprehensible horrors yet somehow finding happiness in moments of joy and love, and doggedly persisting in the effort to be a decent person, and to find meaning in existence."

Vonnegut would chide us for spending too much time on his ideas. His main thrust is to have us look inside ourselves for happiness and meaning. "It took us that long to realize that a purpose of human life (no matter who is controlling it) is to love whoever is around to be loved," a Vonnegut character observes. Vonnegut says this love is embodied by the volunteer fireman, who races to the rescue of anyone, without counting the cost or assessing the victim's wealth, esteem or worth. The volunteer fireman exemplifies "enthusiastic unselfishness." Vonnegut reminds us that we all must cherish the good moments in our lives. Let us close with a few of his favorite words.

"And so it goes! And so it goes!"

Delivered December 3, 1982, People's Church of Kalamazoo, Michigan.

Saint Margaret

The circumstances of her own birth in 1879 were appropriate for the one who led the world on birth control. Margaret Higgins Sanger was the 6th of 11 children born to a poor, unhappy Irish family in Corning, New York. Her mother died of tuberculosis in her 40s, requiring Margaret to drop out of school to look after the family. Margaret recalled that her mother's racking cough forced her to lean against the wall until a spasm stopped. Although her father was an avowed believer in women's rights, there was nothing in his lifestyle to suggest that a man might "wash a dish." His consumptive, everlastingly pregnant wife had to feed and clothe the family, even as her financial management kept the wolf from the door.

Nonetheless, Margaret Higgins Sanger idealized her father, calling him the spring from which she drank. He made a living carving tombstones and was a free-thinking socialist who sponsored the visits of the progressives Robert Ingersoll and Henry George to his conservative Irish Catholic community. His children suffered the scorn and rejection of classmates, who called them "children of the devil." Her father told her, "The one thing I've been able to give you is a free mind. Use it well and give something back to your generation." After her mother's death, Margaret completed a nursing course at White Plains Hospital.

About this time she met and married the architect Bill Sanger, entering what she called with condescending amusement her "suburban interlude." I will deal with this further in closing, but from her youth Sanger longed to live a respectable, middle-class life. The couple bought an acre of land and built their dream home. In their first night there, it caught on fire and burned down. They eventually moved to Manhattan and involved themselves in the social and political life of Greenwich Village. In this Golden Age of radicalism, they associated with Eugene Debs, John Reed, Emma Goldman, Alexander Berkman, Bill Haywood, Max Eastman, Elizabeth Gurley Flynn, and Mabel Dodge. There were now three Sanger children: Stuart, Grant, and Peggy.

But Margaret was longing for a personal destiny of her own. Her husband and father were theoretical socialists; she longed for direct action. She became a nurse, as well as a reporter for the socialist magazine, *The Call.* Her articles on venereal diseases prompted the U.S. Post Office to seize the magazine. Her nursing on the lower East Side brought her into contact with ignorance, poverty, and despair.

One stifling day in mid-July 1912, Margaret was summoned to a Grand Street tenement. Her patient was a thin, Russian-Jew, Mrs. Sadie Sachs, twenty-eight and the mother of three tiny children; her husband, Jake, a truck driver, had come home to find the babies crying and his wife unconscious after a self-induced abortion. Jake had called the doctor, who sent for Margaret. She spent three weeks nursing Mrs. Sachs, in midsummer, in a cold-water flat, with every necessity for comfort and sanitation hauled up and down several flights of tenement stairs, before the patient was out of danger. "Another baby will finish me I suppose?" Mrs. Sachs asked Margaret. Margaret turned to the doctor, "a kindly man, and he had worked hard to save her, but such incidents had become so familiar to him that he . . . laughed good-naturedly," and told Mrs. Sachs to make her husband sleep on the roof. When the doctor had gone Mrs. Sachs turned to Margaret, lifted her thin, blue-veined hands and clasped them beseechingly. "He can't understand. He's only a man. But you do, don't you? Please tell me the secret, and I'll never breathe it to a soul. Please!"

But there was no secret, Margaret claimed, at least none that she knew. Three months later she was called again to the Sachs home; another abortion, the young mother in a coma, the husband sobbing. It was all over within minutes this time. Margaret pulled a sheet over the pale face and went home: "As I stood there the darkness faded. The sun came up and threw its reflection over the house tops. It was the dawn of a new day in my life also. The doubt and the questioning, the experimenting and trying, were now to be put behind me. I knew I could not go back merely to keeping people alive. I went to bed knowing that no matter what it might cost, I was finished with palliatives and superficial cures. I was resolved to seek out the root of evil, to do something to change the destiny of mothers whose miseries were as vast as the sky."

Day after day, women begged Sanger for the secret that rich women used to prevent pregnancies. The case of Sadie Sachs was to change the life of Margaret—and the world. As one biographer writes, "She gave that movement nearly all her productive years. To it she would sacrifice her marriage, and, she may have felt, the life of one of her children."

Compromising between her marriage and new independence, the family took a 1913 trip to Europe, where Bill could paint and Margaret could study "the secret." While Bill painted on the Left Bank and met Matisse and Monet, Margaret learned that there were no legal restraints against birth control or even abortion. The poorest French families tended to be small, so each child had a full share of parental love and affection. Bill wanted to stay in France but Margaret returned to teach slum women to escape the shackles of involuntary motherhood. She did so through a monthly paper called *The Woman Rebel*. It shocked and defied marriage conventions, established religion, and law and order. The Post Office deemed it unfit for the mail. Rather than stand trial, she fled to Europe under the assumed name Bertha Wilson. There, Sanger met Havelock Ellis. They corresponded as long as he lived, and may have become partners but for the fact that "each had work that was far more important than any personal life." On that trip she visited Holland, where the first birth-control clinics were established in 1878 and where the diaphragm pessary device was perfected.

Soon after returning from Europe, her 5-year-old daughter, Peggy, died a death that caused her guilt and grief. She threw herself into her trial, which "presented the anomaly of a prosecutor loathe to prosecute and a defendant anxious to be tried." Liberal newspapers joined radical ones in her corner and socially prominent women began to back her. The night before her trial, 200 guests honored her, including journalist Water Lippmann. The case was dismissed. With birth control a free-speech issue no longer, Sanger began to establish birth-control clinics, evolving from a rebel to a heroine. She launched a national lecture tour, proclaiming "the first right of every child is to be wanted." "It was as if she had been more or less arbitrarily chosen by the powers that be to introduce the new gospel of not only sex knowledge in regard to conception, but sex knowledge about copulation and its intrinsic importance," recalled Mabel Dodge.

She was the first person I ever knew who was openly an ardent propagandist for the joys of the flesh. This, in those days, was radical indeed

... she told us all about the possibilities in the body for 'sex expression' and as she sat there, serene and quiet, and unfolded the mysteries and mightiness of physical love, it seemed to us we had never known it before as a sacred, and at the same time, a scientific reality.

In contrast to Elizabeth Gurley Flynn, who harangued audiences, Margaret was a small, pretty woman of refinement. The Reverend John Haynes Holmes said, "She had the power of a saint." When she was arrested in Portland for planning to start a clinic, she was followed to the jail by hundreds of local women, forcing the police to lock the jail doors—to keep them out.

Returning to New York, she was ready to open her own clinic with her sister Ethel. They found a place at 46 Amboy Street in the Brownsville section of Brooklyn. She sent out 5,000 announcements in English, Italian and Yiddish. When the doors opened in October 1916, Sanger wrote, "Halfway to the corner they were standing in line, at least 150, some shawled, some hatless, their red hands clasping the cold, chapped, smaller ones of their children." Nine days later the police raided. Margaret and her sister refused to ride in the patrol wagon, marching behind it to the Raymond Street jail. When her sister admitted distributing birth-control information, she was sentenced to 30 days in a workhouse. Ethel went on a hunger strike but soon was pardoned through gubernatorial contacts.

Margaret's separate trial was attended by 50 of her clinic clients, as well as by New York society leaders. Rows of limos lined up outside the court. Margaret entered the court carrying an armful of red American Beauty roses. The law stipulated that physicians could provide birth-control information for "the prevention of disease," which was understood to mean venereal disease. The appeals court was unwilling to interpret it broadly to allow physicians to lawfully provide birth-control information to married women for the sake of their health. She informed the judge that she could not honor the law and received a sentence of 30 days in the workhouse. When her time was up, a group of cronies awaited outside singing the Marseilles—with the women in the jail joining in. To give you an idea of Sanger's fame, a British professor wishing to congratulate her on her release, addressed his well wishes to "Saint Margaret, New York."

Soon there were two dozen birth-control clinics in the country. Sanger began to grasp the larger implication of the birth-control movement—eugenics, world famine, delinquency, and overpopulation. Just as she was making her peace with the law, the Roman Catholic Church intervened. The arch-bishop "ordered" police to close a lecture hall to prevent her from discussing indecent and immoral subjects. Again, Sanger marched to the police station behind the paddy wagon. The case was dismissed and the press criticized the church's interference. The archbishop responded that,

> The seventh child has been regarded traditionally by some people as the most favored by nature. Benjamin Franklin was the 15th child and John Wesley the 18th. It has been suggested that the lack of genius in our day is that we are not getting the end of families.

Sanger retorted that Isaac was an only child, as were Samuel and John the Bap-tist. She remained so repulsed by Catholicism that at the age of 80 she threat-ened to leave the country if John Kennedy were elected.

Her divorce was finalized at this time and she rallied an international movement for an upcoming conference on world population. In 1922 she vis-ited Japan, where she granted 500 interviews. Her message resonated less in the Soviet Union, where the expanding economy demanded workers. She de-livered 60 lectures in India. Although she was unable to enlist Gandhi's sup-port, she planted seeds that helped launch India's program to limit its popula-tion. Meanwhile, the American Medical Association broke its long silence on contraception, announcing that physicians had a legal right to provide con-traceptives and those techniques should be taught in medical schools. In 1949, Smith College honored itself and Sanger with an honorary doctorate. But the ultimate triumph was yet to come. Dr. Margaret Sanger, accompanied by the widow of the youngest son of industrialist Cyrus McCormick, called on Dr. John Rock to guarantee that Catholic physician sufficient funds to develop an oral contraceptive. Dr. Rock wrote, "There was no government support, no foundation support. There was nothing but Margret Sanger's influence on a sympathetic lady with plenty of money."

I'd like to close with three observations about Sanger. First, she suffered continual conflict between her desire to have a private life and a public life. Her earliest desire was to wear perfume and promenade with her husband and children in the evening. She once spoke of a kind of "world hunger" for accomplishment and to live at the center of things. "Where is the man, she once asked, to give me what the movement gives, in joy, in interest, in free-dom?" A biographer wrote that she never had a normal family life. "The movement took precedence over all personal claims. It was by her own confession her first thought upon waking every morning and her last thought before she fell asleep at night." I have not spoken of her second marriage to Noah Slee, a wealthy businessman, who gave her everything she had dreamed of as a child in poverty—respectability and a 100-acre estate in Dutchess County. But she was as much an outsider to that world as she was growing up. Sanger exemplifies many who give themselves to social change, sacrificing a private life for a just cause.

Second, biographer Joan Dash wrote, "She was, of course, a fanatic." No one could have accomplished what she did without becoming a rebel, a crusader, a fanatic, a saint. One dominant desire obsessed her. She centered her life around a single-minded goal. I do not find such people especially interesting, but Sanger convinced me that this is the only kind of dedication that transforms society. Her biographer writes of Sanger's second husband, "Margaret had purposely chosen to marry a man whose professed wishes she could ignore, and to live instead a life whose chief rewards came from hard work in the service of others." Let the fanatic speak for herself:

Some lives drift here and there like reeds in a stream, depending on changing currents for their activity. Others are like swimmers knowing the depth of the water. Each stroke helps them onward to a definite objective. As I look back upon my life, I see that every part of it was preparation for the next. The most trivial of incidents fit into the larger pattern like a mosaic in a preconceived design. When once I believed in doing a thing, nothing could prevent my doing it.

Finally, what shall we say of her dream? She died at age 87 in Tucson in 1966. Her *Time Magazine* obituary said, "When she died last week, her vision had been realized beyond her dreams." Her vision was that every child would be a wanted child. After Sadie Sachs died, she had determined that, "I was finished with palliatives and superficial cures; I was resolved to seek out the root of evil, to do something to change the destiny of mothers whose miseries were as vast as the sky."

Observing the contrast between the small, rich families living on the hillsides and the crowded homes of the poor huddled on the river flats, she said,

The fathers of the small families owned their homes; the young mothers had time to play croquet with their husbands in the evening on the smooth lawns. Their clothes had style and charm and the fragrance of perfume clung about them.

She really believed that family planning and birth control would enable the poor to give their children more than they had. "Tell me the secret," Sadie Sachs pleaded. Sanger set that secret free. I wonder if another Margaret Sanger waits in the wings, with a fanatical vision to further mobilize parents—as world citizens—to recognize that our earth is not large enough—even for every wanted child!

Delivered March 15, 1981, Third Unitarian Church of Chicago.

H. L. Mencken

At age nine he discovered "Huckleberry Finn," which he later called, "The stupendous event of my whole life." It triggered a fascination with words, reading, and writing. His father died when he was 18. The day after burial, the son applied to work with one of Baltimore's daily papers. By 25 he was editor in chief of the *Baltimore Herald*, then the youngest person to ever hold such a post with a metropolitan paper. For 40 years, he wrote for the *Baltimore Sun*, published 30 books, wrote 100,000 letters (he regarded the telephone as a contrivance of the devil and felt obliged to answer any letter within 24 hours). He wrote the definitive book on American English, marking its separation from British English. He founded two magazines: *The Smart Set* and *American Mercury*. His heroes were George Bernard Shaw and Frederick Nietzsche. His closest friends were Theodore Dreiser and Sinclair Lewis. He was a man born at the right time to be at odds with his time. He was at his height during the 1920s, ridiculing Prohibition, the Scopes Trial, the Bible Belt, and Harding and Coolidge.

Like Third Church, Henry Louis Mencken had numerous faults. But he also had four virtues that we should covet. He was skeptical, irreverent, nonconforming, and funny.

The skeptical Mencken was always asking impertinent questions. He wrote, "The art of thinking must be a relatively recent acquirement. It was not until skepticism arose in the world that genuine intelligence dawned. When that happened no one knows, but it was probably not more than ten thousand years ago." He adds,

> I'd certainly like to know if it can be found out, who was the first person to doubt the magic of priests, and likewise who was the first to note the vanity of all so-called 'philosophical speculation.' These fellows were enormous benefactors of mankind, they were the real beget-

ters of everything properly describable as sound information and rational thinking.

H. L. Mencken made it fashionable to be a skeptic in America.

"Moral certainty is always a sign of cultural inferiority," Mencken said.

The more uncivilized the man the surer he is that he knows precisely what is right and what is wrong. All human progress, even in morals, has been the work of men who have doubted the current moral values, not of men who have whooped them up and tried to enforce them. The truly civilized man is always skeptical and tolerant in this field as in all others. His culture is based on: "I am not too sure."

Although not a pacifist, Mencken opposed World War I and World War II. What he hated about war was that it always became a moral crusade. "The worst government is the most moral of all," he wrote. "One composed of cynics is often very tolerant and humane. But when fanatics are on top, there is no limit to oppression."

Mencken held to a tragic sense of life. He was too much of a cynic to believe that life could be understood. He was attracted to the fiction of Theodore Dreiser and Edith Wharton because they did not offer simple solutions. He was hardest on those writers, politicians, and theologians who professed to have the answers. He liked people who appreciated human existence as a seeking, without a finding. Dreiser saw the struggle of man as gratuitous and purposeless. There is no grand ingenuity, no moral order in the universe. Man is not only doomed to defeat, but denied any glimpse or understanding of his antagonist. He quoted art critic John Ruskin, "To see truly, is to see dimly," and agreed with Joseph Conrad that the experience of life passes all understanding. Skepticism led him to attack everything that reeked of phoniness, fraud, piety or hypocrisy. He coined the word "balderdash," using it interchangeably with "blather."

He believed that the world would never be decent until we got rid of religion. He wrote, "My objection to religion is that it represents an effort by ignorance to account for a mystery that knowledge simply puts aside as intrinsically impenetrable. The more ignorant the man, the more firm his faith." "If medicine had remained as backward as religion, the doctors would still believe in humoral pathology and their chief remedial agent would be blood-letting." Mencken believed that God is the immemorial refuge of the incompetent, the helpless and the miserable. It was not bad that they found refuge but that this made them self-righteous, setting themselves above others. It was the arrogance, audacity, and self-righteousness of "the religious" that inspired Mencken's vehement attacks. "No one knows who created the visible universe and it is infinitely improbable that anything properly described as evidence on the point will ever be discovered," he wrote. "No one knows what motives or intentions, if any, lie behind what we call natural laws. No one knows why sin and suffering were sent into this world, that is, why the fashioning of man was so badly botched." He equated all religion with astrology and palmistry. But he especially despised the Protestant majority for engendering Prohibition, blue laws, and the censorship of the 1920s. "I have never been to a Jewish home that didn't serve good grub," he observed, "I have never known a Jewish prohibitionist."

One biographer wrote that Mencken put an end to society's hush-hush attitude toward the president, bishops, professors and business executives. He treated them all as human beings with human foibles and prejudices. He enjoyed observing pillars of society the way that others enjoy watching animals at the zoo. He said that the then-Pope looked like a truck driver suffering from varicose veins and hemorrhoids. He said that if you turned President Herbert Hoover upside down, he would look just the same. Mencken said that "a Galileo could no more be elected president of the United States than he could be elected Pope. Both high posts are reserved for men favored by an extraordinary genius for swathing the bitter facts of life in bandages and soft illusion." On the other hand, he respected President Grover Cleveland because he admitted to fathering an illegitimate child.

Like the chicken and egg, it's unclear if the politicians and priests created the dependency of the masses or if people's dependency creates a need for heroes and demagogues. Mencken created the word "booboise" for those who refuse to think for themselves and who swallow the blather and balderdash of their leaders. He felt that the man on the street was as incapable of deciding governmental questions as he was of deciding questions of medicine. Rather than letting a majority of non-thinking people elect the president, Mencken believed it would be far more intelligent to elect the candidate chosen by the least number of people since the minority usually is right. He points out that the "booboise" rejected such great artists as Dante, Goethe, Cervantes, Swift, Molière, Pope, Thackeray and Balzac.

Mencken's only hope was cultivating people who could think for themselves. "The government of Harding and Coolidge was not based on force," he wrote, but depended "upon the credulity of man quite as much as upon his docility. Its aim is not merely to make him obey, but also to make him want to obey." "The capacity of human beings to believe the obviously not true is apparently almost unlimited," he added. "Politicians fall into trouble, not by overestimating it, but by underestimating it." Early in life, Mencken seemed to look inside himself—not to others—for direction and ideas. He wrote, "In a country of pushers and yearners, what a joy it is to meet a man who envies no one and wants to be nothing he is not." He says elsewhere that he has an incapacity for envy. Such a man is not likely to fall for a demagogue, to take anyone else's truth on authority, or need a hero to emulate.

H. L. Mencken believed that life should be enjoyed. He defined Puritanism as, "the haunting fear that someone somewhere may be having a good time." In that vein he wrote that it was "a dull dark depressing day in winter; the whole world looks like a Methodist Church at Wednesday night prayer meeting." He said that "the chief contribution of Protestantism to human thought is its massive proof that God is a bore." He never forgave Bible Belt Christians for imposing 13 years of Prohibition.

Mencken felt that good eating and good drinking was an essential part of life. Describing this appetite, his biographer wrote,

> Then he would have half dozen bratwursts or several slices of pot roast or a dozen small sausages, with one big or two small boiled potatoes and a green vegetable on the side, all coaxed down with several slices of bread and a tall beer. Then a big piece of cheesecake, a cup of coffee and then he would start on his serious drinking for the night, usually amounting to 4 or 5 large beers. If he were questioned, be would say, "Poof! Food never hurt anyone, but only if it's washed down with liquor. Most of the so called trouble from overeating comes from under drinking."

Mencken appreciated anyone who could out-eat and outdrink him. He scorned President Taft's intellect but admired his bulk. He despised the lean look of

Woodrow Wilson. In addition to eating and drinking, he valued companionship around the table. He was fond of the German proverb, "A man is seldom better than his conversation." This exuberance came through in Mencken's writing. Walter Lippmann said of his style,

> When you can explain the heightening effect of a spirited horse, of a swift athlete, of a dancer really in control of his body, when you can explain why when watching them you feel more alive yourself, then you can explain the quality of Mencken's journalistic influence.

He loved to play practical jokes on friends and for them to reciprocate. He would subscribe to Southern Baptist periodicals on behalf of atheist friends, ask a Bahá'í priest to call on them, or send in their names to the prohibition society. He said, "Mirth is necessary to wisdom, to comfort, above all to happiness." This seemed self-evident to him but it also seemed to him as though there was some kind of conspiracy against happiness in life. You can't blame it all on the Baptists. "People make themselves unhappy," he said. "They store away opportunities for happiness the way they save money to spend some other time, and then die not spending it, not happy. It seems that people are afraid to be happy."

Mencken believed that the secret is that a "man who can laugh at himself is never really miserable." Even tackling serious matters, Mencken's style and vocabulary made his writing fun. It was H. L. Mencken who said, "Conscience is the inner voice which warns us that someone may be looking." It was Mencken who said, "How little it takes to make life unbearable, a pebble in a shoe, a cockroach in the spaghetti, a woman's laugh." He defined marriage "as being the most sanitary and least harmful of all the impossible forms of the man-woman relationship." He told a biographer, "You can say anything about me that you please, but that I was a Christian."

I hope that nine-year-olds keep reading *Huckleberry Finn* and acquire the insight to be skeptical, irreverent, non-conformist, and humorous. I leave the last words to Mencken, who wrote his own epitaph. "If, after I depart this vale, you ever remember me, and have thought to please my ghost, forgive some sinner and wink your eye at some homely girl."

September 21, 1980, Third Unitarian Church of Chicago.

Scoundrel Time

Born in 1906, she split her childhood between New Orleans and New York City. She quit college in her junior year. The only degrees she received were honorary. Her first and only marriage was to a Schubert Theaters press agent, who introduced her to her eventual career. That marriage began in New York City and ended eight years later in divorce in Hollywood. There she met Dashiell Hammett, the detective story writer, who created the "The Thin Man" series. Though they never married, their intimate relationship lasted from 1930 until his death in 1961. Her relationship with Dashiell Hammett and life-long friendship with Dorothy Parker led to her most crucial hour—appearing before the House Un-American Activities Committee on May 21, 1952.

Lillian Hellman tells her story in her new book *Scoundrel Time*, a title taken from a line in the book: "Truth made you a traitor as it often does in a time of scoundrels." Hellman is one of America's leading playwrights—only Arthur Miller and Tennessee Williams are in her league. Her career began with the opening of *The Children's Hour* in 1934, followed by 12 plays, including *The Little Foxes*, *Watch on the Rhine*, *Another Part of the Forest*, and *Toys in the Attic*. As early as 1940, her name was associated with two labels: "successful playwright" and "fellow traveler." Like many Americans, she was radicalized by the Spanish Civil War. Yet Hellman was never as political as Dorothy Parker or Dashiell Hammett, who joined the Communist Party in the late 1930s.

In his introduction to Hellman's book, historian Garry Wills reminds us that the McCarthy era predated Joseph McCarthy's inquisition. The first Attorney General's List of Subversive Organizations was compiled by President Truman, Attorney General Tom Clark, and J. Edgar Hoover in 1947 to implement loyalty oaths for government employees. It was a checklist to screen federal employees. Membership in any of the suspect groups would spur an investigation about a person's job fitness. This was expanded beyond formal membership to rope in anyone who attended meetings of an organization branded as "un-American" or who gave them money. By 1949, when the Soviet Union tested its first atomic bomb and Chairman Mao declared victory in China, the State Department had fired employees for nothing more than stating the fact that Chiang Kai-shek was losing. In 1950 the Korean War began, Alger Hiss was convicted on Soviet-spy perjury charges, and McCarthy levied his first accusations. The following year, Julius and Ethel Rosenberg were condemned to death for Soviet espionage.

Hellman writes that there was no communist menace in America at that time but some people "needed to believe" there was. Michigan Senator Arthur Vandenberg told President Truman that to get a massive foreign-aid program through Congress he needed to scare the hell out of people. Hellman argues that some people embraced anti-communism as a way to undermine remnants of the New Deal. People used it to settle scores or further their own careers. Others correctly understood that communism would deprive them of their wealth. Against this background, the radical was portrayed as an immoral threat who deserved prison or execution. Hellman writes,

> If Whittaker Chambers was capable of thinking up a pumpkin [as the ludicrous hiding place where this informant claimed that he stashed government secrets supplied by State Department official Alger Hiss] . . . Mr. Nixon seized upon this strange hiding place with the eagerness of a man who already felt deep contempt for public intelligence. And he was right.

As with many novelties, California pioneered civilian loyalty testing when the House Un-American Activities Committee held hearings on Hollywood notables in 1947. Hellman recalls that each studio asked its employees to sign affidavits swearing that they were not Communists, did not associate with radicals, and that if they had supported suspect organizations in the past, that they would not repeat the mistake. She writes,

> I don't think the heads of movie companies, and the men they appointed to run the studios, had ever before thought of themselves as American citizens with inherited rights and obligations. Many of them had been born in foreign lands and had inherited foreign fears.

Columbia Pictures President Harry Cohn presented Hellman with a new script-writing contract containing a loyalty clause. It demanded that nothing she believed, acted upon, contributed to, or associated with could conflict with what the studio wanted. She refused to sign, exiling her from Hollywood for 16 years.

In a new round of Hollywood hearings in March 1951, Dashiell Hammett—with whom Hellman had been living for 20 years—was sent to jail for contempt. He refused to name the contributors to a "civil rights congress bail fund" on the Attorney General's list. While he served six months in jail, the IRS discovered that Hammett owed $100,000 in back taxes. Hellman knew her time was coming. A state senator had compiled a list of those who allegedly followed or supported Communist Party programs, including the names Pearl Buck, Charlie Chaplin, Dorothy Parker, Danny Kaye, Katharine Hepburn, and Lillian Hellman. When her summons arrived, she sought the counsel of future Supreme Court Justice Abe Fortas. Fortas had a hunch that the time had come for somebody to waive the Fifth Amendment and to tell the witch hunters, "I will testify about myself, answer all your questions about my own life, but I will not tell you about anybody else, stranger or friend."

Fortas was defending Owen Lattimore at the time and referred Hellman to Joseph Rauh. He wanted her to defend herself by pointing out that the Communist press had criticized her. Hellman believed that this played the enemy's game by attacking communists at a time when they were being persecuted. "In my thin morality book, it is plain not cricket to clear yourself by jumping on people who are themselves in trouble." Instead she wrote the committee, staking out her position that she would not inform on others.

On May 21 she testified before the House Un-American Activities Committee for 37 minutes. As her letter was read into the transcript, an unknown voice came to her from the press gallery saying, "Thank God, somebody finally had the guts to do it." Looking back, Hellman writes, "It is never wise to say that something is the minute of your life, but I still think that unknown voice made the words, that helped to save me." "I will not and cannot cut my conscience to fit this year's fashions," she testified. Although the committee dismissed Hellman soon thereafter, the IRS soon found that she was tax delinquent. She was forced to sell her farm in Pleasantville, New York, which had been her refuge from the tensions and pressures of life. Forced to sell quickly, she received a fraction of what it was worth. Still, she and Hammett refused to sell to a subdivision developer. Hammett said, "Let everybody else mess up the land, why don't you and I leave it alone."

Lillian Hellman, who had made $140,000 a year, took a half-day job in a department store under an assumed name. "I was in the grocery department and that was not unpleasant, but I kept it a secret because I knew it would worry Hammett." "Nothing was as it had been, but because it had been so bad, small things seemed better than ever, the occasional rental of a catboat for a day's sail, a canoe for the pond, a secondhand car."

Hammett and Dorothy Parker both died within a short time. Hellman writes of her 30-year relationship with Hammett,

> I know as little about the nature of romantic love as I knew when I was 18. But I do know about the deep pleasure of continuing interest, the excitement of wanting to know what someone else thinks, will do, will not do, the tricks played and unplayed, the short cord that the years make into a rope and in my case, is there hanging loose, long after death.

What I have said so far is not proper sermon material. A sermon causes you to look internally, to analyze your values, and to assess the direction your life is moving. As James Baldwin said in our opening words, "The hope of the world lies in what one demands, not of others, but of oneself." I have chosen Lillian Hellman's story because she exemplifies what private honor looks like in a rotten world.

Garry Wills writes that a popular image of a radical is of a wild, irresponsible bomb thrower.

> But most radicals I have met were extraordinarily civil. They oppose the general degradation, not with a programmatic solution, but with a personal code that makes pride possible in a shameful social order. They do not wish to be implicated in responsibility for society's crimes, which means that they must take a special kind of responsibility for their own acts.

Lillian Hellman was not an overtly political person. She embraced no particular ideology; she simply had a personal code of honor and decency. She was a rare, clean, and upright person, Garry Wills said. She had admiration for every kind of excellence, self-discipline, loyalty, and the determination never to injure others. She attributed her philosophy to Southern individualism. In 1964, she wrote that so much of her had been "molded to last for good" by the black woman who had looked after her as a child. Sophronia was an angry woman and she gave me anger, an uncomfortable, dangerous and often useful gift.

Hellman paid a heavy price for standing up to the Un-American Activities Committee. "My belief in liberals was mostly gone, I think I have substituted for it something private, called, for want of something that should be more accurate, decency." She watched Robert Taylor, Larry Parks, Elia Kazan, José Ferrer, Clifford Odets, Charles Laughton, and Edward G. Robinson recant all they had stood for to cooperate with the committee. She saw men who were cowards become liars, saving themselves at the expense of others. Odets told her the night before his testimony that he would not cooperate, but the loss of a swimming pool or tennis court proved too much to many people. Kazan told Hellman that it was easy for her to resist because she had little money left to lose. When Charles Laughton received a notice of the death of his friend Bertolt Brecht, he went so far as to call the FBI to inform them that he didn't request the death notification, so it should not be counted against him.

Hellman found herself betrayed by both liberals and intellectuals.

> I had up until the 1940s believed that the educated, the intellectual, lived by what they claimed to believe: freedom of thought and speech, the right of each man to his own conviction, a more than implied promise, therefore, of aid to those who might be persecuted. Almost all, either by what they did or did not do, contributed to McCarthyism, running after a band wagon which hadn't bothered to stop to pick them up. In every civilized country, people have always come forward to defend those in political trouble. Certainly the good magazines, the ones that published the most serious writers, should have come to the aid of those who were persecuted. *Partisan Review*, which had through the years published many pieces protesting the punishment of dissidents in Eastern Europe, made no protest when people in this country were jailed or ruined. In fact it never took an editorial position against McCarthy himself. *Commentary* didn't do anything. No editor or contributor ever protested against McCarthy.

What it all boiled down to was that those who had made it were determined to keep it at any cost, and this included liberals and intellectuals. Hellman discovered that the liberal and the intellectual do not necessarily have a personal code of honor and decency. I am talking about our own personal lives, about developing something private that Hellman called "decency." How do we as parents, as Unitarians, raise up a generation of children who will be unable to cut their consciences to fit this year's fashions? The hope of the world lies in what we demand of ourselves. We must not be implicated in society's crimes. We must have private honor—a personal decency. It must be wretched to grow old and not be able to look back on a time when your private code of honor clashed with the world's rotten standards and you confronted it, standing firm. Hellman showed us what it takes to live our finest hour.

Delivered May 16, 1976, Third Unitarian Church of Chicago.

Lenny Bruce

A new Broadway play opened last May, written by Julian Barry and directed by Thomas O'Horgan, who directed the rock musical *Hair*. The opening scene resembles an American Indian pow-pow, in which each member of the tribe is asked to give up something for the Lord. Each tries to outdo the other's sacrifices. Finally, they all are surpassed by a man who offers to give up something that can't be mentioned. The scene suggests that—sometime in the history of religion—zealous worshippers went too far, associating the natural enjoyment of sex with evil.

This new play, *Lenny*, is about nightclub entertainer Lenny Bruce. He was one of the few bright spots in America during the 1950s, when President Eisenhower and Joe McCarthy held sway over a sleepy American public. Lenny tried to wake us up. He was the first entertainer who dared to talk in public the way he talked in private. As he put it, "I have the right to talk in night clubs the way corporation vice presidents talk in their living rooms and board rooms."

Comedians before Lenny had gone after people who were skinny, fat, bald, deaf, or blind. Jerry Lewis imitated a buck-toothed Japanese; Milton Berle portrayed a transvestite. But Lenny lampooned the spiritual bankruptcy of organized religion, the chasm between love and marriage—and between lawyers and the law. He made jokes about white liberals. He questioned the sanctity of the American Medical Association and of motherhood. He had the audacity to tell veterans that we are hated overseas for what they had done to Asian and European women in exchange for chocolate bars. Defending Adolf Eichmann at the height of his Nuremberg trial, he asked American audiences if they felt superior because they could use long-range missiles to incinerate their enemies sight unseen. He made appeals to spare the lives of Eichmann and Caryl Chessman, the "red-light bandit," whom California sent to the gas chamber in 1960 for armed robberies and sexual assaults. Lenny said supporters of capital punishment believe that, "I am so good and I am so pure that I have to murder those murderers."

He relentlessly reminded us of what we did to the Indians. He said he couldn't fathom,

> Why they should have held to the absurd notion that they had some claim to the land just because they were here before us. And the next people we set out to liberate were the Mexicans but we always maintained a sense of justice—we left them a land where holy men could walk the desert.

Lenny spoke about a new drug rehab program that's developing new ways to attack addicts.

> I don't know about you, but I rather enjoy the way my money is spent to arrest, indict, convict, imprison, parole, and re-imprison those who have been caught using drugs. I'd just drink that money up in liquor or spend it on cigarettes anyway.

Lenny said that, "In the halls of justice, the only place you'll see justice is in the halls."

Lenny Bruce was a penetrating critic of our common hypocrisies. He wanted us to face up to life as it really was. He would joke about it so that it would be less painful. He believed that if men look honestly at themselves they are less likely to cast stones at others. He was a Jew who preached to Christians that the essence of Christianity is forgiveness. "Of course there are some people who sell themselves for money," he said.

> That some constitutes 90 percent of the people I've known in in my life, including myself. We all sell out some part of us. Anyone who is married for security is a hooker. Two dollars for a short time, as opposed to a marriage license and a lot of two dollars for a longer time.

"I keep in mind that the only difference between [quiz-show fraudster] Charles Van Doren, [tax-dodging businessman] Bernard Goldfine and [corrupt Teamsters Union boss] Dave Beck and me is that they got caught." Lenny said Teamsters boss Jimmy Hoffa was Christ-like because he hired ex-convicts. He tells his audience that he loves his country and yet would tell every top secret, make shoe shine rags out of the American flag, and denounce the Constitution in order to save his own life. "I have seen ethics erode according to the law of supply and demand," he said. Lenny believed that change was possible if enough people stopped pretending and recognized themselves for what they really are. What made Lenny Bruce funny was that he was a compulsive truth teller.

He was born in New York City in 1926 as Leonard Schneider. After his parents were divorced when he was five, various relatives shuffled the unwanted child around. At the time, Lenny found escape in confusion: power failures; a blizzard that would halt traffic and mail; clogged toilets that overflowed and ran down the hall. He loved anything that would stop the flow, back things up, and open up new possibilities and new directions. Confusion was entertaining. At 16 he ran away and worked on a Long Island farm. He was shocked to discover that the couple he lived with already slept in separate bedrooms in their 30s. "I knew they were tired after working a long day, but I couldn't understand why anyone who could, wouldn't want to sleep in each other's arms."

In 1942 he enlisted in the Navy for a three-year hitch. After seeing early action in the war, he got transferred far from the fighting and grew so bored that he impersonated a transvestite to get discharged. Fresh out of the service, he married the stripper Honey Harlow. Lenny landed a job with the Brother Mathias Foundation. It paid him to solicit money for British Guiana's unfortunate lepers, going door-to-door in wealthy neighborhoods dressed as a priest. To obtain his uniform, Lenny snuck into the closet of a rectory. There he found 12 clerical collars, along with a numbered edition of Henry Miller's *Black Spring*, and seven far-out *Tillie and Mac* porn comic books. After Lenny collected $8,000 dollars in just three days, Honey was badly injured in an auto accident. Lenny promised God that he would go straight if she walked again.

In 1951 Lenny won a prize on Arthur Godfrey's talent-scout show. He began to appear at New York City's Blue Angel, where Harry Belafonte, Mike Nichols, Elaine May, Shelley Berman, Dick Gregory, and Barbra Streisand started out. At the Blue Angel, Lenny would have the house lights turned up to reveal the limited company that his white liberal audience traveled in.

Are there any niggers here tonight? I know one nigger who works here, I see him back there. Oh, there, two niggers, customers and ah, between those two niggers sits one kike. Man, thank god for the kike! Uh, two kikes, three niggers, one spic and two grease balls!

He joked about liberals who cherish Negroes but won't live near them. He said he knew people so liberal that they can prove it by showing you their cancelled checks.

In one act he pretends to ask the Grand Wizard of the Ku Klux Klan if he'd rather spend 15 years with a white woman or a black woman? Upon receiving the expected response, Lenny asks the Klan chief if it would make any difference if the black woman in question is Lena Horne and the white woman is Kate Smith? He winds up telling the Wizard,

> So you are not really concerned with black and white anymore, you are concerned with who is pretty. So let's get basic and persecute those who are ugly. And as far as your sister is concerned, man she would jump over 50 Charles Laughtons to get near one Harry Belafonte.

The name of Lenny Bruce is synonymous with pornography and obscenity. Many of those who accused him of bad taste would think nothing of restaurants refusing to seat someone because of their skin color. Lenny pointed out how afraid people are to even speak words that describe body parts or functions. We tell little boys to wash their ears, feet, and little ga-ga. People rarely say "Where is the toilet?" We prefer such euphemisms as "little boy's room" or "powder room." Lenny said that God made his body and, if it's dirty, then the imperfection lies with the manufacturer.

He pointed out the hypocrisy that requires contraceptives sold in America to bear a label saying, "For the prevention of disease only." He saw irony in punishing homosexuals by imprisoning them with a bunch of sex-deprived men! He would challenge men in his audience to a lie-detector test, promising $1,000 to anyone who had not been actively or passively involved in a homosexual experience. The purpose of Lenny Bruce's uncomfortable humor was to stop people from casting the first stone.

He ridiculed the film raters and the parents who allowed children to see Alfred Hitchcock's *Psycho* but shielded them from nudity. Lenny said he never saw a stag film where anyone was killed—or even slapped in the mouth. "It is my belief that you can't do anything with anyone's body to make it dirty to me. Six people, eight people, one person. You can do only one thing to make it dirty—kill it. Hiroshima was dirty."

Lenny believed that the purpose of words is to get as close as possible to the object that a speaker is describing. He used a lot of four-letter, eight-letter and 10-letter words. He was first arrested for obscenity at Chicago's Gate of Horn in 1962. The arresting officer said that his offense had as much to do with what Lenny said about religion as the words that Lenny used. In America, we do a better job of protecting the right to worship than the right of a citizen to say what he pleases.

The first religious joke Lenny told was about trying to find a priest to listen to his problems. They were all too busy. Finally, he found a priest who had time for him, but before he could recount his troubles the priest tried to sell him a chance on a new Plymouth. Lenny said he hoped to see the day when General Motors would auction off a 1958 Catholic Church. Lenny said he also asked a rabbi, "Is there a God?" The learned rabbi answered, "We are not here to talk of God; we are here to sell bonds for Israel." The audience's nervous laughter told Lenny that he had hit another sore spot that needed probing. He saw religious hypocrisy wherever a rich church or synagogue stood adjacent to poverty. "I know in my heart," he explained, "that any man who calls himself a religious leader and owns more than one suit is a hustler—as long as there is one man who has no suit at all." He once said that, thanks to the Catholic Church, "there'll still be freaks—the thalidomide babies will grow up and get a good tie-in with the Barnum & Bailey sideshow." But Lenny did not despair. It filled him with hope that people were leaving churches and going back to God.

No prominent figure of the 1950s escaped his wit. "Tell you what a bad guy Castro is. Since Castro came, you can't get no narcotics, no abortions, and there're no prostitutes there. He's really screwed it up for vacationers." Back when U.S. House Speaker Sam Rayburn was still just 78, Lenny asked why anyone would take a chance on electing him to another term when Mutual of Omaha and Allstate turned him down for life insurance years ago. He said that those following Adlai Stevenson's campaign from New York to Alabama might suffer a nervous breakdown trying to keep up with his gyrating positions.

"I could never visualize Eisenhower even kissing his wife, not on the mouth anyway," he said. "And even Nixon—well, he kissed his wife, but on the forehead, and only on Thanksgiving, in front of his in-laws." He does a routine where a bell boy who barges into Eleanor Roosevelt's hotel room complements her breasts. Far from offended, Eleanor is rather pleased. Lenny's aim was not to be obscene but to show that, aside from her intellect and humanitarianism, Eleanor Roosevelt was a woman who took pride in her body like anyone else. Lenny said that *Time Magazine* photos of Jackie Kennedy during her husband's shooting were obscenely dishonest. One showed her climbing out of the limousine over the caption, "Going for help." A caption to another photo suggested that the First Lady was helping a Secret Service agent climb aboard the limo. Lenny didn't buy it. He countered that Jackie panicked like any normal person and tried to flee, as the secret service agent endeavored to keep her onboard.

Albert Goldman of Columbia University recently previewed a Lenny Bruce biography that he is writing.

> Relentlessly collapsing the distance between a cat and a king, dragging every legendary figure down to the level of common humanity, with its grossness and cupidity, cynicism, cowardice, and anger, Lenny peopled his imaginary world with preposterously deflated heroes.

Lenny, who spent $500 dollars a week to satisfy his habit, died of drugs at the age of 40 in 1966. One thousand people jammed the Judson Memorial Church in New York City for a funeral officiated by Baptist Minister Howard Moody, counterculture journalist Paul Krassner and beatnik poet Allen Ginsberg. They took Lenny's words as their theme. "I have to live with my own truth, whether you like it or not." Even the conservative *National Review* wrote that, "Lenny, like D. H. Lawrence and Walt Whitman, was basically moved by a sincere vision of the sacredness of life and, like them, he used obscenity to express it." *The New Yorker* eulogized, "The purity of his filth would have earned him a halo in any well-regulated heaven."

Lenny called America out for professing Christian love and democratic goodness while dispensing death, hate, corruption and lies. He cared deeply about dishonesty and injustice. Biographer Albert Goldman said, "What he saw as simple, true, and terribly funny was this: The great world of social, political, and religious power, authority and dignity is nothing but a gigantic racket run by petty hustlers and Broadway agents."

Delivered June 9, 1974, Third Unitarian Church of Chicago.

Part Three

Bear Others' Burdens

The good we secure for ourselves
is precarious and uncertain until
it is secured for all of us.

JANE ADDAMS

Witches in Your Britches

U nitarian General Assembly delegates in Quebec recently urged us to focus on "civil liberties." Denomination President William Sinkford reaffirmed, "Unitarians' loyalty to the freedom of the mind to believe and of the tongue to speak what the mind believes." He added, "Our national security is guarded more through freedom and constructive criticism than it ever could be through the silence of conformity and fear."

Provisions of the new counter-terrorism U.S. Patriot Act expand the power of the federal government to conduct secret electronic surveillance and "sneak-and-peek" searches that:

- Access records of libraries and bookstores, while authorizing criminal prosecutions of librarians or bookstore owners who reveal that their records have been searched;
- Empower the attorney general to detain non-citizens without probable cause, hold them for seven days without charges, and to detain them indefinitely without judicial review; and
- Permit the attorney general to designate domestic organizations as terrorist groups based on a vague definition of "terrorism."

The *New York Times* recently wrote about the Orion Electronic Systems that American cities are acquiring. Denver Police already have used this system to create files on 3,400 citizens and organizations, including the American Friends Service Committee and an 84-year-old Catholic nun who works with destitute Mexicans. The police superintendent explained that officers use their own judgment to determine who merits surveillance. The Department of Defense's Total Information Awareness program allows federal agencies to share information to catch terrorists. Overseen by Iran-Contra-scandal veteran John Poindexter, this program can combine financial, education, travel, medical, criminal, and other government records to create risk profiles on millions of U.S. citizens.

No wonder membership in the American Civil Liberties Union is up by 20 percent! A Gallup Poll a year ago, asked people if the government should violate civil liberties to protect the nation; 49 percent said "No," and 47 percent said "Yes." The tide turned by this past September, when 62 percent opposed violating civil liberties to protect the nation. We would like to think that public opinion prompted the administration to scale back its plans to force postal workers and meter readers to report suspicious behavior.

Columnist Leonard Pitts writes that we have been here before. The 1798 Alien and Sedition Acts made it a crime to criticize the government. President Lincoln suspended habeas corpus during the Civil War. In World War I, Congress passed the Espionage Acts, which criminalized anti-war protests, imprisoning Eugene Debs and deporting Emma Goldman. President Roosevelt placed 110,000 Japanese-American citizens in internment camps. During the Vietnam War, the Chicago Police Department's Red Squad infiltrated our congregation and kept files on many of our members. In the most chilling part, Pitts writes,

> I could call the FBI tomorrow and tell them you're involved in terrorist activities, maybe manufacture some evidence against you. And no lawyer, no one-time phone call, no Miranda rights, no compulsion for the government to account for your whereabouts, or lay out the case against you, no chance to tell your side of the story.

During the 1692 Salem Witch Trials 150 people were arrested and 20 were killed. The intriguing thing about the trials was that the accusers were presumed innocent but defendants who would not confess to consorting with the devil were convicted. One saved one's life by confessing. A person was either with the prosecution or against it. Last month the *New York Times* ran an article about how our justice system is based on the premise that a prisoner's acknowledgement of guilt mitigates his responsibility. Sentences are reduced for prisoners who take responsibility for their crimes. A contrite criminal has a better chance of parole than innocent people who refuse to confess to crimes that they never committed.

Arthur Miller wrote his 1953 play *The Crucible* about the Salem Witch Trials to protest history repeating itself under Joe McCarthy. Miller showed that there are periods of hysteria and irrational exuberance, when people lose their perspective, don't think clearly, and don't listen to their own consciences. He used words like "silly," "daft," "fraud," and "panic," followed by phrases like, "the fever died." One critic noted that the 20 "witches" executed in Salem are "a microscopic number compared to the millions who have died in the species of witch hunts peculiar to our rational, scientific times." What happened at Salem and in the McCarthy era was mild compared to recent mass brain washings and indoctrinations.

Yet we are always surprised by the megalomaniacal aspirations of a cynical demagogue and the appalling ease with which such methods succeed. Joe McCarthy held two presidents captive and struck saintly Illinois Senator Paul Douglas dumb. Just one senator, J. William Fulbright of Arkansas, voted against funding McCarthy's witch hunt. McCarthy denounced General George Marshall's role as an instrument of Soviet conspiracy. He said that Marshall would sell his own grandmother for any advantage. He categorized preceding Democratic administrations as, "20 years of treason." He accused Eisenhower, who defeated fascism, as being weak, immoral, and cowardly, with a foreign policy of appeasement, retreat, and surrender. Fifty percent of the American people had a favorable impression of McCarthy; 21 percent had no opinion of him at all.

But the fever died and the hysteria passed in 1692 and in 1952. People could not believe they had been duped. The governor of Massachusetts reprieved the eight remaining convicted "witches" before they were executed. Within five years, a judge and 12 jurors formally apologized as the colony declared a day of fasting and prayer to atone for the injustices they committed. In 1711, the state compensated the families of the victims. Last year, Massachusetts formally cleared the names of the convicted witches—more than 300 years after the fact.

So, too, with the Witch Trials of the 1950s. Arthur Miller, who was summoned before McCarthy's committee, said, "Astounded, I watched men pass me by without a nod, men whom I had known rather well for years." Finally, however, the playwright Lillian Hellman testified, "I will not and cannot cut my conscience to fit this year's fashions." Missouri Senator Stuart Symington told McCarthy, "I want you to know from the bottom of my heart, that I am not afraid of anything about you." A woman a few blocks from here, at Central and Race Streets, dared to sue the House Committee on Un-American Activities Committee for itself being un-American. And a woman from Maine wearing a red rose stood on the Senate floor and introduced a Declaration of Conscience. The resolution condemning McCarthy passed 67–22. But for three years he held a razor to the nation's jugular vein. The fever died. The hysteria passed. The witches were exorcised from our britches.

I urge each of you to watch or re-watch the movie *High Noon*. That Western allegory pays tribute to one brave man who stands up to a gang of killers. The church, the judge, the good people of the town all have excuses for why they won't join the fight. The movie stands on its own, but when you view it knowing that it is about those who stood tall or cut bait during the 1950s, it gives you goose bumps. *High Noon* screenwriter Carl Foreman was blacklisted, of course, and had to go to England.

Albert Camus's allegorical novel *The Plague* represented the Nazi occupation of France from 1940 to 1944. The novel deals with how different people reacted to the pestilence. Some became collaborators, feeling that the plague was too strong to combat. The novel's hero is the doctor who does what he must to fight the disease. Camus's definition of a hero is simply one who expresses individual moral responsibility.

I want to switch gears to say that this sermon has nothing to do with Salem, Joe McCarthy, *High Noon*, *The Plague*, *The Crucible*, or even with Attorney General John Ashcroft. Men and women have always had witches in their britches. There are times when we don't think clearly, nor see straight, when we are confused and befuddled. In Miller's words, when we are silly, daft, when we panic, when get caught up in a spell. Jesus tells the story of a man who wasn't himself, whose head was spinning, who did foolish things, who had witches in his britches, and so went off to a far country and squandered his inheritance (perhaps an apt description of America today). I believe that we have known the experience of wandering off to a far country. We have done those things which we ought not to have done and left undone those things which we ought to do. Please don't get too literal here, like the reporters who tried to pin Dr. King down about which mountaintop he had visited. Few of us have been to the mountaintop, but many of us have visited that far country, where neither religion, psychiatry, family, nor friends could bring us home until we came to our senses.

Do you remember Peggy McMartin Buckey? She was the center of the Satanic-abuse scare that gripped this country in the early 1980s. At the time, average Americans believed that devil worshipers had invaded daycare centers. Children were raped and sodomized and ran around naked drinking blood and eating feces—all without attracting the notice of parents, neighbors or authorities. I hope some young Arthur Miller will write a play about this and hold the world premiere at Oak Park's Circle Theater.

It all began in 1983, when a Los Angeles woman reported to the police that her two-year-old son had been sodomized. It didn't matter that the woman was later found to be a paranoid schizophrenic. She convinced other parents that the daycare teachers took their children on airplane rides to Palm Springs, where they were dressed as witches and flew in the air. The therapists who descended upon the daycare center praised children who "disclosed," while telling those who denied the abuse that they were dumb. Although a horse reportedly had been killed at the daycare center, none of the parents could remember seeing signs of equine slaughter. The black "satanic robe" seized by the police turned out to be Peggy's graduation gown. It was then the costliest trial in American history, lasting six years and costing $15 million dollars. In Peggy's obituary a couple of years ago, *The New York Times* wrote, "When you once believed something that now strikes you as absurd, it can be almost impossible to summon that feeling of belief again."

More than 50 years ago, McCarthy nemesis Lillian Hellman wrote a play called *The Children's Hour*. In it, two girls accuse their teachers of being lesbians. Both teachers are fired and one commits suicide. Who can ever forget Sherwood Anderson's story *Hands*? It is about a kind of Mr. Chips character who placed his hands on the hair of one of his students. A piano teacher I know well told a colleague that one of her teaching methods involves placing her hands over the hands of her students. Her colleague cried out, "Oh my God, you can't do that." One outcome of the satanic daycare trials (many such trials followed that first one) is that today's daycare workers hesitate to hug children or to change a diaper without a witness!

The *New York Times* reported that Harvard has raised the standards under which it will bring charges against students in its campus court. The reform followed years of complaints that students were put though disciplinary hearings for crimes like sexual assault based on little more than an accusation. The new policy will require students to present sufficient corroborating evidence before the campus disciplinary board will hear accusations against another student. Harvard's Thought Police are not dormant, however. The current *New Yorker* reports that the university revoked a speaking invitation to poet Tom Paulin because he might offend Jewish students because Paulin had written a poem with the intriguing title, "*On Being Dealt the Anti-Semitic Card*." Standby. The African American Studies Department has invited New Jersey Poet Laureate Amiri Baraka (a.k.a. Leroy Jones) to speak in the spring.

Do you sometimes read something—and go back and read it again? This article was about an African American law professor at Vanderbilt University.

She said, "I think [Republican Mississippi Senator] Trent Lott should lead the national debate on race. If we're going to have a serious discussion, we need people to say what's on their minds. I don't think he should step down. If we attack these people when they put their feet in their mouths, we can never get to the root of the problem." Cincinnati Reds owner Marge Schott was fined $25,000 for making racial and ethnic slurs in a private conversation. She also had to take a course in multi-cultural sensitivity training. Rev. Jesse Jackson was all but crucified for making a comment in private about "Hymietown." Is it better to silence such comments or to allow them to be discussed and contradicted? "Let the tongue speak what the minds believes." One of the values of free speech in a free church is that it lets every emotion hang out—but hang out to dry in the light of scrutiny.

This is usually the time when *Tinker Hammack* whispers to her neighbor, "What the hell is this sermon about, anyway?" I have been attempting to say that in our nation, social organizations, and in our individual lives, "spells come over us." We suffer periods of irrational exuberance when we get witches in our britches. Eventually, the fever breaks as an individual here and there bravely lets the tongue speak what the mind believes.

A play about the Nuremberg trials is running in Chicago. The scene that I remember from the movie is when the Nazi judge on trial asks, "How did we ever get to this place?" The American judge answers, "The first time that you rendered an opinion that you did not believe." At the end of the relentlessly tragic play *Rosencrantz and Guildenstern are Dead*, one protagonist says to the other, "There must have been a time, in the beginning, when we could have said—no." The Greek Orthodox Church has an unusual annual service. At 3 a.m. on October 28, 1940, Mussolini's ambassador to Greece knocked on the door of Prime Minister Ioannis Metaxas. The Italian ambassador advised the Greek leader that Greece should refrain from resisting the invading Italian troops. Metaxas said "No," and shut the door. To this day, they celebrate.

You know how I love obituaries. A couple of months ago I read one for Stephen Cary, a former head of that terrorist group the American Friends Service Committee. Cary was a conscientious objector who would not fight in World War II. "I have no illusions that my pacifist views are going to prevail," he said. "But every great change in expanding the dimensions of human freedom has come from very small original beginnings: someone said no." Or as Dr. King said, "Our lives begin to end the day we become silent about things that matter." When our *Bernetta Howell* ran for public office, her motto was,

"No bricks on my tongue," and we all wore little bricks on our lapels. What a motto for a politician: to let the tongue speak what the mind believes.

Oh hysterias will come again. High fevers will rage with "spells" that cannot soon be broken. The Reichstag burning, the Dreyfus affair, the Inquisition, the Red Squads, the Nazi plague, the Scopes Trial, the McCarthy period, Elián González, Monica Lewinsky, O. J. Simpson, and repressed-memory syndrome. The best of us will have witches in our britches and will know what it feels like to wander aimlessly in a far country. To come to oneself must be one of the most glorious experiences. The old Shaker hymn says that when we "come down where we ought to be . . . 'Twill be in the valley of love and delight." All of us make the journey to find ourselves. It doesn't matter much what else we do find if we don't find that. D.H. Lawrence said that that was the only thing that he would fight for—that bit of inward peace where he was at one with himself.

After the terrible Watergate experience, Senator George McGovern appealed to our sanity. "Come home America," he urged, from military spending so wasteful that it weakens our nation, from special-privilege entrenchment and tax favoritism. Come home to the affirmation that we have a dream and can see a new world. Let us be joyful in that homecoming, when America comes home to itself . . . again, and again, and again.

> Grim Cotton Mather
> Was always seeing witches
> Daylight, moonlight,
> They buzzed around his ear,
> Pinching him and plaguing him
> With aches and pains and stitches.
> Witches in his pulpit,
> Witches by his bed.
>
> Nowadays nowadays,
> We'd say that he was crazy,
> But everyone believed him
> In old Salem town
> And nineteen people
> Were hanged for Salem witches
> Because of Cotton Mather
> In his long black gown.

Old Cotton Mather
Didn't die happy.
He could preach and thunder,
He could fast and pray,
But men began to wonder
If there had been witches.
When he walked in the streets
Men looked the other way.
STEPHEN VINCENT BENET

Delivered January 26, 2003, Third Unitarian Church of Chicago.

Ordinary People

Originally established to remember those who died in the Civil War, Memorial Day has become a day to remember those who have died in all wars or even those who have died, period. In a community such as this, it is an occasion to understand how and why the young men of one nation kill those of another, as well as women, children and elderly.

Let's begin with World War II's German Reserve Police Battalion 101. Detailed records on this unit enable us to study them as individuals. These men were too old to be drafted into the regular military but were deployed in something akin to the police and national guard. Their average age was 40; most were from the city of Hamburg. They came from middleclass backgrounds. Most identified as Roman Catholic or Lutheran. They were the baker, tailor, pharmacist, milkman, and postman. They had never seen the enemy nor enemy fire. They had not lost any fast friends in the war that might have incited a thirst for revenge. They grew up before Hitler came to power and could judge the Third Reich by different standards than the young recruits who grew up in Nazi youth organizations. They were the kind of men whom no one would believe could become mass killers.

The Nazis sent this battalion's 500 men to the small Polish town of Józefów at a crucial time in July 1942. The Nazis were barely holding their own on the Russian front. Major Wilhelm 'Papa' Trapp briefed his men on their "special assignment." They were to surround this Jewish village, sort out men fit for work camps, and take everyone else to the forest and shoot them. Reading this assignment, Major Trapp had tears in his eyes. He told his men that those who were unable to carry it out could step forward and receive other duties. Ten or 12 men did. By the time the sun set on Józefów on July 13, 300 "work Jews" had been boarded on trucks for work camp and they heard shots as the 1,500 other members of their community were shot in the forest at the edge of town. The orders for this brutal assignment contained this addendum, "Company commanders are especially to provide for the spiritual care of the men who participated in this action. The impressions of the day are to be blotted out though the holding of social events in the evenings."

Twenty years after the war, 210 of these men were located and interrogated. They were back at their old jobs, attending their old churches, and living ordinary lives with their families. One said,

> Through the point-blank shot that was thus required, the bullet struck the head of the victim at such an angle that often the entire skull, or at least the entire rear skullcap, was torn off. Blood, bone splinters, and brains sprayed everywhere and besmirched the shooters.

For 16 months, Battalion 101 went from village to village in Poland. By the end, they had executed 38,000 people with a bullet through the back of the head and packed 45,000 people into cattle cars bound for the gas chambers, for a total body count of 83,000. There also were "forest patrols" or "Jew Hunts," in which Battalion men "tracked down and killed their prey in direct and personal confrontation." They were assisted by Polish Christian civilians, who blew the whistle on where their Jewish neighbors were hiding. Many Poles believed that Hitler had one redeeming feature: liberating Poland from the Jews.

Christopher Browning, a history professor at a Lutheran seminary, tells Battalion 101's story in the book *Ordinary Men*. This sermon is titled "Ordinary People," because today Battalion 101 would have both men and women. There is no record that the mothers or wives of these 500 men disapproved of their mission. When one newlywed officer brought his bride to one of the villages, she sat in the town square and watched the entire mop up.

Our most pressing question is: Why did just 12 of the 500 men refuse to participate in a civilian slaughter when they were offered a choice by a teary commander who appeared to have his own qualms about the assignment? One objector, Heinz Bachmann, said that under no condition would he participate in an action in which defenseless women and children are shot. Others stated that if they did not do it, someone else would. Most said they did not step forward for fear of being isolated, rejected, or ostracized by their comrades. Refusal meant that you were not really a man—one tough enough to kill women and children. Many of those who did opt out belittled themselves, confessing that they were too weak to follow orders. They did not see themselves as good. Rather, they failed to live up to the standards of the day. Although those interviewed after the war never expressed overt hatred for Jews, they did communicate a feeling of us versus them. Jews were somehow outside the pale of humanity—something less than human.

It was amazing how accustomed the men grew to their orders. As the year wore on, these ordinary men became increasingly efficient and calloused executioners. About a third of them enjoyed their new powers to behave cruelly and arbitrarily, inventing new forms of harassment. Reading the book, I often thought of the response my mother would have had. "Well, Donald, what do you expect of Germans?" I wonder what she would have thought of what Charlie Company did on March 16, 1968. Charlie Company was made up of 105 American boys with an average age of 20—the kid next door. There are many similarities between Charlie Company and Battalion 101. In one significant difference, the 500 Vietnamese that Charlie Company annihilated in four hours were not just killed. They were raped, sodomized, and mutilated.

Charlie Company had only been in Vietnam for three months but already had suffered 28 casualties, including the deaths of five men. It was near impossible to distinguish who was the enemy; buddies were killed by snipers, mines and booby traps. They were primed for revenge. It was time to settle the score. "When you have lost 21 from your company," one of them later said, "you tend to want something back for it. We actually wanted heavy contact out there. We were hoping for it." They welcomed the assignment to destroy the village of My Lai. The assignment was to kill the pigs and drop them in the wells to pollute the water supply, cut down the banana trees, and burn every hooch. There were to be no prisoners.

Some of the Charlie Company boys must have been disappointed when they encountered no enemy fire. As with the Polish Jews, "the enemy" consisted entirely of unarmed civilians—mostly women, children, and older men. One Charlie veteran later wrote, "That day in My Lai, I was personally responsible for killing about 25 people. Men and women. From shooting them, to cutting their throats, scalping them too. Cutting off their hands and cutting out their tongues. I did it." Some of the men were "double vets," GI slang for the dubious honor of raping a woman then murdering her. Many women were raped, sodomized, mutilated, and had their vaginas ripped open with knives and bayonets. One woman was killed after the muzzle of a rifle barrel was inserted in her vagina and the trigger pulled. "Soldiers repeatedly stabbed their victims, cut off limbs, sometimes even beheaded them. Some were scalped, others had their tongues cut out, or their throats slit, or both." Other victims had C Company's signature Ace of Spades carved into their chests.

A GI who was not at My Lai but who heard about it wrote numerous people seeking an investigation. A year later, Arizona Congressman Morris Udall pushed for a trial and journalist Seymour Hersh took the story to the American people in April 1969. A photographer had been present; *Life Magazine* ran color pictures of the atrocities. The 71-day trial focused on Lt. William "Rusty" Calley. Every psychiatric test was given to him. The tests found no psychiatric disease and indicated that he knew right and wrong. Lt. Calley used much the same defense as the Germans. He "did not feel that he was killing human beings but rather that they were animals with whom one could not speak or reason." *Time Magazine* quoted a My Lai vet saying, "We are here to kill dinks. How can they convict Calley for killing dinks? That's our job." In the process of dehumanizing the Jews and the Vietnamese, German and American soldiers dehumanized themselves. More recently, did the four L.A. police officers who savagely beat Rodney King—or the "L.A. Four" goons who savagely beat white truck driver Reggie Denny—think of their victims as human beings?

Sixty-five percent of the American people say that massacres like My Lai are bound to happen in war and that it is wrong to prosecute an American soldier for "doing his duty." President Nixon blamed the scandal on the Jews. "It's those dirty rotten Jews from New York who are behind it," he said, referring to the reporting of the *New York Times*. A popular song was written about Lt. Calley:

> My name is William Calley, I'm a soldier of this land
> I've vowed to do my duty and to gain the upper hand
> But they've made me out a villain,
> they've stamped me with a brand.

This is hard to believe and so I will quote from the book *Four Hours in My Lai* by Michael Bilton and Kevin Sim.

> "A Rally for Calley" was held in Columbus, Georgia when he came home and among the speakers were [segregationist] Lester Maddox, George Wallace, and John Williams (the Governor of Mississippi). Governor Jimmy Carter organized the "American Fighting Men's Day," exhorting the citizens of Georgia to drive with their headlights on and honor the flag as Rusty had done.

The only C Company soldier to do time, Lt. Calley was court martialed, convicted and sentenced to life in prison for the premeditated murder of 22 civilians. The next day President Nixon ordered him transferred to house arrest in his apartment. Three years into his house arrest, Judge J. Robert Elliott overturned the conviction, saying, "War is war and it's not unusual for innocent civilians such as the My Lai victims to be killed." Writer Jonathan Schell wrote, "If we learn to accept this there is nothing we will not accept."

I found two Charlie Company soldiers who refused their orders. Michael Bernhardt and Harry Stanley said, in effect, "The orders were that we were going into an enemy village and that they were well armed. I didn't find that when I got there. And ordering me to shoot down innocent people, that's not an order, that's craziness to me, you don't. I didn't feel like I have to obey that."

In both Battalion 101 and Charlie Company the extraordinary few conducted themselves in a moral fashion. We need more research on how we shape those who have the presence of mind and the strength of character to act responsibly. Some Germans and American soldiers under pressure and provocation committed atrocities, while a tiny minority resisted these pressures to maintain their integrity. "Following orders" is no excuse. There is always an opportunity for individual moral responsibility. Charlie Company was composed of boys, the kid next door. Battalion 101 had 40-year old men, fathers and husbands with careers. The Lutheran professor who wrote the book on Battalion 101 closes with these words:

> The collective behavior of Reserve Police Battalion 101 has deeply disturbing implications. There are many societies afflicted by traditions of racism and caught in the siege mentality of war. Everywhere society conditions people to respect and defer to authority, and indeed, could scarcely function otherwise. Everywhere, people seek career advancement. In every modern society, the complexity of life and the resulting bureaucratization and specialization attenuate the sense of personal responsibility of those implementing official policy. Within virtually every social collective, the peer group exerts tremendous pressures on behavior and sets moral norms. If the men of Reserve Police Battalion 101 could become killers under such circumstances, what group of men cannot?

In both Battalion 101 and Charlie Company we learn that it was easier for the men to kill than to break ranks as non-conformists. This leaves us then with the question: How do we raise children with the inner resources to be non-conformists, and how do we teach an appreciation for dissent? Lt. Calley's name is widely known but not the men who refused to join the My Lai massacre.

This is a community that identifies with dissent. We feel comfortable walking picket lines for open housing or to bring the troops home. We refused to take loyalty oaths in the 1950s. We voted to provide a sanctuary for Central American refugees whom the government seeks to send home. We supported inter-racial marriages long before they were tolerated by others. We have voted for Robert La Follette, Henry Wallace, Eugene Debs, Norman Thomas, and Barry Commoner. We welcome humanists, atheists, and agnostics. We have young people who have been conscientious objectors or draft resisters. We called a woman minister 75 years ago; women often have a majority on our board of trustees. We raise children to be individuals and to discover their own sexual orientation. Yet, we are not good. We are not the answer to the world's evil.

As I said in my opening words, the line dividing good and evil cuts through each human heart. All I am saying is that if you are a part of a community of dissenters, it may make it easier to dissent when the time comes and you must choose between stepping forward and breaking ranks—to refuse to take part in cruelties or atrocities.

Delivered May 24, 1992, Third Unitarian Church of Chicago.

The Spirit of Survival

You may know Gail Sheehy's book *Passages* about the stages of adulthood. This divorcee now has a new book titled *The Spirit of Survival*. It opens with her only child, a daughter named Maura, leaving for college. This event coincides with a trip that Sheehy makes to refugee camps in Southeast Asia. There, she catches the eye of a 14-year-old orphan named Mohm. Frightened with the thought of suddenly being alone, Sheehy adopts Mohm, hoping that they can fulfill each other's mutual needs. The book is also the story of the destruction of a fourth of Cambodia's population by Pol Pot and the Khmer Rouge, which is depicted in the film *The Killing Fields*. Sheehy's new book, *Spirit of Survival*, tells how a child orphaned by the destruction of her village—along with her parents, grandparents, brothers and sisters—manages to come through four years of war and start a new life on New York's 5th Avenue.

Mohm is a 10-year-old child who persevered despite being deprived of all normal sources of support. She runs by day under falling Vietnamese bombs and she lies down in the woods at night, covering herself with leaves.

> "Now and then I remember something of that time," Mohm told Sheehy, "especially the mines. People go through there before us, it's a trail of the dead. You see a body, another, another. A mine blows up in front of you—phhssh-swok! Then a finger floats by. Natural as a leaf blowing in the wind."

"You become accustom to it," she said. "You even see people killed in front of your face, shot by the big-guns or blow up; you see it all the time."

Although the book is almost 400 pages, Mohm's story could have been told in 50. Gail Sheehy also writes about her love life, her daughter in college, and an evening she spends with Gore Vidal. The book reminded me of how Margaret Truman inserted herself in the biography she wrote about her father. Beneath a picture of President Truman at Yalta, Margaret wrote "That is me on the left, I felt awful that my slip is showing." I stuck with Sheehy's book, nonetheless, because I am fascinated with how and why some people become survivors—and others do not.

Mohm did not survive by chance alone. There were too many incidents along the way where she made choices that shaped her destiny. Moreover, the more that she survived adversity, the more special she felt about herself, growing in self-confidence and self-esteem. She emerges with what Sheehy calls "a victorious personality." During the period that Mohm is on her own, from age 10 to 14, three attributes seem to enable her to survive where others did not.

Mohm has the ability to bend according to circumstances. There is a plasticity in her approach to life. Her mother disappears and life goes on with her father. He does not come home and she manages to look after her young brother and sister. Part of the book has Mohm speaking when she was just learning English.

> My sister body look like an old dry chicken, the skin hangs off, all wrinkly. My little brother swell so much he can't walk. The sadness it give to look at them, there is nothing to compare it with. I take out the rice and try to push it into my sister's mouth. She make a sound so dry, like palm leaves rattle. The rice come back out. My brother is numb and swollen. His face only bone, sunk in like monkey. Maybe no use.

When they die, she goes to another village to find her grandmother. When grandma dies, she sets off with some refugees heading toward Thailand. The book quotes a German Jewish Holocaust survivor, "Everything I did was by the seat of my pants. When it was necessary to be a thief, I was a thief, when it was useful to be a mechanic, I presented myself as a mechanic."

Sheehy talks about other survivors closer to home. An impoverished girl—whose lunch was two slices of bread with a slice of bread in the middle—laughs about her "bread sandwich" with classmates in the lunchroom. A boy whose mother and father are mentally ill makes a room for himself in the basement where he can escape to maintain his own sanity. Plasticity—the ability to bend according to circumstances—seems simple. But it is rare. People will say, "I always pictured myself as a grandmother," and they fret over it long after it has become a biological impossibility. Another says, "I always pictured myself married," and can't go on when that doesn't happen. Others say, "I didn't think I would ever grow old and feeble."

Mohm tells about when she and a group of kids spent the night in the woods alone, whimpering in fear of ghosts and wild animals. Another day a gust of wind blew up the sarong of one of the girls, revealing the ugly brown shorts that they all wore.

Everyone laughed at once. I was laughing so hard, I couldn't stop. The wind blew up her skirt and I think, "Must have come from God." God knew we needed a breath of joy. So he put a breath of joy on the wind and blew it our way.

Mohm's second survival skill was self-trust. She looked to her own intuition and she trusted her own instincts. There was no one else whom she could really trust. She lived at a time when children spied on their parents. Everyone owed primary allegiance to Pol Pot.

Part of this self-concept comes from "a private family myth" that serves as a defense against those who persecute you. Mohm recalled that she had been somebody before Pol Pot. She used this as a shield against the shame of being degraded and treated like a slave. Malcolm X similarly reminded Harlem cleaning ladies that they were descendants of African kings and queens. Jews have survived countless atrocities holding to the belief that they are "chosen people." Bill Berry, when he spoke here at my installation in 1969, told how his mother would holler after him each Saturday as he left home for the Chicago Loop with his shoe-shine kit, "Don't forget that you are a Berry." He was through college before he realized that that didn't mean a damn thing. Jessie Jackson says that, to succeed, you have got to believe that "I am somebody."

This is so foolish that I hesitate to tell it. My grandparents, who died in rural Kentucky in 1950, lived in a house without electricity or indoor plumbing. They carried their water from the spring house in a bucket. Nonetheless, they raised their five children to believe that they "descended from the highest flower, of the tallest stock, of the oldest Virginia aristocracy." What a gap between a family's myth and its primitive lifestyle! Psychologist Robert Coles tells the story of Ruby, the young black girl escorted through the white picket lines when New Orleans schools were integrated. Ruby's home had a picture of Jesus on the wall and she identified her own life with his. She felt that she was anointed to lead her people to a better life. You can endure a great deal if you feel that you are anointed, chosen, or that you descend from royalty—or the oldest Virginia aristocracy!

Ted Lampert shared with me a book about a Jewish refugee who travels through war-ravaged Europe with her son. She pays their way by selling off pieces of the family's silver—except for the silver teapot. She tells her son that he will need that when he becomes an ambassador. This crazy, autobiographical novel was written by French Resistance fighter Romain Gary—who did, indeed, become a French ambassador after the war.

Although it played less of a role in Mohm's story, most survivors with a victorious personality have a mentor or a pole star. This person recognizes the younger person's worth, provides him or her with purpose and direction, and inspires hope that things will improve. This can be a parent, teacher, counselor, minister, or a peer. At one fateful moment, Mohm is traveling with a group that has been ordered to dig their own mass grave. The group selects her to trick their captors, persuading them that they have been ordered to move on to another village. Another time, Mohm met a dying woman, who encourages Mohm to hurry on because she looks like a girl who has what it takes to reach the Thai border.

It is amazing how frequently people recount how someone intervened in their lives, changing the whole direction in which they were moving. Our *Hank Hansen* had dropped out of high school to find work when he chanced upon a man on the street in his home town in Minnesota who encouraged him to finish school and get his diploma. Perhaps the most athletic-looking man in this congregation told me that he was a skinny runt until a scoutmaster challenged him to lift weights and change the way that others perceived him. Secretly, I wanted to be a minister from an early age. But I don't believe that I would have kept at it if a particular adult had not reinforced that passion, saying that he, too, believed that's what I should do. It sounds ridiculous that it takes such a person in our lives, but most many of us have had such an experience.

The poet Sara Teasdale wrote that victorious personalities are found in those who, "make the most of all that comes and the least of all that goes." Those with victorious personalities seem to suggest that the unchallenged life is not worth living. In the Old Testament, *Moby Dick*, and *The Odyssey*, survivors pass through three stages. First, they are uprooted from home, family, security or health. Next, they are cast off into an internal or external wilderness or darkness, where they confront danger, uncertainty or evil. Finally, comes a reunion or reconciliation into a new home, better than the one they had been driven out of.

The human spirit has the resources to prevail over tremendous adversity, to heal itself, and to emerge strengthened. For too long we assumed that disturbing childhood experiences inevitably result in a neurotic adulthood. Children of trauma can be far more resilient than we thought. Mohm convinced Gail Sheehy that children exposed to risk are better off than those who are over-protected. "The experience of knowing one has survived what seemed unsurmountable offers a shield of 'perceived invulnerability' against future disasters in adult life," she writes. "It is even becoming respectable to suggest that children may need challenges and high-risk conditions in order to develop the self-generated immunity to trauma that characterizes survivors. To be tested is good. The challenged life may be the best therapist." Since stress is inevitable, those who learn to cope with it early on are better prepared for life.

Sheehy's earlier book *Pathfinders* plumbs the common characteristics of hundreds of successful adults, finding that most of them endured some kind of trauma as children. "They may have been born into poverty, or have lost a parent through abandonment, divorce or sudden death, or had an alcoholic or mentally ill parent," she writes. "Yet those who were to become the most resilient adults overcame childish limitations and found themselves performing—temporarily—on a level of maturity well beyond their years."

Robert Louis Stevenson wrote that,

> For 14 years I have not had a day of real health. I have awakened sick and gone to bed weary, yet I have done my work unflinchingly. I was made for a contest and the powers that be have willed that my battlefield shall be the dingy, inglorious one of the bed and the medicine bottle.

One of the Old Testament's most intriguing stories tells how, "Jacob was left alone; and a man wrested with him until the breaking of the day." This man, assumed to be God, said, "Your name shall no more be called Jacob but Israel, for you have striven with God and with men and have prevailed." I cannot think of any mature person who has not figured out that life is a contest or a battlefield. The sooner we realize it, the better equipped we will be for the struggles ahead.

One amazing thing about survivors is that they tend to emerge from battle not only with victorious personalities but also with a sense of gratitude. A holocaust survivor said,

> Having escaped persecution by the Nazis, I have always had the impression that life has been 'granted to me a second time' and so I had to show

that I deserved that life, that I was worthy to live it. It was no longer even mine; I was living, in a way, by proxy.

If you are visiting today, seeking a place to raise your children in the presence of survivors with victorious personalities, look no further. One of our members begins his witness with these words,

> We had just finished playing, put our violins away, looked into each other's eyes, happy, young, and satisfied. We were not quite 17 and very much in love. Suddenly the windows of the fourth floor apartment started to vibrate and the deep noise of an explosion permeated the room.

It was September 1, 1939. Warsaw fell 27 days later and this 17-year-old Jewish boy would travel alone by cattle train, by horse and buggy, and by foot until he reached the border. *Eva Terveen* was no older than Mohm when her family was wiped out by a Russian Tsarist pogrom. She saw her baby brother killed before her eyes. She and her sister traveled alone through Russia and Poland, 12- and 13-year-old girls, determined to join an older sister in the United States.

Our flowers today are in memory of *Mary's* good-looking, intelligent, socially committed son, whom she lost just out of college. *Hazel and Hank's* 21-year-old son, Christopher, was president of his senior class at Rockford College when leukemia struck. *Denise Gaynor* was pretty, fun-loving and had just discovered the delights of dating when she was killed on a highway downstate. *Len* was 17 and his younger brother was six when their father ended a long-suffering military injury by committing suicide, leaving his eldest son to be "the man" of the family. *Marvin Wolberg* was swimming in Belmont Harbor on a summer Sunday afternoon, when a motorized pleasure boat struck. Some of you attended this morning's forum talk by Lupe Lozano. Her husband, union organizer Rudy Lozano, was assassinated in 1983 while her two-year-old son looked on.

Time does not permit us to tell of: *Isaac Schwab* and his family in the concentration camp; *Reid's* struggle with alcohol; *Barry's* loss of hearing as a young man; *Bob Sanders's* determination to travel and "see the world" without eyesight; *Ann Gaynor*, the woman who didn't have any time for cancer; *Ruth Thompson*, who faces a future without relatives following the death of her parents and both of her brothers. These are the ones who make the most of all that comes and the least of all that goes. We don't need books or therapists or sermons to know that our human spirits can prevail over tremendous adversity, heal themselves, and emerge strengthened.

I have been criticized for not publicizing my sermon topics in advance. In my defense, I invoke William Ellery Channing, who said, "No matter what subject I announce, my only theme is the dignity of human nature." Anyone who has spent time here knows that I just have one sermon that I dress up to fit the occasion. Neither athletic powers nor intellectual giants greatly impress me. What moves me is the spiritual power that some people marshal into victorious personalities to conquer adversity. Someone attending *Georgia Mottelson's* memorial service said, "I never heard of a funeral ending with 'The Hora.'" The passing of a victorious personality demands the Hora, the Hallelujah Chorus, the brass section of the Chicago Symphony Orchestra, or *"The Internationale."*

Delivered September 7, 1986, Third Unitarian Church of Chicago.

Freedom of Choice

Worried about speaking too often on the same topic, I checked: this is only the third time in 16 years that I have spoken on self-deliverance. I firmly believe that there is a time to live and a time to die. We ourselves know better than anyone else when the time to die has come.

Two events bring this to the fore again. First, I have waited 12 years for the film *Grace Quigley's Solution*. I was delighted to hear that the author of this story threw the script over Katharine Hepburn's fence in 1973. Hepburn comes from an independent New England stock of free thinkers and nonconformists. It comes as no surprise that she invested $80,000 to help produce this film. At age 75, this could be the last of Hepburn's 45 films.

The film deals with a woman who feels that her life has been spent, that she has nothing more to live for, and that in—*Emma Twigg's* words—she would "like to check out." She happens to see a mafia hit man kill someone and, eventually, offers to pay him to kill her. Word soon spreads, and Grace Quigley's friends also want to engage the man's services. In one of the most realistic scenes, Grace takes her hit man to visit a nursing home and the hardened assassin cannot believe that such "death houses" really exist. Hepburn for the first time is communicating to a wide American audience that there are those who rationally prefer death than to go on living. That point is ruined, however, when Grace Quigley becomes irate at a dishonest cabbie and wants the hit man to kill him, too. At this point, you can almost hear the Vatican say, "You see where such a philosophy leads." Those who are against self-deliverance leave the theater with their greatest fears confirmed and those favoring self-deliverance feel that Katharine Hepburn betrayed their trust in her good judgment.

The second event was the *Chicago Tribune's* review of the book *Last Wish*. It's written by Betty Rollin, who also wrote the book *First You Cry* about her experience with breast cancer. *Last Wish* is about her mother's self-deliverance. It begins with these words,

Two hours before my mother killed herself, I noticed she had put on make-up. This shocked me, but it shouldn't have. Whatever the occasion, my mother liked to look her best. That was her way. Just as it was her way to die as she did. Not when death summoned her, but when she summoned death.

Betty writes that the memory of her mother's illness with ovarian cancer is terrible but the memory of her death is wonderful. The cancer was detected in early 1981, two and a half years before she died. Ida Rollin was the type of person who did not believe in a happenstance or topsy-turvy world. She believed that if you did things right, they came out right. In the 1930s she studied nutrition. She took it personally when even the flu afflicted her daughter or husband. True, her husband of 49 years did die of a heart attack one evening when getting up to change the channel. But Ida told everyone at the wake, "My Leon died healthy."

Following the death of her husband, Ida had gone into what she called her selfish period. With her daughter raised and husband dead, she did things for herself. She took piano lessons. She took up bridge. She joined a folk dance group. She joined a theater group that performed for under-privileged children. And she dropped a lot of her old friends and relatives. "All she does is complain. She is boring, who needs it." Betty writes of her mother, "She was smart enough to know that life had been good to her, so she went about feeling grateful. Her gratitude took the form of a kind of continual merriment." Ida had been raised an Orthodox Jew but sent her daughter to the Ethical Culture Society in New York City. She still defined herself as a theist because she needed someone to thank for all the good things in her life.

Ida Rollin was 75 when her ovarian cancer was discovered. She still clung to the idea that if she just ate right she would be all right. Ida entered into chemotherapy with all the optimism that her kind of life implies. She suffered the treatments without complaint because she believed that they would help her. She wore her wig and continued to pursue her activities on the "good days" between treatments. After a year's remission it returned in a more extreme form. One day she said to her daughter, "I know how some people suffer and still they cling to life. But to me, this isn't life. If I had life, I'd want it. I don't want this."

The second half of the book tells how Betty Rollin accepted her mother's decision and helped her end her life. It's an exaggeration, but it seems like she asked every physician and pharmacist in New York City what medication and dosage would give her mother the deliverance she sought. Finally, she called a doctor in Holland, who told her about Nembutal. Ida asked her doctor casually for a prescription, saying that it previously had helped her sleep.

Ida then proceeded to plan her last days. "Here is the check for the November rent. Here is my safety deposit key. All that I have is in bearer bonds; remove them at once." "What do people do who don't have children?" Ida asked. "What if you want to 'check out' but you have no one to help you?" Finally, the appointed day came. Dressed in a new gown and wearing makeup, Ida looked over the family photos one last time with Betty and her husband. Ida washed down the precious red pills with club soda and said, "Remember, I am the most happy woman, and this is my wish. I want you to always remember that." Betty began to cry but knew that her mother was closing "the door" she had been looking for gently behind her.

Each person has his or her value system. Whether life has meaning at any given time can only be answered by an individual. We each have different prerequisites for what we require to choose to go on living. I will mention three examples from my own experience. First, I conducted the memorial service for the mother of a young woman who attended this church. Her mother was not terminally ill. I do not know all the details but essentially it was impossible to fit her with dentures. She was around 60, attractive and still dated. She tried to eat in the corners of dark restaurants but found that too embarrassing and humiliating. She defined life on the basis of such social amenities. Deprived of them, she choose to overdose on sleeping pills.

Another incident occurred a year and a half ago to a woman who had made her adjustment to a nursing home. She loved reading and was able to adjust to the confines of four walls and living in the midst of people whose mental capacities and whose social amenities were far more limited than her own. Then her eyes began to fail. This was all she had left of what she considered "real living." One day, she called a cab and was dropped off in her wheel chair at an apartment building. There, she wheeled herself into the lobby, took the elevator to the top floor, and pushed herself off.

In my first church there was a young man who probably would have lived 40 more years but an illness left him impotent. He was not a Purdue University "All American." But he was made of the same kind of good looks, pleasing personality, bedside manner, and well-endowed physique. No one who knew him believed that it really was a "hunting accident."

When Sigmund Freud was dying of cancer he asked for—and received—a lethal drug. Dr. Christiaan Barnard, who performed the first successful open-heart transplant, tells in his book *Good Life, Good Death* how he instructed the physician attending his mother that she should receive no antibiotics nor feeding tubes. He tells how he and his brother, also a physician, visited a patient slowly suffocating from an advanced lung carcinoma. As the brothers left the bedside they vowed to each other that they would never permit the other to linger in such a condition. They agreed that they would leave pills by the bedside or, if necessary, administer a fatal overdose to the infirmed brother.

I get sick to my stomach when I read about Dorothy Healy of La Jolla, California. Her 92-year-old husband was suffering from emphysema, arteriosclerosis, a stroke, and hallucinated that he was being attacked by birds. She strangled him with her nylon stocking. She pleaded guilty to voluntary manslaughter, saying, "Walter would have thanked me." She received five years of probation. Hans Florin visited his wife in a nursing home in Hollywood, Florida, where she was suffering from advanced Alzheimer's disease and irreversible degeneration of the brain with symptoms of severe senility. She lived in her bed, would not talk, and spent most of her time screaming. Hans took his wife to an empty room at the end of the corridor and shot her. The district attorney called it a classic first-degree murder. A grand jury refused to return an indictment, setting the 79-year-old man free.

I do not think that one has to be a Marxist to see class distinctions in how we die. Dr. Christiaan Barnard's mother is not going to suffer. He will not have to strangle her with a stocking nor will he have to wheel himself off a tall building when he goes. Dr. Freud died a gentleman's death thanks to the lethal solution that his physician gave him. There was no need to smother him with a pillow, as the character Chief does to his lobotomized friend Randle McMurphy in that *One Flew Over the Cuckoo's Nest* scene that stands out for its great violence and compassion.

In ancient Greece, before the rise of Christianity and its gospel of love, anyone who was suffering beyond their ability to manage it could obtain hemlock from the magistrate. In Sir Thomas More's vision of *Utopia*, suicide is accepted when one no longer has the desire or will to go on living. Francis Bacon in *New Atlantis* depicts a society where one's physician will assist with "the good death."

Dr. Christiaan Barnard chides colleagues who act shocked at the thought of helping an incurable patient find release from great pain. If the medical profession is so dedicated to the preservation of life, why didn't the American Medical Association condemn World War I, World War II, the Korean War, or Vietnam? Does that trade group expend its money and prestige crusading against capital punishment?

We live at an exciting time when dying patients and their families are no longer passive. We are going to be hearing a lot more about patient's constitutional rights. The right to die is not going to be settled by physicians but by the courts. People are fed up with hearing, "We would be playing God if we turned the machine off." Angry family members respond, "You played God when you turned it on."

There was a landmark 1976 ruling by the New Jersey Supreme Court, ordering Karen Ann Quinlan's respirator to be turned off at her parents' request. Two years ago a presidential commission concluded that mentally competent adult patients who have little hope of recovery should be allowed to make this decision themselves. The commission held that family members, or others acting on behalf of so-called incompetents, should be able to decide whether or not artificial measures should be used. This year a Gallup poll found that 81 percent of Americans supported freedom of choice on whether or not to use life-support systems for those thought to be terminally ill.

An article describes resuscitation this way,

It is a noisy, brutal process, hard on the medical staff as well as on the patient. Doctors pound the chest, needles jab for arteries and veins, tubes are rammed down the air passages. There are electric shocks, needles in the heart, broken ribs and terse orders in the air.

Is it any wonder that a woman sued physicians for battery when they resuscitated her aged, dying husband? Her attorney said,

Do we use a technology just because it exists? What is this technology designed for? It was designed for the unexpected heart stoppage, for the emergency room to gain time to help a victim. It was not designed to take a cancer-ridden elderly man with six weeks to live and, when his heart stops, to get him going again so he can live six more weeks in a painful fog. We should justify technology in each individual situation. To treat every patient with every technology is to treat him for the doctor's benefit, for his fear of malpractice, not for the patient's well-being.

I urge you to read the papers. The time of nylon stockings and wheelchairing off 10-story buildings is passing. A California court recently ordered a hospital to permit a patient suffering from five usually fatal diseases to refuse further treatment. It recognized his constitutional right to die. It said that the patient's wishes were paramount to the interest of the patient's hospital and doctors. The *New York Times* editorialized, "the court is very clear on the patient's right to say 'enough is enough' and that hospitals must respect these wishes or be sued." A day after this, a New York judge ordered that a respirator keeping a Long Island man alive to be disconnected at his family's request. Charles Perricone had been declared brain dead, and one doctor said that the machine had been merely ventilating a dead body. The hospital had refused the family's plea to turn it off. Medical technology has brought us a long way; we can ventilate a dead body to Armageddon.

Edna Leach was admitted to the hospital in Akron, Ohio with Lou Gehrig's disease. She was placed on a respirator without consulting the family and remained in a chronic vegetative state. Probate Judge Bill Spicer sided with the family and ordered the hospital to disconnect the system. The doctor refused; the family found another physician who would. Edna—who had been in the hospital for 162 days—died 20 minutes later. Mr. Leach then filed a $1.26 million lawsuit against the hospital and the doctor, charging that their extended, unwanted treatment violated Edna's constitutional rights. What is important about these cases is that doctors, who always claimed that they must do everything to keep patients alive to prevent lawsuits, may be held legally responsible for providing treatment that exceeds the wishes of patients or their families.

I believe that one of our inherent rights is to summon death ourselves if we no longer find joy, meaning, or purpose in life. The Greeks believed that it was not possible to describe a person as happy until he died happily. That is not only my wish for you—but my promise. I hope that no member of this congregation ever has to take a wheelchair to a tenth-floor balcony, or use a nylon stocking, or spend months seeking a Dutch doctor who will tell you which medications will give you release. I shall do everything within my power to see that you can leave this world happily, as quickly and as painlessly as Dr. Sigmund Freud or Dr. Christiaan Barnard's mother. I have assisted in self-deliverance before and I shall do it again. This is our great covenant—to help one another.

Delivered October 6, 1985, Third Unitarian Church of Chicago.

Abandonment of the Jews

The *Chicago Tribune* recently reviewed *The Abandonment of the Jews*, about America's role in the destruction of European Jewry. It's a story of silence, indifference, inefficiency, and insensitivity. Don't regard it as something out of the past. Instead, look for parallels to what is happening today.

The story of the annihilation "of a people" was never first-page news. If and when it was covered, it was buried in the back pages. What are the key events of our times relegated to the back pages? What were our parents, teachers, and ministers doing during the final solution? Were they preoccupied with some counterpart of the game of Trivia Pursuit today? Why didn't they write letters in civics class or collect money in church school for the French Jewish children orphaned when their parents were deported? The most important question the book poses is, "Would it be any different today? Would Americans be more sensitive, less self-centered, more willing to make sacrifices, less afraid of differences than they were then?"

Author David Wyman is chair of Jewish studies at Amherst College. He is a Protestant of Swedish descent. He says that the book was difficult to write because one simply does not want to believe the documented facts—a strange confession for a historian.

Nazi leaders decided on July 31, 1941 to pursue a "complete solution to the 'Jewish problem.'" Three months later, Jews were forbidden to leave and the emigration gates to America already had closed. In January 1942, three grave diggers who had managed to escape from one of the death camps provided documented reports to the Polish underground about what was happening.

There were many reasons why people discounted such reports. The British had spread extreme anti-German propaganda during World War I and people suspected more exaggeration. It also seemed inconceivable that a civilized nation could commit such barbaric acts. It was more plausible to believe that the Germans were shipping the Jews to work camps needed for the war effort. When the camps were liberated, General Eisenhower purposely entered with as many reporters as possible because the stories still seemed unbelievable.

Another factor working against the Jews was that in 1941 America was still coming out of the Great Depression. People who had been out of work clamored to severely limit immigration. Veterans groups wanted to ensure that our soldiers would find jobs when they returned home. Surveys at the time revealed that three out of four Americans opposed increasing immigration rates. As a disincentive, visa application forms were four feet long, had to be filled out on both sides, and submitted in six copies. The government added a Catch-22 requirement that a refugee had to be in "acute danger." Where refugees were in acute danger (i.e. in Germany), there were no American consuls to issue visas. And Jewish refugees who escaped Germany into Spain and Portugal were disqualified because they were no longer in "acute danger." There also was fear that Nazi agents would apply to emigrate. In a sign of the times, Congress overwhelmingly defeated a bill that merely sought to ease naturalization procedures for those living in the U.S. who had sons in our armed forces.

A U.S. Jewish paper editorialized in late 1942 that,

It was during the first few months of this year that the pitiless, horrifying word 'extermination' became commonplace in our vocabulary. It was in that year, too, that all our cries and pleas for life-saving action were shattered against walls of indifference until we begin to stifle in the black realization that we are helpless. It was the year of our endless, bottomless helplessness.

During the three and a half years between Pearl Harbor and the end of the war in Europe, approximately 21,000 refugees entered the United States. This amounted to 10 percent of the legally available quota from Axis-controlled European nations. In other words, while the "final solution" was unleashed, 190,000 legal immigration openings went unused.

One idea was to use "free ports." In commerce this means that goods from overseas can be temporarily stored inside a nation's borders. A *New York Times* editorial proposed that refugees be granted a few acres of the poorest land in America—land that they would give up as soon as they could return home. President Roosevelt issued an executive order allowing an abandoned Army base at Oswego, New York to accept 1,000 refugees. Journalist I.F. Stone wrote that America's contribution was "a kind of token payment to decency, a bargain-counter flourish to humanism." The smallness of the offer "destroys the value of the gesture," said Charles Joy of the Unitarian Service Committee.

"If the United States with all its resources can take only 1,000 of these people, what can we expect other countries to do?" With one twentieth of our population and land, Sweden answered this question eight months later by welcoming 8,000 Jews from Denmark.

The author writes of the Jewish camp in Oswego,

> Within a month of the refugees' arrival, anti-Semitism began to increase rapidly throughout the city. Oswego residents who befriended the refugees encountered social ostracism. There was some ganging-up on the refugee children in the public schools. Malicious rumors circulated persistently, especially claims that the government furnished luxury items for refugees and had drained the area of such scarce commodities as ration foods and cigarettes in order to pamper them. A physician in Syracuse told colleagues that the refugees had steak twice a week, despite the meat shortage.

Having considered immigration policy, let's turn to the responses of the press, religious groups, Congress, President Roosevelt and the American Jews, themselves. The *New Republic, the Nation* and the columnist Dorothy Thompson stand out as rare exceptions who labored to keep the Holocaust before the American people. "The information was not readily available to the public because the mass media treated the systematic murder of millions of Jews as though it were minor news." "Roosevelt's failure until March of 1944 to mention the Jewish extermination in his press conferences may have led editors to conclude that the issue was a minor one. And reporters did not ask him what he was doing about the situation." American filmmakers avoided the subject. Although Hollywood released numerous feature films on refugees and Nazi atrocities, none dealt with the Holocaust.

The popular "March of Time" news series running in movie theaters during the war did not touch on extermination, nor did the official U.S. war film series, "Why we Fight." The first American paper to carry a story on the final solution was the *Boston Globe*. It ran that story on June 26, 1942 with the headline "Mass Murders of Jews in Poland Pass 700,000 Mark." The *Globe* buried this scoop at the bottom of page 12! One wonders what its main headline was that day. The *Seattle News* ran the *Globe* story on page 30. Carrying "all the news that's fit to print," *The New York Times* published the story five days later on page six.

The author writes, "Efforts by the United States and other governments to persuade the Vatican to voice public condemnation of Nazi atrocities against civilians came to nothing." Pressed by America's representative, the papal secretary responded, "the Vatican could not condemn particular atrocities publicly, but that it had frequently denounced atrocities in general." The author adds, "In the United States both the Protestant and the Catholic churches remained nearly silent and seemingly indifferent in the face of the crisis in Western and Christian civilization." *The Christian Century*, normally the voice of liberal Protestantism, suggested that New York Rabbi Stephen Wise, the lead spokesman for the Jewish cause, was exaggerating the situation. "No major denomination spoke out on the issue. Few of the many Christian publications cried out for aid to the Jews."

The earliest rescue effort in Congress came from Emanuel Celler, a Jewish Democrat from New York. His bill called for opening America's door to the French Jews, who were about to be rounded up by Vichy authorities. The bill languished in the Committee on Immigration until the French crisis was over. The Jewish chair of that committee, Rep. Samuel Dickstein, never held hearings on the bill. When American Jewish leaders asked Congress to urge the United Nations to rescue the Jews, the best that they could get was an 11-nation joint resolution condemning Nazi atrocities and saying that the guilty would be held responsible. "The State Department had shown itself to be entirely callous," the author writes. "Most members of Congress seemed to know little, and care less."

Jewish hopes centered on a conference to be held in Bermuda by British and American leaders. It passed resolutions to encourage neutral nations to take more refugees and to find a way to evacuate the 5,000 Jews living in Spain. Szmul Zygielbojm, a Jewish member of the Polish national council, committed suicide a week after the conference. In one of his last letters, he wrote,

The responsibility for this crime of murdering the entire Jewish population of Poland falls in the first instance on the perpetrators but indirectly it is also a burden on the whole of humanity, the people, and governments of the Allied States which thus far have made no effort toward concrete action for the purpose of curtailing the crime. By the passive observation of the murder of defenseless millions and of the maltreatment of children, women and old men, those countries have become the criminal accomplices . . . As I was unable to do anything during my life, perhaps by my death I shall contribute to breaking down that indifference.

American Jewry did not present a united front. The divided Zionists and the Anti-Zionists fought over which group should speak for the rest. Of the seven Jews in Congress, only Emanuel Celler persistently advocated government rescue actions. Samuel Dickstein joined the struggle from time to time. Four others seldom raised the issue. Rep. Sol Bloom sided with the State Department throughout. The book's author wrote, "Overall, Jewish intellectuals remained as uninvolved as non-Jews. To note one example among many, Walter Lippmann, a highly influential news columnist who dealt with practically every major topic of the day, wrote nothing on the Holocaust."

Supported by perhaps 99 percent of American Jews, President Roosevelt did almost nothing for the cause. He, of all people, could have placed the issue before the American people. He held press conferences twice a week and spoke not a word about the mass killings for at least a year after the news first broke. Rabbi Stephen Wise's unlimited trust in the president was misplaced. After Wise urged Roosevelt to rescue those who had not yet perished, the most that Roosevelt would say was that "the perpetrators of the crime would be held accountable." Wyman writes, "In the end, the era's most prominent symbol of humanitarianism turned away from one of history's most compelling challenges."

The most amazing part of this history involves the obvious need to rescue those who were next in line to die. Eleanor Roosevelt, when pressed, seemed to say that all that we could do was win the war, or that those guilty of crimes would be punished, or a Jewish state would be established in Palestine after the war. Even requests to bomb the train tracks taking victims to Auschwitz were denied. The War Department said,

> It is not contemplated that units of the armed forces will be employed for the purpose of rescuing victims of enemy oppression unless such rescues are the direct result of military operations conducted with the object of defeating the armed forces of the enemy.

Although bombs were dropped within 30 miles of Auschwitz, the War Department said that destroying the rail lines would take crews away from "decisive missions" essential to the war effort! It noted that the military appreciates the humanitarian importance of the mission but that the most effective relief to the victims is the defeat of the Nazis.

The unpleasant topic that I have avoided to the end is the real reason for

American silence, indifference, inefficiency and insensitivity. The sociologist David Riesman writes that anti-Semitism hit a historic peak in 1944. A rumor that I recall hearing in grade school was that the Jews shirked military service, staying home to prosper while Christian boys went off to fight and die.

Office of War Information surveys revealed that the impact of atrocity information on the average American was seven times greater when it involved general atrocities rather than those perpetrated against Jews. The U.S. and Britain rescued 100,000 Yugoslav, Polish and Greek refugees from disastrous conditions. It was not a lack of workable plans that stood in the way of saving thousands more Jews. Nor was it insufficient shipping, the threat of infiltration by subversives, or the possibility that rescue projects would hamper the war effort. The real obstacle was that there simply was no strong desire to rescue Jews.

I wish that someone would go through our church records during the period when European Jewry was destroyed and do the same at the two synagogues on Harlem Avenue, along with the surrounding Catholic and Protestant churches. What a sordid tale it would reveal! How trite and petty are many of our activities as the main events pass us by. We know that 10,000 people met to express outrage in a Chicago stadium in 1942. Did this congregation charter a bus to go? Were we a sponsor? Did we contribute money for refugee assistance?

As I said at the beginning, the chief reason to retell this story is that it has relevance now. There are refugees who seek sanctuary today and church boards and finance committees are scared shitless that activists will press the issue and demand a response. There's not a Jew in this congregation who believes that the issue before us today has only to do with him or her. It has to do with that ancient question that Cain asked God and that we each must answer again. "Am I my brother's keeper?" Let us answer that question with: "Never again."

Delivered December 16, 1984, Third Unitarian Church of Chicago.

A Community of Survivors

Survivors of Nazi concentration camps have written at least 80 books about their experiences. I am indebted to Terrence De Pres of Colgate University for summarizing their accounts. Life offers no more extreme testing than the concentration camps. Here was life at its worst and some managed to stay alive in body and spirit. We will perhaps never be tested to the extent that they were—never called upon to suffer as they suffered—yet many of us find it difficult just to survive ourselves.

I used to quote William Faulkner's Nobel Prize acceptance speech, "Man will not just endure—but man will prevail." Or the words of Jesus, "I am come that they might have life, and might have it abundantly." The more my life becomes enmeshed with others, the easier it has become for me to eulogize someone at a memorial service for just managing to survive. Someone who has been able to keep his or her body and soul together for 60 or 80 years. If we can go beyond surviving, fine. But it is no small thing just to be a survivor.

I want to deal with three specific lessons learned by the concentration camp survivors. The first lesson concerns personal dignity. A survivor writes, "This is the first step to the grave. It was almost an iron law: Those who failed to wash every day soon died. Whether this was the cause or effect of inner-breakdown, I don't know; but it was an infallible symptom." The turning point toward life or death was something so basic as one's personal appearance!

I went not long ago to visit a friend in an institution for the mentally ill. Those of you who have visited such places are aware of the personal appearance of the patients. Their outward appearance almost always testifies to the confusion and the depression that exists inside. People in nursing homes often have to be forced to bathe. The young widow does not care to even brush her hair. The jilted lover often begins to overeat and takes little interest in his personal appearance. Our appearance is in many ways our declaration as to how we feel about ourselves and about life.

Concentration camp prisoners were forced to wet and soil themselves.

Psychologist Bruno Bettelheim concludes that this excremental crisis made it impossible for camp inmates to see themselves as full adults. Imagine how camp prisoners looked and smelled, especially those who had given up the will to live. An enormous revulsion and disgust naturally arose among the prisoners. The prisoner was made to feel subhuman, to see his self-image in the dirt and stink of his neighbor. They destroyed their dignity, every vestige of humanity, reducing prisoners to the level of wild animals. They filled prisoners with horror and contempt toward themselves and their fellow prisoners. SS guards appeared superior, not only by virtue of their guns and assurance, but also by their elegant apartness from the filth of the prisoners. This made it easier for them to do their jobs. SS guards didn't think of themselves as killing "people."

In this environment, each prisoner had to decide to give up or to resist. And the first step of this process had to do with personal dignity and personal appearance. A prisoner wrote,

> I began to look around me and saw the beginning of the end for any woman or man who had the opportunity to wash and had not done so, or any woman or man who felt that the tying of a shoe was wasted energy.

It wasn't simply that millions were murdered. First, they were murdered in spirit, as a means of killing them in body. A survivor said that if we were to put all the evil of our age into one image, it would be the face with dead eyes.

The first step to keeping life and light in the eyes is to wash the body, comb the hair, brush the teeth, and exercise so far as possible. I am personally amazed that this is the first lesson to be learned about surviving. Again, it makes more sense if you visit—or occupy—a prison, hospital, or nursing home. A substitute teacher enters a classroom where children have meager possessions. Yet here is a child who walks differently, who wears clothes with a sense of pride, who has a light in his eyes. There are children in sections of this city that have become human dumping grounds who have made a decision that they are superior to their environments.

The second concentration camp lesson is that we must extend care to others. A Treblinka survivor writes, "In our group we shared everything; and the moment one of the group ate something without sharing it, we knew it was the beginning of the end." Elie Wiesel records the advice of a veteran inmate to a recent arrival. "We are all brothers, and we are all suffering the same fate. The same smoke floats over all our heads. Help one another. It is the only way to survive." Terrence De Pres, who has researched 80 survivor books, summarizes their story. "Prisoners survived through concrete acts of mutual aid, and over a period of time these many small deeds, like fibers in the shuttle of a clumsy loom, grew into a general fabric of debt and care."

The survivors testify over and over again that the need *to* help is as basic as the need *for* help. Another survivor writes,

> Working with us were weaker men who grew exhausted after a few trips of carrying sacks of cement from the storeroom to the building site. The younger of us, myself included, pitched in to help them. We had agreed among our group that we would help one another to whatever extent was possible, rather than surrender to the dog-eat-dog philosophy which poisoned the minds of some prisoners.
>
> Ilse worked on the day shift and came back at noon. She turned away from me so that I could not see what she was doing, and dug into her pocket. "I have brought you a present!" she announced triumphantly. There, on a fresh leaf, was one, red, slightly mashed, raspberry.
>
> It was astonishing to see how anxious these hungry men were to share what they had . . . There was half an orange on all the beds in the room. One of our friends had received a parcel. He had not even been able to wait for our return.

A survivor of Majdanek writes,

> I thought of my arrival and my first impressions of the camp. I knew that a person coming to a camp was afraid of everything and everybody; that she was distracted and terrified. The first word was so important. I decided to be patient, to answer all questions, to calm them, and give them courage. My life at that point began to hold meaning.

It was not ruthlessness that enabled them to survive, but a decision to use their lives to help others. Life in extremity is radically social. Those who could not share were not able to survive.

Compare these stories to the bestseller lists. *How to Be Your Own Best Friend. Your Erogenous Zone. Looking Out for Number One.* Millions of people are looking for ways to survive and buying the wrong messages. Just satisfy yourself. Don't worry about anyone else.

The third death-camp lesson is that survival depends upon solidarity. Self-centered and isolated individuals didn't live to tell about it. Survivors organized themselves. They had to learn to live collectively.

> The great individualists of our free days, the unorganized and backward workers, the cynics, not to mention businessmen who knew nothing of organized action ... all disintegrated morally. They became witless tools for the Nazis. They groveled for favors although their groveling degraded them further. And they did not live long in Buchenwald.

"Survival could only be a social achievement—not an individual accident." Collective action is more effective than individual effort—solidarity becomes power in proportion to the degree of discipline in the group. One of the prisoners wrote, "As soon as one of us is alone he thinks, 'What's the use? Why do it? Why not give up?' But with others, one keeps going."

Austrian scientist Konrad Lorenz argues that man is a social creature.

> If it were not for a rich endowment of social instincts, men never could have risen above the animal world. All specifically human faculties, the power of speech, cultural tradition, moral responsibility, could have evolved only in a being which, before the very dawn of conceptual thinking, lived in well-organized communities.

"I soon realized that alone one could not possibly survive. It was necessary therefore to form little families. In this way we looked after one another." I do not believe that it is any more possible to survive by oneself in Chicago today than in one of the concentration camps. Only communities of love can confront the hatred, the division, the suffering of this world. Peevish individualism simply will not work. Survival is a social achievement in Chicago or in Auschwitz. In extremity, life depends upon care for others. It depends upon solidarity.

I read these lessons in bed last week. I read them at a time when I had little energy and, as snow piled up outside my window, somehow I was unconvinced! I felt something of the coldness and powerlessness of those prisoners and yet I felt that I myself would never have survived. They are good lessons. I believe them. And I believe they are valid for us. Yet, there is something missing. As one reads of Nazi concentration camps, one is convinced that horses and other beasts would not have survived where humans did.

When the human form lies shrunken to a childish form, when arms and legs have become like twigs, when the mouth is parched and puckered, when every bite of food causes the return of dysentery, when the very smell of the camp soup brings on nausea, when there is no help, no care, no medicine—whence comes this magic will to live? Where is it born? In which recess of the human body does it bud and blossom—so strongly that it can conquer death in so many shapes? Whence comes this imperishable willpower to find the means of going on? Wasn't there something else the survivors of hell could tell us—something else that they could testify to—something else they found at the end of their ropes?

All the survivors seemed to have experienced the same thing. After we have used up all that there is in us, there is something that can only be described as "life itself." It is greater than, and other than, ourselves. "The reference is always made to something like a 'reservoir of strength,' which in extremity becomes active and is felt as the deeper foundation of selfhood." Stripped of everything, the survivors found themselves falling back upon some biologically determined "talent," long suppressed by cultural deformation—a bank of knowledge embedded in the body's cells. Something innate within the life process—the ingrained inheritance of all life experience in a particular line of descent.

Human ancestors split from chimps fewer than 13 million years ago. In the deepest sense, man's inheritance goes back to the appearance of life on earth. There is something within us that could be called "survival behavior." With millions of years of surviving packed into our genes, it would be strange if there were not, at some deep involuntary level, special capacities geared to enabling us to cope with extremities. Des Pres writes, "Something innate—let us think of it as a sort of biological gyroscope—keeps men and women steady in their humanness despite inhuman pressure." Something that enables them not just to survive physically but to survive as human beings. Everything going on around them was gauged to turn them against each other but, in a multitude of ways, men and women persisted in social acts. The more pressure from without, the more solidarity. There was a return to community as an inborn reaction to danger and stress.

How often we hear people say that just the thinnest veneer of civilization keeps us from turning into animals. What would we do if pushed to our very limits? These survivors testify to the fact that, at the heart of the human psyche, there is something that is life-sustaining and life-affirming. Something takes over when we have used up all we have inside us!

- Those who failed to wash everyday soon died.
- The moment one of the group ate something without sharing it, we knew it was the beginning of the end.
- I soon realized that alone one could not possibly survive—it was necessary therefore to form little families.

Delivered January 29, 1978, Third Unitarian Church of Chicago.

Canary in the Coalmine

With a membership that is 20 percent Jewish, our church is a bridge between Christians and Jews. Yet this message is directed primarily at those of us with Christian backgrounds. We are the ones who must most remember that anti-Semitism is "the canary in the coalmine" that signals impending danger to society as a whole.

The Holocaust is the unfinished business of Christian churches. The single most important event in recent church history is the Holocaust. Yet it is virtually ignored in church schools and carefully avoided by preachers in the pulpit. I recommend to you a book titled *New Lives* about Holocaust survivors in America. Their great fear is that the Holocaust was a matter of indifference to everyone but its victims, that the world has taken no lessons from it, that it changed nothing, taught nothing, and meant nothing. One survivor says,

> We were fighting in Auschwitz—fighting for life each day—and the greatest fear of the people I knew was not just death; but the idea that every last one of them would die, and there would be no one left to tell what had happened to them.

Today we remember the victims—and also what caused them to become victims. It is not my intention to indict contemporary Christians so much as to remind ourselves of the dangers of anti-Semitism in our tradition. It is my presupposition that the acid test of Christianity is its treatment of the Jews. The Christians of the world have not acknowledged—let alone repented—for the mass murder of Jews by Christians in the heart of Christendom. What happened on Christianity's watch between 1942 and 1945 is so outrageous and scandalous that Christianity has made itself incredible to Jews, humanists, and even to some Christians.

Methodist minister Franklin Littell, a former professor at Chicago Theological Seminary, wrote a book titled *The Crucifixion of the Jews*. He writes, "The Jews who have experienced the cross on a vast scale, with the loss of one-third of their total world population in three years, see the cross as something that Christians do to others." Littell says that the Christian church has "gotten itself off the hook" by popularizing such extraordinary Christians as Dietrich Bonhoeffer, Alfred Delp, Franz Jägerstätter, Paul Schneider and Kurt Gerstein. If Germany had 80 million people, it is a gross misrepresentation to concentrate on a few Christian martyrs! Littell says, "The vast majority of the martyrs for the Lord of History were Jews."

As we know, Christianity came out of Judaism. Peter, Paul and Jesus all would have perished at Auschwitz. Jesus's disciples and earliest followers were Jewish. But by the time of the Emperor Cyprian in the 3rd Century, Christians were blaming the death of Jesus on both the Romans and the Jews. Littell writes, "By the year 258, theological anti-Semitism had reached the polished form, which prevailed through succeeding centuries." Some Unitarians believe that theology has few consequences. Yet when Vatican II chose to "forgive the Jews for killing Christ" circa 1962, for example, Arab League governments pressured Catholics not to eliminate this from their teachings!

To appreciate anti-Semitism's reach, I will quote a couple famous Christians. Martin Luther proposed a plan of action for Jews.

> First, to set fire to their synagogues or schools . . . Second, I advise that
> their houses also be razed and destroyed. Third, I advise that all their
> prayer books and Talmudic writings, in which such idolatry, lies, cursing,
> and blasphemy are taught, be taken from them. Fourth, I advise that their
> rabbis be forbidden to teach henceforth on pain of loss of life and limb.

Luther continues in this vein through seven points. I leave the rest to your imagination.

Rev. Dietrich Bonhoeffer, who was hanged by the Nazis for attempting to assassinate Hitler, wrote,

> The church of Christ has never lost sight of the thought that "the chosen
> people" who nailed the redeemer of the world to the cross must bear the
> curse for its action throughout a long history of suffering . . . The conver-
> sion of Israel, that is to be the end of the people's period of suffering.

Hitler, who died a Roman Catholic, and Hermann Göring, who died a Lutheran, were not aberrations of Christian theology. They were political manifestations of it. Rev. Littell writes,

> Adolf Hitler, the Third Reich, the Aryan paragraphs, and the death camps, these were not accidental appearances in the heart of Christendom: They were not strange and inexplicable manifestations of some sudden revolt and of demonism, eruptions out of the abyss which defy intelligent appraisal. Neither were they uniquely German or Teutonic, as though some racial explanation might serve to take the curse from the rest of us. They were the legitimate offspring of a Christian civilization which, underneath the cosmetics of official creeds and public displays of piety, was formless and heathen at heart.

The question is not how could Judaism survive the Holocaust but how could Christianity?

There is something that intrigues me that may relate to the Catholic Church's concern with fetuses today. I am referring to the fact that the Catholic Church used its political clout to save those who were confined to institutions for mental and physical deficiencies, yet never exercised that clout to save healthy Jewish children, nor brilliant Jewish scientists and authors.

The Vatican signed a "concordat" treaty with the Nazis that gave Hitler his first major diplomatic victory and an entree into "decent international society." The accord was engineered by the man who became Pope Pius XII. Hitler wanted the Vatican treaty to give his regime respectability and to eliminate the Centre Party. Although Hitler was elected to office by a majority, the Centre Party retained sufficient power to block legislation granting him absolute power. On July 20, 1933, Hitler and the Pope signed their agreement. One provision stipulated that priests could no longer participate in politics, effectively gutting the priest-backed Centre Party. In return, the Nazis guaranteed the Catholic Church the right to run Catholic schools, exempt theology students from military service, and allowing the Vatican to nominate theology professors at German universities. A French paper editorialized that,

> The main feature of the concordat is the transformation of all Catholic associations into purely spiritual and religious bodies, without political or economic existence. This is a triumph for the National Socialist gov-

ernment. It took Mussolini five years to achieve this; Germany has done it in a week. Catholicism in Germany has lost everything to save its life.

Within six months of its birth, the Third Reich had received full approval from the highest spiritual power on earth.

A German scholar wrote,

> The wiping out of the Jews would be inconceivable without the coop-eration and the participation of the Christians. It came neither sud-denly nor unexpectedly . . . it is no accident that the ideologues of anti-Semitism have borrowed their weapons extensively from the arsenal of churchly teaching and terminology.

In seizing anti-Semitism as a political weapon, the Nazis built upon the theo-logical and cultural anti-Semitism that churches had assembled over centuries.

Hitler wrote in *Mein Kampf* that it is easier "for people to believe big lies than little ones" (especially if they build on predisposed beliefs). He told the German people that they had been defeated in World War I not so much by the Allied forces as by international Jewish bankers. He invoked the Red Men-ace and denounced Socialists and leftists as Jews. He blamed the traditional legal order of the Weimar Republic on Jews. He appealed for the preserva-tion and cleansing of the "pure Aryan blood stream." Hitler wrote of "the nightmare vision of the seduction of hundreds of thousands of girls by the repulsive, crooked-legged Jewish bastards." Posters depicted the black-haired Jewish boy, diabolic joy on his face, waiting to ambush the unsuspecting girl, whom he defiles with his look.

On April 1, 1933, three months after coming to power, Hitler called for a boycott of all stores owned by Jews. Next, they were barred from civil ser-vice—from teaching, the stage, the media, medicine and dentistry. Books by Jewish authors were burned. Jewish children were banished from public schools. Those with even 25 percent Jewish blood were forbidden to play the music of Bach, Beethoven, Mozart and other Aryan composers. In 1938, the Nazis began to sequester all remaining Jewish wealth, allowing just $2,000 per Jew. Jews who had been allowed to purchase immigration papers now were re-duced to paupers.

When a Jew killed a German secretary in the embassy in Paris, Hitler un-leashed his first real pogrom on November 9, 1938. All 500 synagogues were burned; 50,000 Jews were sent to concentration camps. Every Jewish home was smashed; Jewish men, women and children were savagely beaten. The German Jewish community was fined $400 million for the resulting damages, for which, after all, they were responsible. On January 1, 1939, all Jewish businesses were liquidated. Scores of scientists were employed to demonstrate the "racial inferiority" of Jews. Hitler offered to sell 150,000 Jews as hostages. He also planned to ship them to Madagascar. But when war was declared against the USSR, he felt compelled to move faster, hitting upon the "final solution."

Roman Catholic Gordon Zahn wrote, "the German Catholic who looked to his religious superiors for spiritual guidance and direction regarding Hitler's war, received virtually the same answers he would have received from the Nazi ruler himself." Commenting on American churches today, Franklin Littell says, "Much Christian congregational life is dull in worship and in culture, it is virtually indistinguishable from the Rotarians or the country club." He continues, "Liberal Protestantism in America . . . is very little different from the liberal Protestantism of Germany which accommodated so readily to Nazism."

There is no way to generalize about the Holocaust. But I am suggesting that the Jews were destroyed because they were a "peculiar people" and Christians cooperated in that destruction because European Christianity had gone mainstream. This marks a change from our roots. When the New Testament told the faithful "you are a peculiar people," it meant that both the Christians and the Jews had been "called out," were unique and special groups. Both Jews and Christians were called to be a counter-culture. But in recent centuries in America and Germany, Christians no longer were in the minority. The U.S. director of the National Council of Christians and Jews discovered that the most liberal churches had the most anti-Catholic, anti-Fundamentalist and anti-Semitic curricula. In America, we seem to prefer religions that do not make us conspicuous or set us apart.

Littell suggests that part of Christian anti-Semitism stems from guilt. "Jews who persist in maintaining a counter-culture are an unpleasant reminder that New Testament standards require Christians to be counter-culture, too." I hope you do not think that I am mistaking the forms of religion with its contents. Orthodox Jews in America are the least likely to speak out against Vietnam, racial injustice, poverty, or inequality or discrimination. Like their Christian counterparts (i.e., Nazarenes and Southern Baptists), they maintain the forms of religion without its contents.

If I have had a theme during the last nine years, it is that Unitarians have left the American mainstream. There is a counter-culture here at Third Church, as much as there is in an Amish community, a hippie commune, or a monastery. Those who are faithful to the prophets should carry signs identifying themselves as a people who will not be assimilated. Both the New Testament and the Old Testament reiterate over and over again that, "You are a peculiar people."

When I'm done I hope that you will tell each other, "He didn't say anything I haven't heard before." For this is a message we need to hear many times. We must remember the victims of the Holocaust—and the theology that facilitated it. It is a sign of hope that the public schools in Philadelphia and New York City require each child to learn what happened in the Holocaust. A highlight of my life was hearing Simon Wiesenthal speak last fall about bringing Nazis to trial. He is not interested in revenge but, rather, that justice be done. Isn't it strange, he said, that I am told to forget what has happened in the Holocaust by those who continue to remind Jews of what they did to Jesus 2,000 years ago?

Let us remember the victims of the Holocaust—and to be realistic about human nature. The limit of man's evil exceeds our imaginations. There seems to be no point beyond which we will not go to hurt others. From the memories of the Warsaw Ghetto comes this message, "What defeated us, ultimately, was Jewry's indestructive optimism, our eternal faith in the goodness of man, or rather, in the limits of degradation." Even Hitler exaggerated man's goodness. He feared that each new anti-Semitic decree would be met with an outburst of righteous indignation. It never came. One survivor writes, "Confidence trapped and killed the Jews of Europe." A confidence that believed that it couldn't happen.

Wiesenthal says that there are 85 Neo-Nazi parties in America today. There are 7 million German Nazis who are still alive. The *New York Times* reported recently on our rightward swing. Forty-seven percent of Americans now consider themselves right of center, with 10 percent in the middle of the road. I simply cannot believe in the coincidence of what I found in the mail this week. While I was researching death camps, I received a packet of the most horrible anti-Semitic materials—worthy of Hitler himself. They came from a Joseph Dilys, who lives in Chicago at 3607 S. Union.

Emil Fackenheim writes,

Jews are forbidden to hand Hitler posthumous victories. They are commanded to remember the victims of Auschwitz, lest their memory fade. They are forbidden also to despair or to escape into cynicism, lest they cooperate with Hitler in delivering the world over to the forces of Auschwitz.

As Christmas draws near, let us remind our Christian brethren of the words of Bonhoeffer. "Only he who cries out for the Jews may sing Gregorian chants." The canary in the coalmine flutters his wings. Brown shirts march in the streets of Skokie. Swastikas appear on black leather jackets. A Northwestern University historian writes that the Holocaust is a hoax.

First they came for the socialists, and I did not speak out—
Because I was not a socialist.
Then they came for the trade unionists, and I did not speak out—
Because I was not a trade unionist.
Then they came for the Jews, and I did not speak out—
Because I was not a Jew.
Then they came for me—and there was no one left to speak for me.

Delivered December 11, 1977, Third Unitarian Church of Chicago.

Editor's note: This essay was delivered months after the U.S. Supreme Court ruled that neo-Nazis had a right to march in the Chicago suburb of Skokie— home to thousands of Holocaust survivors. The Nazis were led by Frank Collin, the son of Dachau survivor Max Collin (born in Munich as Max Cohn). In the end, Collin and a small band of followers rallied outside a Chicago federal building—drowned out by thousands of counter-protesters.

Is Unearned Suffering Redemptive?

As two women left church, one asked, "What was he talking about today?" Her friend replied, "I don't really know. But it seemed to do him a world of good." Today's topic falls into that category. I always wanted to make the concept of "the cross" understandable to atheists. One does not have to be a Christian or a theist to appreciate its symbolism. Ironically, if more people who consider themselves to be Christian really understood the cross, they would reject it. At the risk of offending Jew and Gentile alike, I will address the symbolism of the cross.

By chance, today marks the anniversary of Dr. King's death. I do not believe that anyone in modern American history understood the cross as well as Martin Luther King, Jr. He said,

> We must somehow believe that unearned suffering is redemptive. I pray that recognizing the necessity of suffering, the Negro will make of it a virtue. To suffer in a righteous cause is to grow in our humanity's full stature.

This idea of the cross was foolishness to the Greeks and a hurdle for the Jews. Neither group was interested in a religion that celebrated unearned suffering. It is almost unbelievable that American blacks who have suffered so much were willing to follow a leader who made a virtue out of suffering. Some people believe that Dr. King died at the right time. Near the end of his life there was a growing restlessness with his insistence that the way to full manhood or womanhood was to deliberately embrace suffering to further a righteous cause.

Dr. King surely realized that most people seek to reduce their suffering—not expand it. No other religion has had the stupidity to use a negative sign as their symbol. Buddhists chose the lotus flower; the Jews, the Star of David; Unitarians, the flaming chalice; and so it goes. Yet Dr. King used the symbol of the cross to its utmost, inviting his followers to join him in discovering that unearned suffering is redemptive.

I believe that the key word here, is "unearned." For something to qualify as a cross experience, it has to be freely chosen. It has to be something that you could walk away from. There are some troubles that we can avoid and others that are unavoidable. King promoted that awkward third category— troubles that we could avoid but choose not to. The cross that Jesus bore at Calvary and the crosses that Dr. King and his followers bore in Birmingham were freely chosen. Both leaders could have lived comfortable, carefree existences. Instead, they voluntarily shouldered the cross of unearned, redemptive suffering.

Sometimes people refer to their mother-in-law, their alcoholic husband, or their teenage daughter's pregnancy as "the cross they have to bear." That misuses the term. A "cross experience" must be deliberately chosen suffering. True Christians take upon themselves the burdens of others. The average Christian might look upon this as insanity, but I believe that this is what conversion means.

Dr. King said, "There are some who still find the cross a stumbling block. Others who consider it foolishness. But I am more convinced than ever before that it is the power of God unto social and individual salvation." If the word "salvation" turns you off, "fulfillment" is an acceptable synonym. If someone wants to find fulfilment, to reach humanity's full stature, then they must shoulder responsibilities that they could easily avoid—thereby discovering for themselves that unearned suffering is redemptive. This idea makes most of us uncomfortable, although the experience is not foreign to us. The murals around this room primarily depict individuals who made unearned suffering redemptive (Dr. King, Harriet Tubman, Jane Addams, Gandhi and Tom Paine). Visitors might conclude that we honor masochists.

Obviously, no healthy person wants to suffer. Life has plenty of unavoidable suffering. Why add to it? The reason is that, thus far, we have not found any other way to achieve progress. There have to be some people who are strong enough to bear the burdens of others if there is to be any kind of civilization at all. From the moment of birth, someone must immediately bear the burdens of a newborn. Wherever ignorance or evil would destroy human life, there is only one way out—through the sacrifice of someone willing to live and die for others.

The point of T. S. Eliot's play The *Cocktail Party* is that if evil is to be put right there must be expiation and reparation. Marc Connelly dealt with this theme in his play *Green Pastures*. God looks down from above and sees evil throughout the world. He says to Gabriel, I've sent a flood, I've sent plagues, I've sent prophets. What can I do to deliver them?

Force, coercion and laws won't fully transform society. They can help, and Dr. King advocated laws for voter registration and against lynching. Yet he knew that real change would come only as some people voluntarily offered to bear the burdens of others. I keep searching for a short cut. Consider something as simple as teaching a child to read. Who in their right mind wants to spend every Tuesday and Saturday here at church to help a child improve this one area of his life? Isn't there a short cut that doesn't involve one person bearing the burdens of another? The price of creativity, growth, and human progress is someone's pain and suffering.

Was it the historian Eugen Rosenstock-Huessy who said that if anyone makes a complete sacrifice, history goes forward one millimeter? Quaker civil rights leader Bayard Rustin said, "Nothing that is good, personal or social can begin to occur so long as there is any effort to pursue security." Yet we all go on in the pursuit of security, seeking whatever will protect us from the pain and suffering of others. The idea that unearned suffering is redemptive was not only foolishness to many ancient Greeks and Jews, it is the babbling of an idiot to most Americans—and most Unitarians.

Consider a hostile, lonely, crotchety person—the kind of person most of us go out of our way to avoid. There is no way back into society for that person unless someone bears his burdens, takes his crap, and leads him back into the human family. As the psychiatrist William Glasser puts it, the person who is sick or losing, changes only as he has a relationship with someone who is healthy and succeeding.

Christians have a tough sell with the idea that unearned suffering is redemptive. Too few healthy, successful people are willing to take on the burdens of others. Nor is this principle limited only to personal relationships. Dr. King applied it to suffering for a righteous cause. Dorothy Day, Roger LaPorte, James Reeb, Scott Nearing, Clarence Jordan, Martha Tranquilli are some of the names of those who have embraced unearned suffering and found something strong, vital and sustaining in the experience. The activist A. J. Muste said, "Whenever love that will suffer unto death is manifested, whenever a true crucifixion takes place, unconquerable power is released into the stream of history." Thousands of us are still being nourished and undergirded by the sacrifices of those who have gone before us.

What many Christians don't understand is that Easter and Good Friday are the same thing. The crucifixion was the victory. The cross is not a de-tour—or hurdle—on the way to the kingdom, nor is it even the way to the kingdom. It *is* the kingdom come. Bearing the burdens of others, laying down one's life for friends is the ultimate. Any approximation of it is to be prized and treasured.

Dr. King believed that the only hope for mankind was to recognize the need for suffering and to look on it as a virtue. Only as we are willing to vol-untarily assume the burdens of others can we find the ultimate value in our own lives. If we do this, Dr. King told his people, future historians would say, "There lived a great people—a black people—who injected new meaning and dignity into the veins of civilization." This has been and always will be the hu-man condition. Poet James Russell Lowell wrote, "Truth forever on the scaf-fold, Wrong forever on the throne." Only unearned suffering keeps alive a dream of something better. Pain and progress are linked together. Hence it is critical that a sufficient number of people embrace the philosophy that un-earned suffering is the path to human fulfilment.

I believe the Nazarene was right on this point and that his understand-ing of life will finally triumph. In country after country there is a growing be-lief "that he who would be the greatest of all must be the servant of all." That's the difference between Mao and Chiang Kai-shek; between Ho Chi Minh and Ngo Dinh Diem; between LBJ and César Chávez; between Nixon and MLK.

I have been trying to deal with the complex symbolism of the cross. If we eliminated that symbol, we would need another one to convey the need to bear the burdens of others and to find fulfilment through suffering on their be-half. There is much in Christianity that is irrational, ridiculous and erroneous. Those of us born into it found it necessary to separate ourselves from it. But, as Unitarians, we are free to draw on any teaching that is true and good. I believe that there are more people here who are committed to the idea of unearned suffering than there are in traditional Protestant and Catholic churches. I hope this is always a place where the great treasures of all the world's religions are honored. Let this be a community that understands the cross as one of the great insights into how human life is sustained and nurtured. Let us remem-ber Dr. King's words, "If a man has not discovered something that he will die for, he isn't fit to live."

Delivered April 4, 1976, Third Unitarian Church of Chicago.

A Service of Repentance

n prosecuting the Indochina War, the U.S. Government demands two things of its people: warm bodies and cold cash. And so we have the draft and taxes. The young men who oppose the draft have exhibited great courage and bravery. Thousands have left their native land and are now exiles. Thousands more have served in prison. And thousands of others have declared themselves conscientious objectors, taking an unpopular position in our society. A mother told me that she didn't feel there could be anything good about the draft—until her playboy son became a man by confronting it and deciding that his life's purpose did not include killing.

Those who have supplied the cold cash have not wrestled with this war like those told to supply the warm bodies. With few exceptions, we have paid for this war graciously. We have somehow felt that our role was to compliment the young men who resisted, the Berrigan brothers, Army Captain Howard Levy, Chaplain William Sloane Coffin, Dr. Benjamin Spock and Daniel Ellsberg. We voice disapproval of the war but our deeds have not been consistent with our words nor our actions reflective of our beliefs.

The Roman Catholic theologian Gordon Zahn wrote a book on Franz Jägerstätter, the German peasant who went to his death rather than support Hitler. Zahn found among Jägerstätter's possessions a handwritten essay. It offered the hypothetical case of two men, each performing substantially the same services for the Nazi Reich. One believed in the movement and thought that what he did was right and proper. The other rejected the Nazi's ideology, goals and policies yet considered himself to be the better of the two because he did not share the other's commitment to National Socialism. Jägerstätter recognized that the non-Nazi's actions arguably were worse because he knew that what he was doing was wrong.

Some members of Third Church look down upon those who are unenlightened about this war. Jägerstätter would say that it is worse for we who know better to finance the war. I hope that some who have come here today to thank God for their enlightenment will leave here asking for forgiveness, if not from God then from those who have suffered for refusing to support this war, and those who have suffered from the bombs that our money purchased.

I want to make clear that I distinguish between draft dodgers and draft resisters. The true man of conscience confronts the system. While some of us have counseled young men on the draft, I wonder if they should have counselled us on resisting war taxes? They should have turned on us as Jesus turned on the maudlin women who followed him to his crucifixion, saying, "Don't weep for us, weep for yourselves."

Several of us attended a dinner last month honoring Karl Meyer on his release from prison for tax resistance. I sat there thinking, "Damn you, Karl, you are right, and if you did not exist, I would not feel guilty." Karl chides us for passing the buck and blaming the war on others. We are always writing to Senators Charles Percy and Adlai Stevenson, telling them how to vote. April 15th is the day that we vote, casting dollar ballots for or against the war. You've heard the chant, "LBJ, LBJ, how many kids did you kill today?" Karl would ask why we don't put that question to ourselves.

Isn't there a point at which we will have had enough? The seamstress Rosa Parks was riding home from work when a white man asked her to give up her bus seat. She broke the law and refused. Is there some point at which justice and humanity will mean more to us than the law of the land? We should respect what is right more than the law. Our actions should be governed by justice rather than legality. Thoreau wrote that if the injustice of the law,

> is of such a nature that it requires you to be the agent of injustice to another, then I say break the law. Let your life be a counter-friction to stop the machine. What I have to do is to see, at any rate, that I do not lend myself to the wrong which I condemn.

Albert Camus wrote in this vein that the willingness to violate the laws of the state for humanistic reasons is a mark of political maturity.

After Dachau and Auschwitz, no person of conscience can believe that authority has to be obeyed blindly. Each citizen must ask himself whether or not he wishes to participate in the annihilation of the people of Vietnam. Even *Life Magazine* wrote in an editorial after the 1945 bombing of Hiroshima,

> Our sole safeguard against the very danger of a reversion to barbarism is the kind of morality which compels the individual conscience to the

group, right or wrong. The individual conscience against the atomic bomb? Yes, there is no other way.

Tax resister Milton Mayer writes,

In so far as there is any worldly sovereign in the United States, it is not the general will or the Congress or the president. It is I. I am sovereign here. I hold the highest office in the land, the office of citizen, with responsibilities to my country heavier by virtue of my office, than those of any other office, including the president. I cannot abdicate my right because it is inalienable.

Our own government recognizes that in the domain of conscience there is a moral power higher than the state. We do a disservice to our country and to humanity if we violate our conscience. Thoreau reminds us we are men first and subjects afterwards. Often people say that they voted for Johnson and got the foreign policy of Barry Goldwater, as if they have done all they can do. Our leaders know that all but a handful of citizens will continue to finance the war in exchange for the right to be left alone.

Gandhi wrote that every citizen is responsible for every act of his government. We may not be able to stop others from killing but we can stop our part in it. Mario Savio, leader of Berkeley's Free Speech Movement, said,

There is a time when the operation of the machine becomes so odious, makes you so sick at heart, that you can't take part. You can't even passively take part! And you've got to put your bodies upon the gears and upon the wheels, upon the levers, upon all the apparatus, and you've got to make it stop!

It is as old as Antigone, the question of whether to comply with conscience and violate the law, or violate your conscience and obey the law.

In this generation as in all generations, there are those who follow their consciences:

Dear IRS: I am told thou shalt not kill while my government says I must support the butchery in Vietnam or go to jail. By paying for bullets I am as guilty as the man who pulls the trigger or the president who orders the slaughter. I am 35 years old, a factory worker. I did my share of commie killing in Korea only to see Korea turned over to a hand-picked military dictatorship of the worst kind. I mention this only so that you would know it is not only the young who have had a belly full of power-crazed, corrupt insensitive leadership. You sir may choose to remain an instrument of a government gone mad, that is your affair. You may claim that you were just following orders, but I have finally reached a point in my life when I must begin to follow my conscience. —William Cox-Dunn, Colorado.

A young solider back from Vietnam noted that activist Angela Davis was imprisoned for buying guns used in a killing hundreds of miles away. She wasn't present at the killing, but she's being tried as a murder accomplice for allegedly paying for the guns. Drawing a parallel, the soldier asked, "Who bought the gun that I used and Lt. William Calley used at the My Lai massacre? Who is buying the bombs that are being dropped right now?"

The Nuremberg trials held that international law imposes duties and liabilities upon individuals, as well as upon states. It ruled that war crimes are committed by men, not by abstract entities. Only by punishing individuals who commit such crimes can the provisions of international law be enforced. Individuals as well as states must be held responsible for committing international crimes. The essence of the Nuremberg principle is that individuals have duties that transcend national obedience. It established further that a superior's order does not release a person from responsibility under international law, provided a moral choice is possible. There is a distinction between morality and legality. If the law asks you to be less than human, then it makes you an agent of injustice. Frederick Douglass wrote that the limits of tyrants are prescribed by the endurance of those whom they oppress. Isn't there some point where we will draw the line and refuse to be accomplices in the evil that our government is doing in Southeast Asia?

It is only if men follow their consciences that the law improves. It is only men of conscience who enable the gap between law and justice to close. The Supreme Court declared that Dred Scott was property and not a person. But men of conscience refused to accept that decision. I cannot conceive of what American history would look like if we removed the chapters in which men followed their consciences rather than the laws. The underground railroad, the suffragettes, the birth-control movement, the labor unions, the refusal to take loyalty oaths, the tea tax, interracial marriage laws, segregation in lunchrooms and streetcars, abortion laws, laws against homosexuality. Time and again, society moved forward only because people followed their consciences rather than the law.

Now you know what you are getting for you tax dollar today. You do not need to be told that 70 cents of your tax dollar is going for war-related purposes. You know that in a country the size of Texas we have dropped 6 million tons of bombs, three times more than the total dropped in World War II, 22 tons for every square mile in Indochina, 300 pounds for every man, woman, and child. Our newest automated air war now deliberately seeks to maim rather than kill because it inflicts greater psychological impact on the enemy to mutilate his child rather than kill him. Your tax dollars are at work dropping six million pounds of bombs today—4,000 pounds each minute. You know that we are destroying their ecology for 20,000 years, that we have wiped out species of mammals, birds and fish, that our bombs have formed craters that are filled with a mosquito malarial scourge.

You know Dwight Eisenhower was right when he said: "Every gun that is made, every warship launched, every rocket fired signifies in the final sense a theft from those who hunger and are not fed, those who are cold and are not clothed." Thoreau said that we meet our government or it's representative face to face once a year in the person of its tax collector. And it is at this time that we can let our government know how we feel about what it is doing. At bare minimum, we can express our disapproval when we pay our taxes, stop paying the federal Vietnam-War tax added to our phone bills, or we can hold back $5 to register disapproval. We can keep our income below the taxable level. A family of five can make $4,400. A couple past 65 can earn $3,500 without paying taxes. Karl Meyer, who has now chosen this route, writes, "If we choose to work only part time and live more simply we can have extra time to grow, create and do more things for ourselves or offer our work as a gift to people in need." There are many alternative routes open for those whose conscience will not permit them to kill. We do have a choice on April 15th and there is no way to escape responsibility. We may not be able to change others or our government, but we can change the way that we live and how we relate to the annihilation of the Vietnamese.

If there is any hope for our society (and I believe there is) then it depends upon a restoration of the ideal of individual responsibility. Each individual must renounce for himself those loopholes that have served him so well in the past (escapes into helplessness and rationalizations). Society can exist if we can rely upon man's moral nature, on his ability to choose the right course from the wrong. We can only exist if we recognize man's right and duty to follow his conscience, even if this leads to civil disobedience. Civil disobedience is not disrespect for society but deep concern for it. It is a letter to society that says, "I love you so much that I cannot cooperate when you do wrong. So I stand in the way of your wrong steps, requiring you to step over me to continue." Men of conscience are the true patriots. They are the true sons of Frederick Douglass, Henry David Thoreau and Eugene Debs. Those who violate their consciences to comply with the law are the sons of Grover Cleveland, Billy Graham, and Warren Harding. Someone asked the Quaker William Penn how long he should continue to wear his sword? Penn replied, "As long as thou canst. As long as thou canst."

It is my hope that on April 15th next year that we will have a great celebration of conscience rather than repentance. This congregation went on record five years ago to condemn this illegal, immoral, and insane war. The time has come to condemn it in both words and acts. Those of us told to supply the cold cash must be as faithful in our resistance as those asked to supply the warm bodies. The true discovery of America lies before us. I believe that every draft and tax resister shall be granted amnesty and that we shall experience a new birth of freedom. The Nuremburg judgment was not based on the philosophy that governments would stop war but that individuals would stop following leaders who wage unjust wars. We have a moral choice. Not to decide is to decide . . .

Delivered April 16, 1972, Third Unitarian Church of Chicago.

Part Four

Enjoy Life

Happiness never decreases
by being shared.

BUDDHA

(SIDDHĀRTHA GAUTAMA)

Blind Fate

ike many of you, I grew up believing, "Jesus loves me, this I know, for the Bible tells me so." The Bible was not questioned in my home, nor the fact that Jesus loved us and that the heavenly father was looking out for us. St. Matthew preached, "Even the hairs of your head are all numbered." The Psalmist proclaimed,

> A thousand may fall at your side, ten thousand at your right hand but it will not come near you. You shall not fear the terror of the night nor the arrow that flies by day, not the pestilence that stalks in darkness, nor the destruction that wastes at noonday.

"The eternal God is your dwelling place and underneath are the everlasting arms." We were not religious kooks in Dayton, Ohio. One of the two ministers that I knew before going to college attended Yale Divinity School; the other came from Harvard Divinity School.

When I was at Hiram College, a minister with a Ph.D. from the University of Chicago spoke. Dr. Duncan Littlefair of the Fountain Street Church in Grand Rapids asked,

> Does anything have meaning? What is the meaning of a cat or a cow or a carrot or a carbon atom? It seems a stupid question. All things just are. They exist, that's all, and so do you. You simply exist like a cow or a carrot or a carbon atom, except that you are not content with that. You want, you need, something more. You need purpose and meaning and significance. But the universe doesn't provide any. It just rolls on, changing, ever changing, ever experimenting with new forms, ever using old forms. On and on it rolls, and it creates and destroys you.

That was my introduction to humanism at the age of 19. Sir Julian Huxley defined the term at a 1959 celebration of Darwin's centennial at Third Unitarian Church of Chicago.

I use the word Humanism to mean someone who believes that humans are just as much a natural phenomenon as an animal or a plant; that our bodies, minds and souls were not supernaturally created, but are productions of evolution, and that we are not under the control or the guidance of any supernatural being, but have to rely on ourselves and our powers.

The idea that our whole species was an accident came as a shock. I suppressed Dr. Littlefair's message, attending the University of Chicago Divinity School myself and becoming ordained in the Christian Church. I served two Christian parishes before switching to Third Unitarian in 1969—almost 15 years after hearing Rev. Littlefair. As individuals and as a species, we emerge here on Earth without a script. We have to improvise as we go. We can neither comprehend nor master the art of living. We are broken by powers and forces beyond our control. The second phase of my religious journey brought a belief in benign indifference—the realization that the universe is indifferent to my health or to my happiness.

I cannot remember the date when I entered the third stage. I no longer believe that the universe is on our side and I no longer believe in the benign indifference of Albert Camus's humanism. At some point in the last five years I concluded that life has it in for us; that blind fate waits in ambush; that life mocks us and destroys us. Job, Prometheus, Oedipus, Ahab, Lear—they are representative of our fates. A basic disharmony in the universe is not conducive to our well-being. In Walter Kerr's words, "We find in the natural order, in the cosmos itself, disharmony in the makeup of things, and perfectly innocent man is broken." In the words of Prometheus, "I am wronged," and in the tragedy *Medea*, "Many of the things we think will happen, yet never happen. And the things we thought could never be, yet the gods contrive." Hamlet said, "The times are out of joint."

I am saying that some of the fault doth lie in the stars, and not all of the fault lies with Brutus. The universe was not created with our happiness in mind. This is not the best of all possible worlds. There should be a 50–50 chance that half of the people would experience lives of fulfillment and serenity. For years I was embarrassed by the fact that my parents's marriage was dysfunctional—that our family seemed to be messed up. The longer I live, the more typical I see that we are. We do not seem to be able to master the art of living, and it is not just us. "I can will what is right, but I cannot do it," St. Paul said. "The whole creation groaneth in travail." Life seems to be at cross purposes. It never seems to run smoothly. People seldom marry and live happily ever after. We all suffer from the slings and arrows of outrageous fortune. We all know the heartaches and the thousand natural shocks that flesh is heir to.

A great proponent of reverence for life also recognizes the duality of life. Albert Schweitzer writes:

All thinking must renounce the attempt to explain the universe. What is glorious in it is united with what is full of horror. What is full of meaning is united with what is senseless. The spirit of the universe is at once creative and destructive. It creates what it destroys and destroys what it creates. And therefore it remains to us a riddle, and we must inevitably resign ourselves to this.

The Good Book itself tells us, "Man that is born of woman is of few days and full of trouble. He cometh forth like a flower, and is cut down." Time and chance happen to them all. Jesus consoled us by saying, "Let the day's own troubles be sufficient for the day." You ain't seen nothing yet! It is not just that Macbeth is ambitious, or that Othello is jealous, or Oedipus rash, or that Lear is proud. We all have our blind spots—our Achilles heel. T. S. Eliot, an orthodox Christian Anglican, wrote, "The best of a bad job is all any of us make of it, except, of course, the saints." Arthur Miller raised the question that haunts me, "Oh God, what unfits us all for life?" I am saying that the game is rigged, the cards are stacked, the dice are loaded. The odds are not in your favor— the universe is not healthy for children, or for any species. Comedian George Carlin noted that it is horrible what we have done to the earth. We deserve the headline, "Mother earth raped again." But because of the floods, droughts, tsunamis and earthquakes, we might also say, "She asked for it!"

Writer Donald Ogden Stewart wrote,

Once upon a time there was a prince and princess: that's exactly how a description of the Murphys should begin. They were both rich; he was handsome; she was beautiful; they had three golden children. They loved each other, they enjoyed their own company, and they had the gift of making life enchantingly pleasurable for those who were fortunate enough to be their friends.

The Murphys were friends of F. Scott Fitzgerald who based characters in *Tender Is the Night* on them. When Gerald Murphy proposed to Sarah, he told her that they would "create a life for themselves of creativity and beauty." "Do you know," he wrote, "I think we shall always enjoy most the things that we plan of our own accord, and together, even among others, but in our own way." In other words, their life would be fresh, new, and invented. It would be of their own creative imagination.

Fitzgerald wrote to Sarah Murphy, "The love of life is essentially as incommunicable as grief." Most everyone would say that they are glad to be alive, but love of life is stronger than that, and it was in this respect that the Murphys are remembered. They, in their own way, mastered the art of living. John Dos Passos, a life-long friend, wrote, "People were always their best with the Murphys." Sarah Murphy said, "One secret I learned was that the ability to know what another person feels in a given situation will make or ruin lives." In order to live their own invented life, Sarah and Gerald had to free themselves from their surroundings, including their strong-willed parents. With their three children, they sailed for Europe in 1921 and remained there until 1933. Gertrude Stein said that Paris was where the twentieth century was. They went to Europe to reinvent themselves.

Poet Archibald MacLeish wrote of their Europe years, "Person after person, English, French, Scandinavian, everyone who met them, came away saying that these people really are masters at the art of living." Those closest to the Murphys found it almost impossible, however, to describe the special quality of their life, or the charm that it had for their friends. They made any place they lived a revelation of their own personalities. Gerald said of Sarah, "She has remained so essentially original—I have no idea what she will do or propose." Their friends included Picasso and his wife, Olga, Igor Stravinsky, Cole Porter, Amy Lowell, Ernest Hemingway, Erik Satie, Gertrude Stein, Alice B. Toklas, Dorothy Parker, e e cummings, Rudolph Valentino, Man Ray and Joan Miró.

Gerald Murphy gave this clue to Fitzgerald, "I believe you have to do things to life to make it tolerable." Good things are not going to come to you. Life is not only indifferent to you, it has it in for you. We will not escape the 4 D's: Decline, Dependency, Desertion, and Death. The title of a biography about the Murphys is taken from a Spanish proverb, "Living Well is the Best Revenge." In Gerald Murphy's words, "Only the invented part of life is satisfying—you are in for a bad time if you only take what life deals out." The things that just happen to you can be disappointing so you have to invent, create, and stage the pleasures that life can give. The Murphys made an art of life itself.

One night when the florist was closed, Sarah Murphy decorated her dinner table with the children's toys. Picasso loved it. At an army-surplus store, Gerald Murphy found some T-shirts once worn by Greek sailors. These became his standard attire for a whole summer. When their son Patrick was in a sanitarium in the Swiss Alps, the atmosphere was so depressing and gloomy that the Murphys bought an abandoned dance hall, did it over American style, and engaged a five-piece band from Munich to play on Friday and Saturday nights.

The invented life of the Murphys is not an option for us. All we can do is to take the concept and use it as we can. You make an event out of each day. Or if you work 9-to-5, five days a week, you make an event out of the weekend. E. B. White wrote of his aunt:

> There was something about Aunt Poo which was always exciting. Poo was the member of the family who had thrown off conventions and become an artist. She had been to Paris. She was Bohemia in suburbia. Strong-minded, sentimental, domineering, she had a flair for giving life a certain extra quality. She was a great one to make 'an occasion' of a day. Any sort of anniversary inflamed her. It would suddenly occur to her that today was Lincoln's Birthday, or the Ides of March, or Decoration Day, and in no time at all the house would tremble with the violence of redecoration or cookery or charades. She had the gift of celebration. There was no day so drab but, under Poo's fiery tutelage, could be whipped into a carnival.

My friends chide me that I never read the same book twice. But the Murphys charm me as much as they charmed their friends. I read *Living Well Is the Best Revenge* about eight years ago and reread it this summer. I said that the Murphys sailed to Europe with their three small children in 1921. But they returned home in 1933 with only their daughter. One son died of tuberculosis; the other of spinal meningitis. Gerald Murphy wrote to Fitzgerald,

> In my heart I dreaded the moment when our youth and invention would be attacked in our only vulnerable spot, the children. How ugly and blasting it can be, how idly ruthless. I know now that what you said in *Tender is the Night* is true. Only the invented part of our lives, the unreal part, has any scheme, any beauty. Life itself has stepped in now and blundered, scarred and destroyed.

They experienced life in two dimensions—what it will do to you, and what you do with it.

Their biographer writes, "The Murphys' refusal to 'go under' was profoundly moving to their friends." One friend wrote,

> The memory of a night with the gay Murphys of Paris in that rarefied cold silence and atmosphere of death is one of the most terrifying of my life. But I am prouder of them for that fight for Patrick's life than for anything else in their lives. The point is, they were not only the most alive, the most charming, the most understanding people; they were, when the roof of their dream house crashed into their living room, the bravest.

The best revenge, even for the death of one's sons, was to go on living well for each other, their daughter, and for their friends.

The concept of "living well" is too vague to be helpful. We must each decide what "living well" means for us. For Gerald Murphy it included painting. Before he died of prostate cancer in 1964, one of his paintings was exhibited in the Museum of Modem Art in New York City—alongside a Picasso.

Now the Sabbath lies before us and we each must decide what living well means for us! As the poet said:

> Enjoy the present smiling Hour;
> And put it out of Fortune's Pow'r . . .
> Happy the Man, and happy he alone,
> He who can call today his own:
> He who, secure within, can say
> Tomorrow do thy worst, for I have liv'd today,
> Be fair, or foul, or rain, or shine,
> The Joy I have possess'd in spite of Fate are mine.
> Not Heav'n itself upon the past has Pow'r;
> But what had been, has been and I have had my Hour.

Delivered October 6, 1996, Lake Shore Unitarian Society, Winnetka, Illinois.

87 Times

hope that you used your imagination and had fun with the title announced for today's sermon. September 1933 went down in history for two repeals: The repeal of Prohibition and the repeal of the legal compulsion for literary squeamishness. For that is when Judge John Woolsey lifted the ban on James Joyce's *Ulysses*.

That novel is 783 pages long. Of the few who have read it, fewer still have understood it. The entire novel takes place in Dublin in just 16 hours on June 16, 1904. The novel is not so much about outward events—what someone said or did. Rather, it is composed of internal dialogue. Joyce introduced "stream of consciousness" literature. The book ends with a 45-page monologue as Molly Bloom looks back over her life. There is little punctuation; it has just eight sentences. Molly Bloom leaves little to the imagination and her musings are uncensored (hence the ban). The beauty of it is her total acceptance of life. In that monologue, Molly Bloom says "yes" to life 87 times.

> And all the queer little streets and pink and yellow houses and rose gardens and the jasmines and geraniums and cactuses, and Gibraltar as a girl where I was a flower of the mountain yes . . . yes that would do your heart good to see the rivers and lakes and flowers of all sorts of shapes and smells and colors spring up, even out of the ditches and primroses and violent nature it is as for them saying there is no God I wouldn't give a snap of my two fingers for all their learning and why don't they go and create something . . .

And so, for 45 pages, Molly Bloom goes on listing all the things that she said "yes" to in her life.

Bloom reminds me of that line in Dag Hammarskjöld's diary. "But at some moment, I did answer 'yes' to Someone—or Something—and from that hour I was certain that existence is meaningful, and that, therefore, my life, in a self-surrender, had a goal." Hammarskjöld's diary has inspired people since it was published 30 years ago. Yet his single affirmation of saying "yes" to life pales next to Molly Bloom's 87 affirmations—all occurring in less than an hour after midnight.

I recommend a book by an English professor at Northwestern University titled *The Art of Celebration*. Dr. Alfred Appel conceived of the book while recovering from a heart attack. Its subtitle is "20th century painting, literature, sculpture, photography, and jazz." Even if you just look at the pictures, you capture its essence. Dr. Appel wrote this book in hopes that each of us will have a place where we keep a collection of music recordings, paintings, prints, photographs, poetry, novels, and videos that affirm life. It could be a Molly-Bloom celebratory shelf with 87 affirmative entries.

Obviously, this shelf is subjective. Dr. Appel has reproductions of Matisse, Calder, and Léger. He has poetry by William Carlos Williams, Wallace Stevens, Marianne Moore, and Richard Wilbur. He has recordings of Louis Armstrong, James Johnson, Artie Shaw, Count Basie, Duke Ellington, Benny Goodman and Tommy Dorsey. He has films of Fred Astaire, Ginger Rogers, Charlie Chaplin and Buster Keaton. He believes that to survive in this world we need daily contact with powerful images and voices of affirmation. Most of the prints in this book are in brilliant colors. Dr. Appel evaluates any work of art by whether it affirms or negates life. He may have works in his home by Kafka or T. S. Eliot, but not in the corner devoted to the celebration of life. There, he only permits that which is joyous and life embracing.

He tells the stories of some of "his artists." For instance, Fernand Léger made a painting of the city that is not only optimistic but utopian. Lord knows we need affirmations of the city. Léger painted it after he had spent four years as a stretcher-bearer in World War I. He was gassed at the Battle of Verdun, where 700,000 men were killed or wounded in nine months. Léger returned from the war determined to place his artistic gifts in the service of creating hope for our human future. He tells the story of Paul Klee, who would warm up before painting by playing Mozart or Bach on the violin. Matisse loved to play works by Louis Armstrong and Sidney Bechet before working. It makes a great deal of difference if we start our day with Louis Armstrong or Bach or if we start our day as our forefathers did with morning prayers and Bible reading.

Many years ago I initiated my own morning routine. From about 6:30 to 8:00, I read the *New York Times* and the *Chicago Tribune*. By the time I finish I am almost too weak to go to work. I am in no mood to say "yes" to anything. I have read about five teens who set fire to a homeless man out of boredom. The Montreal judge who "let off" a man who sodomized his nine-year-old step-daughter after finding that he had preserved her virginity. A Detroit father glued his daughter's eyes shut because his wife would not give him money for crack cocaine. A Florida man had sex with a corpse but there is no law on the books to prosecute him. A law student in Tallahassee was charged with so-liciting a hit man to kill a secretary who had accused the student of trying to steal a copy of an exam. Within eight minutes of a judge suffering a heart at-tack at 4500 Madison, eight people rushed to his side—looting everything of value from him and his car.

There is lighter news. A Round Lake man has chosen his dog to be his best man at his wedding. A 64-year-old woman in Detroit has been ordered out of her retirement complex for spewing obscenities at her neighbors. A Har-vard professor has written a book about the sexual experiences that Ameri-cans have had while abducted by aliens.

It is the fortunate ones, who—after reading the morning news—go to work. Pity those who then turn on the morning talk shows. It is not unusual for them to feature women who have had sex with their daughter's teenage boyfriends, men who have breasts larger than their wife's, or senior citizens denouncing the discrimination they have suffered at nude beaches. On the ra-dio you can listen to the rap lyrics, "Kill a cop, beat a bitch."

Now you have heard it here—not just from the religious right. The world is going to hell. We do not have to go with it. I am going to ridicule some of this idiocy and suggest what might sound like a trite solution. But it is a start. We need someplace in our home where we can go for daily sanity and renewal. Ann Arbor Unitarian minister Ken Phifer tells of a member of his congrega-tion. At age 80, Bessie began collecting a box full of notes, cards, photos, po-etry, news clippings and bits of philosophy about brave and virtuous people. She calls it her "good box." Lord knows, that's a start.

We are going through a period that recalls Senator Joe McCarthy's philos-ophy that there is no objectivity or truth. Knowledge is politically construed. It is an extension of power. All stories are valid and all cultures are equal. If you feel strongly that something is true, then it probably is. A repressed mem-ory therapist told PBS' *Front Line,* "I don't care if it is true. What actually hap-pened is irrelevant to me." After several men were falsely accused of rape at Vassar College, a college counselor said, "If they weren't actual rapists, they should explore their potential for becoming rapists." In Arthur Miller's play *The Crucible* about the plague of McCarthyism a character cries out, "Is the accuser always holy?" Must every repressed memory vilify another person?

I am collecting the experiences of people who repressed joy and then suddenly recollected something good that happened to them long ago. In 1942 my sister married a man whose parents were poor. Yet, somehow, they managed to give the newlyweds a check for $75. When she cleaned out their home after they died, she discovered documents showing that they had taken out a loan on their old car before the wedding. There is not a person here who has not been the recipient of such kindness and generosity. Do whatever's necessary to recover these repressed memories. Go to an acupuncturist or a hypnotist. Get a friend to beat you with a rubber hose. Dredge up the materials that you need for your "good box."

Dr. Appel writes of an Eastern European country where the saxophone was banned as a "decadent" jazz instrument. Czechoslovakia's Velvet Revolution was sparked by dissidents defending the right of a rock band to perform. Václav Havel, the playwright who became president, writes,

> Who could have foreseen that the persecution of one obscure rock group would have such far reaching consequences? The freedom to play rock music was understood as a human freedom and thus, as essentially the same as the freedom to engage in philosophical and political reflection, the freedom to write, and the freedom to express and defend the various social and political interests of society.

Shakespeare writes that "we strut and fret our hour upon the stage." We must choose if we are going to strut or fret! It is hard to fret to jazz, rock or Mozart. There are many harsh things that life does to us. Bad hands are dealt and we must play them. But there are also areas where we can design our lives, where we can choose what we want to do in this hour or this day. The script is not all written. There are moments when we can choose to fret or to strut. You can design a day tailor-fit to yourself. Dr. Appel tells us that he would go to an art exhibit, then browse old book stores, lunch at his favorite restaurant, go to Birdland and hear Charlie Parker and Dizzy Gillespie, and then go home totally exhilarated. It is possible to plan an exhilarating day in Chicago without spending a cent. But how many times does that happen in our lives? How many movies have you seen lately that left you exhilarated about our species and our future?

Most of us came out of the Judeo-Christian tradition. We were taught that we had been created "just a little lower than the angels." "What a piece of work is man, how noble in reason, how infinite in faculties, in form and moving how express and admirable, in action how like an angel, in apprehension how like a God!" Does the morning news encourage that Shakespearian concept of what you are or what you could be?

My grandmother in Kentucky used to sing the old gospel song, "I am the child of a King." That makes you strut. Alan Watts, the Episcopalian priest who died a Buddhist, wrote, "How is it possible that a being with such sensitive jewels as the eyes, such enchanted musical instruments as the ears, such a fabulous arabesque of nerves, can experience itself as anything but a God?" He continued,

> And when you consider that this incalculably subtle organism is inseparable from the more marvelous patterns of its environment, from the minutest electrical designs to the whole company of the galaxies, how is it conceivable that this incantation of all eternity can be bored with being?

I hope the Molly Blooms here have been saying "yes, yes, yes," as they listen to these descriptions of our species. We are made like the nightingale. One nightingale will not sing its song unless it first hears it from another nightingale. If "yes" is our song, others will take it up. I want it said of us what D. H. Lawrence said of Walt Whitman. "He drove an automobile with very fierce headlights . . . through the darkness of this world."

Emerson wrote, "Give me health and a day and I will make the pomp of emperors ridiculous." All of us are more upset by illness than we are delighted with health. We are here today. Most of us have use of our eyes and ears and we can touch and taste and smell. Abraham Maslow wrote that,

> All you have to do is go to a hospital and hear all the simple blessings that people never before realized were blessings—being able to urinate, to sleep on your side, to be able to swallow, to scratch an itch, etc.

Austrian director Max Reinhardt boasted that he took pleasure in everything, including brushing his teeth in the morning. I am asking you to say "yes" to brushing your teeth, being able to scratch, to urinate, to sleep on your side. I have an ulterior motive in that I believe that happy and appreciative people help others. Those who feel good, do good.

"But Reverend Wheat," someone says, "what about 'the heartache and the thousand natural shocks that flesh is heir to?' What about 'the road winding upward to the very end?' 'Luck's a chance but trouble's sure.' 'Train for ill, and for good.' 'The storms and floods are going to come to all of our houses.' You sound like Norman Vincent Peale, today." Let me be perfectly clear. We must not only say "yes" to the good things in life but also to aging, to dentures, to hip replacements, and death. May Sarton, the Unitarian poet who spoke to our universal experience, died this summer. One of her poems is tacked up above my typewriter.

> I am not ready to die,
> But I am learning to trust death.
> As I have trusted life.
> I am moving
> Toward a new freedom born
> of detachment. And a
> sweeter grace learning to let go.
>
> I am not ready to die.
> But as I approach sixty
> I turn my face to the sea.
> I shall go where the tides replace time, where
> my world will open to a far horizon.
> Over the floating, never-still flux and change.
> I shall go with the changes,
> I shall look far out over the golden grasses
> And blue waters.
>
> There are no farewells.

A member of our congregation also died this summer. A woman so quiet and so content that it will be hard to notice her passing. I said at her memorial service that I had known others who had lived as well—but no one who equaled her in dying. She said "yes" to cancer. She said "yes" to the inevitability of death. When we say "yes" to life's journey, it is with the understanding that it has an end. Socrates said that the unexamined life is not worth living. Nor is the unlived life worth examining.

Albert Camus wrote, "If there is a sin against life it lies in despairing of it, and evading the implacable grandeur of it." This sin must not be tolerated here. We agree with the Greek Bishop Irenaeus, who wrote in the third century, "The glory of God is the human person fully alive." And let that glory always radiate from our lives as we say "yes" to life, as we strut to Louis Armstrong or Mozart's Country Dances, as we feast our eyes on a Monet exhibit or our bodies on Thanksgiving turkey, as we stand by the cradle of our first grandchild, or at the grave or our dearest friend.

"Yes," "yes," "yes."

Delivered September 10, 1995, Third Unitarian Church of Chicago.

Blessings on You

spoke here in September on the assigned topic of Science and Religion. This morning, it's Wheat 101—the very basis of my religion. I have an old-fashioned concept of religion as the art of counting blessings. This is not just my opinion. I can prove that religious people are grateful people. (Did you ever know anyone, of any faith, who was religious but not grateful?) And the more grateful they are—the more deliberate they are in the art of counting blessings—the more generous they are. The religious person is the grateful person. The grateful person is the generous person. Ministers today have the same unpleasant task that religious leaders had in Old Testament times. The book of Deuteronomy reminds us,

> You are living in great and goodly cities which you did not build and houses full of all good things which you did not fill, and cisterns which you did not hew, and vineyards and olive trees which you did not plant.

This is so un-American that Senator Joe McCarthy would have called Deuteronomy's author before the House Un-American Activities Committee. We consider ourselves self-made men and women. Most of us live out our lives devoid of any sense of grace. As some of you remember from your catechism, grace is whatever comes into our lives unsought, unearned, unexpected.

None of us would be here today without grace. It has come to us in the form of friends, dividends, opportunities, forgiveness—even our births. Each of us has reaped what we have not sown and that is the best kept secret in America today. The humanitarian James H. Robinson asks,

> Can the most complacent reactionary flatter himself that he invented the art of writing or the printing press or discovered his religious, economic and moral convictions, or any of the devices which supply him with meat and raiment or any of the sources of such pleasure as he may

derive from literature or the fine arts? In short, civilization is little else than getting something for nothing.

Emerson said that we are all born with a mortgage. The gift of life makes debtors of us all. Dr. King said, "Whether we realize it or not, each of us is eternally 'in the red.' We are everlasting debtors to known and unknown men and women." Einstein put it this way,

> Many times a day I realize how much my own inner and outer life is built upon the labors of my fellow man, both living and dead, and how earnestly I must exert myself in order to give in return as much as I have received.

Indeed, it is arrogant to assume that even Einstein could return as much as he received.

Gratitude is the enemy of the ego. It is hard to be proud or arrogant when one experiences grace and acknowledges what has come into your life unsought, unearned, and unexpected. Describing one of her characters, Flannery O'Connor writes, "Mr. Head had never known before what mercy felt like, because he had been too good to deserve any, but he felt he knew now." The self-made person is too good to acknowledge the grace and mercy that has been freely given. We are living in a state of denial. We do not want to admit how good life has been to us—and this is not just because we are ornery. Jesus said, "For everyone to whom much is given, from him much will be expected." The more we receive, the more we deny it so that less is expected of us.

> My 50th year had come and gone
> I sat a solitary man
> In a crowded London shop
> An open book and empty cup
> On the marble table top.
>
> While on the street I gazed
> My body for a moment blazed
> And twenty minutes (more or less)
> It seemed so great my happiness
> That I was blessed, and I could bless.

W. H. Auden is describing a secular experience with grace. It comes out of the blue and almost makes predestination necessary. It causes us to wonder why some feel blessed and others do not. Perhaps it was his age. I believe that the older we are, the more we feel blessed. Did you ever know a grateful teenager? Maybe it was the book that he had been reading that raised some real or philosophical questions in his mind. The point of the poem is that he walked out of that crowded coffee shop aware of his blessings and filled with resolution. "Now I could bless."

One of my favorite sections in Sunday's *New York Times* is "Metropolitan Diary." Recently it discussed an artist who was having his paintings packed and placed in storage to go live in Italy for a year. As the packer went about his work, the artist thought, "What a monotonous job, day after day." The two men took a coffee break together and the packer asked if the other man was an artist. Then he asked, "Do you do this every day?" The artist nodded. After a silence, the packer said, "It must be boring." Neither man understood that the other felt blessed in his life's work.

Recently I saw Ingmar Bergman's adaptation of Ibsen's *A Doll's House* at the University of Chicago's Court Theater. After a silence after the play ended, I turned to my wife and said, "I don't ever want to see any better drama than this." I read of a literature professor who taught *A Doll's House* in a women's prison. Nora did not make sense to the women there. Not one of those prisoners felt that Nora should have walked away from Helmer. "What if he did call her his 'little sparrow' and treated her like a brainless child, put his own interests first? No one in her right mind would walk away from all that." "He could call me any fucking thing he wanted to, as long as he is paying the bills," one of the prisoners said. Another said, "She musta been havin' her period. She be back in the morning." Whether we feel blessed is relative to how we experience life. With two people living in nearly identical conditions, one can feel blessed and the other not.

I want to project Auden's 50-year-old man into his future. How does a person who feels blessed tip the waitress? How does he respond to the Salvation Army bell ringer? How does he affect others when he goes to work? I believe that the best days and years of his life lie before him. I find myself attracted to those who have discovered that life is a blessing.

Most of us know what it is like to be around those who have not had this realization. John Steinbeck described his experience with a waitress in another coffee shop.

Strange how one person can saturate a room with vitality, with excitement. Then there are others, and this dame was one of them, who can drain off energy and joy and suck pleasure dry and get no sustenance from it. Such people spread grayness in the air around them.

She got through to Steinbeck and she made him want to curl up and die. "What a date she must be, what a lover. I tried to imagine that last, and couldn't."

Now I believe that all groups have made their contributions. The French with their cuisine, the Lutherans with their chorales, the Amish with their quilts. But the Jews deserve the prize for making the bestowing of blessings into a fine art. That's the message of Auden's poem:

It seemed so great my happiness
That I was blessed, and I could bless.

The Jews of Eastern Europe grew up in the ghettos or shtetls. They were forbidden to own land or to practice certain crafts, skills and trades. They were barred from universities and any kind of government job. Inside the ghettos they were "beyond the pale" of the simplest amenities of life. When they left the ghettos, they were beaten, spat upon and killed. Their synagogues and cemeteries were desecrated. What they did have was a religion. God had said to Abraham, "And I will make of you a great nation, and I will bless you and make your name great so that you will be a blessing. And I will bless those that bless you, and him that curses you, I will curse."

The basic Jewish orientation to life was that it is a blessing. And so they lubricated their miserable lives with blessings. These blessings were uttered reflexively without thinking. They peppered their conversations with them. They blessed their children; and children blessed their parents. They blessed the living and the memory of the dead. They blessed friends and strangers. There were blessings for getting up and for lying down. There was a blessing for daughters popularized in *Fiddler on the Roof.* The parents place both hands on the head of the child while pronouncing the blessing, which they administer to adult children, too. There was a blessing before the meal and when the meal ended. There were blessings to be recited before the smell of flowers and spices. Blessings to be recited before the ritual washing of one's hands. Blessings to be recited upon seeing lightning, the new moon, or a scholar. Rather than take credit for the goodness in their lives, these blessings made the Jews conscious that they were living in cities they did not build, drinking from cisterns they had not hewn, and drinking from vineyards which they had not planted. They were supposed to utter 100 blessings a day. This habit helped overcome the cleavage between the holy and profane. It enabled them to see life in its entirety as a blessing.

Muslims teach that the original sin is forgetfulness. "Be we not all guests of Allah?" The philosopher Martin Heidegger reminds us that thinking and thanking share the same root. I grew up in a home where my mother's favorite saying was, "Bless your heart." She said it when she greeted us at the door and when we departed. She said it whenever we did something good and thoughtful. She didn't thank people for a gift; she blessed their hearts. Yet I have had only one *formal* blessing in my life. It was during the 1964 Mississippi Summer Project. A friend of mine and I attended a Black Baptist church. The minister invited us to stay after the service. Now, Protestants don't usually kneel. But I knelt at my ordination and there I did, again. The Baptist minister placed his hands on our heads and bestowed a blessing that, obviously, I remember 30 years later.

The alternative to living life as a blessing is Hamlet's question, "To be or not to be?" Albert Camus says that this is the only philosophical question. Life is a free choice. No one should have to go on living against his or her will. My approach to life is like the right-wingers approach to America. Love it or leave it. But once we have made the decision to live, then we want to live well. And this is where religion as I defined it at the outset comes in. If religion is the art of counting blessings, then our chief religious task is to become grateful and generous people.

Thomas Wolfe wrote from Harvard in 1921, "When I retire at night, when I wake in the morning, I am conscious of the weight of my gratitude; it is the spur that drives me on." That spur drove the man from the coffee shop. Conscious of his own blessings, he was going to bless the world. Einstein says, "There are two ways to live your life; one is as though nothing is a miracle, the other is as though everything is a miracle." Asked if she believed in miracles, Israeli Prime Minister Golda Meir replied, "I depend on them."

I'll close with a story told by Rebecca Parker, president of our Starr King seminary. She was walking theology professor Charles Hartshorne to his dormitory after a conference. In that urban environment he would pause to discover a flower in a cranny, point out the artistic formation of a bare tree, comment on the north wind that was blowing paper along the street. It was as if the world was his and he felt himself a part of it. When Rebecca left him at his dorm, rather than bid her "Good night," he said, "Be a blessing to the world." That beautiful concept is yours for the taking. Yet another experience of grace that comes to you unsought, undeserved and unexpected.

L'Chaim!

Delivered December 4, 1994, Third Unitarian Church of Chicago.

Forcing Ourselves to Be Happy

Let us begin this morning where we have so many times—with Camus's observation that there is but one truly serious philosophical problem: suicide. "Judging whether life is or is not worth living amounts to answering the fundamental question of philosophy." I think it is apparent what our answer is as we gather here to celebrate life. Obviously, one can decide that life is worth living and still not discover how to enjoy it. It is my thesis that the purpose of religion is to help us enjoy life. And no matter how much we enjoy it now, to expand those parameters. I hasten to add that we want to live in a way that increases—not diminishes—other people's enjoyment of life, too.

If you want to be lawyer, or to get to California, or to throw a Christmas party, you need to have a plan to achieve it. Too many people assume that the enjoyment of life "just comes naturally" and takes no philosophy, effort or plan. I am not speaking of a philosophy on the scale of Nietzsche, Tillich or Buber, but simply your own private, personal, practical plan to derive more enjoyment from life than you do now. The purpose of life is the enjoyment of life. Yet much of life is dull, brutish, nasty, mean or petty. We are living in a world where nature shakes the dice of chance. Any single day is filled with jerks and jolts and jars. We have to wrestle with what surrounds us to salvage our enjoyment.

Stuart McCarrell gave me a book for my birthday by John Cowper Powys, an Englishman who wrote what he called "a philosophy for everyman." It was written when all of Europe had fallen and England stood alone during the blitz. Powys wrote,

> We are assuming that you are not one of these happy-go-lucky, reckless, thick-skinned pirates who need no chart, no calendar, no North Star, no map, no mainsail, no lifeboat, no mascot, as they chance it by wind and wave. No, we are those who must have some interior method of keeping up our spirits and retaining some sort of chart to sail by or even drift

by, as fate tosses us about. Some method between you and your own heart by means of which you create the only thing any of us can create, namely, our shield of reception for "the slings and arrows of outrageous fortune."

Powys addressed war-weary Britain but his philosophy of life also applies to us. He writes, "When we enter life, we enter war." We are going to be under attack so long as we breathe. Much of our fate is a result of the way that the dice fall. We live in an arena where we have to force ourselves to wring enjoyment from life.

Powys believes that the beginning of wisdom is:

> to have acquired the habit of wrestling with life as if life were our personal enemy, and of regarding every moment when we forget our pains, discomforts, humiliation, disgusts, horrors and terrors, as a satisfactory victory over a vicious, malicious and demonical antagonist!

Very little is going to be given to us and we are going to have to struggle for what we get. Fate, chance, necessity will place us in situations that are not of our choosing—not of our liking—and we are still going to have to find a way to wring some enjoyment from life. Powys, though the son of an Anglican priest, is not a theist. He does not see the fate of homo sapiens as that much different from the rest of nature. And he advises us to observe other animals, the trees, the flowers, to learn how they endure.

St. Paul writes that the whole of creation is groaning in travail. We must derive some of our enjoyment from fighting and defying the slings and arrows that are indiscriminately sent in our direction. Now I would wager that some of you are turned off by the idea of forcing ourselves to enjoy anything. Yet did anyone here really enjoy that first cigarette, cup of coffee or beer? So many of the habits that we have formed, things that we take for granted as a part of our lives, we had to learn to enjoy. A teenager in this congregation owns a horse and told his mother about how it was to arrange for it to mate. He said, "Mom, I wanted him to like it so he would want to do it again." Yet how often is that "first time" so terrific that it seems better than ice cream, jitter-bugging or hitting a home run?

Swiss playwright Friedrich Dürrenmatt died this week and his obituary quoted him saying that the purpose of theater is "to show us on stage, our foolishness, blindness, our lack of judgement! We ourselves must see in the heroes of the play how our own behavior is often wrong." I doubt if many of us enjoyed that kind of theater when we first were introduced to it. A person who had acquired the taste for classical music said that, at first, "I pretended to like Bach's music." There are many instances in which we trained or forced ourselves to like something—and there are stretches when we must force ourselves to enjoy life. Especially when life is flat, ugly mean or repulsive, we have to develop the habit of finding some endurance and enjoyment.

Powys writes that each of us can have a "trap door," through which you can escape when your situation is unbearable. In that secret reservoir, a smile actually comes across your lips where minutes before there was only a scowl or a frown. The *New York Times* ran an article this week about how anger ranks with—or exceeds—cigarette smoking, obesity and high-fat diets as a cause of early death. One-fifth of the population (30 members of this congregation) possess the bitter, angry reactivity that can harm health. A scientist involved in that study said, "By recognizing irrational anger at the outset and coping with it intelligently, a person can perhaps block the cascade of stress hormones before it tumbles out of control." The scientist said that a person who senses a fit of anger coming can seek distraction by reading a magazine or taking a walk. I quote, "It's not easy to stop those cynical tapes from going off in the head but there is no darn point in them, and it's worth the effort to shut them down."

You can defend yourself from that which would ruin your day and rob you of enjoying life—which is the purpose of life. How often we hear someone say, "I got myself under control." We need to know what is their method of accomplishing that which kings, millionaires and philosophers long for? Jesus said that the kingdom of heaven is within us. We cannot enjoy life properly until we develop a method, a practice, a habit, for getting ourselves "under control." There are those who believe that this is impossible.

My ideal weight should be 165 pounds. Some years back I tipped the scale at over 200. I had a low-key doctor who simply asked, "Were you planning on living?" He placed me on a "last chance diet." I remember driving home with tears in my eyes, believing that there was no way I could abide by the limits of that liquid diet. If I sound like Norman Vincent Peale, so be it. I am saying that the greatest hindrance before you today is your lack of belief in your own power—in your own self-control. Ours is a religion of faith. And humanism has been that since 500 BC, when Protagoras said, "Man is the measure of all things." Not an act of faith in Jesus Christ or Buddha, but faith in our own willpower. As always, you are free to disagree. You can insist that you have no faith in your will power. If that's your position, I wish you luck. You're going to need it!

Powys says we need "faith in ourselves as creatures who are able to create our own private, independent, and personal way of life, in defiance of every obstacle." The psalmist asked, "From whence cometh my help?" Our help must begin with faith in ourselves and our creative power. Well, I can hear *Tinker Hammack* in the balcony laughing, ready to burst out, "This beats anything I have ever heard here. It is nothing but wishful thinking to believe that people like us are going to control ourselves!" My answer is that wishful thinking is one of the most powerful of all cosmic forces. We need every trick, every device, every gimmick we can muster to shield ourselves from the slings and arrows of outrageous fortune. We need a trap door, a shield, a kingdom of God within, so that when others despair, we can stand firm with fortitude.

God, how we can get on each other's nerves! And I am not just talking about the loud-mouth lady in the restaurant, or Uncle Lennie's loose dentures making awful noises at the Thanksgiving table. I am not talking about the cousin who phones to tell you today what she told you yesterday, or the neighbor who brags about her family and puts everyone else down. This is minor compared with how our own spouses, children and parents get on our nerves. That's why I support gun control. I don't want to be shot by a member of my own family—for I have some irritating habits myself. Is there a person here who does not honestly believe that if we could get ourselves under control, life would be much more enjoyable?

I read the other day how rare life-long friendships are between men. I quote,

> Old men grow prouder, vainer, more conceited every year of their old age, and this intensification of their personal importance in their own estimation is accompanied in precisely equal stages by their alienation from their friends. How rare when two men go down to their graves in mutual admiration, consideration and affection.

In 32 years in the ministry I can recall just one older man grieving for the loss of a friend. The purpose of life is to enjoy it. We cannot do so if we cannot control our pride, vanity, and conceit. There are a lot of lonely people out there.

Too many of them are searching for someone who will make them happy. We know where that search ends. The only reasonable search is to find someone with whom we can share the happiness that we have within ourselves.

If only the fault were within the stars! I am asking you to believe that you have the power to enjoy yourself in whatever condition life places you. Our own frame of mind determines whether we are going to cope with fortitude or not. Last year I preached a sermon on a young doctor who had been a tennis champion before he was paralyzed by polio. He then learned to find enjoyment in the way that the sun and shadows made designs on the walls beside his iron-lung machine. That is not too far-fetched from the day that awaits most of us. I think this morning of *Mary Ann Benson* in her room at the Baptist retirement home, of *Hazel Hanson* banished to the cornfields of Indiana, *Ruth Evans* miles from here in Michigan, *Jan Weeks* at Oak Lawn Hospital, *Barney Heinrich* in a Quaker home in Philadelphia. Did their humanism prepare them for that small room? Can they force themselves to find something to enjoy in each day?

Powys writes, "There is only one important question for us, and that is whether we are (or are not) enjoying this life of ours, into which, willy-nilly, and without giving us any choice, we have been incontinently and arbitrarily flung." How to enjoy being alive, in whatever circumstance, is the nitty-gritty of our religion. We have to believe that our enjoyment of life lies in our own hands. We must believe in our own willpower to shape our sensations and feelings. We must steer our own boat through the shallows and between the rocks and reefs of life. Whether we are happy or miserable has got to be our decision. Life with a capital "L" is not interested in our personal happiness.

I suppose it's time to tell the story of the birthday that *Ruth Schutt* faced alone, with her two sons in distant places. She would certainly have become more depressed had she "not taken control of herself." She baked a cake and took it over to the *Becks'* home, where *Clarice* was confined to a hospital bed after a hideous stroke. We are going to decide, and we alone, how we are going to react to every situation that confronts us. I would be unworthy to stand in this pulpit if I offered you false hope. But over and over again, we hear the testimony of people in this congregation who discovered inexhaustible reservoirs of power within themselves, testimonies of the discovery of strength that they had no idea existed. There are 25 widows in this congregation alone. They need to heed the widow who wrote,

We have been conned into believing that happiness marched two by two and anything less is loneliness. Daughters are not taught to be widows, love songs never hymn the quest for self. Where are the songs of the love for the life we love; and the joy of achieving it single-handedly?

The widow affirms the person she discovered buried under so many layers of daughter, wife and mother.

Our house poet, *Stuart McCarrell*, wrote that, "We must make love to life itself—with all of our senses." Here we sing the love songs, not to another person or a deity, but to life. Here we celebrate the belief in ourselves and in our own creative power to decide ourselves how we will respond to fate and chance and necessity. When we call this service a "celebration of life," we are not celebrating art, literature, music, friends, family, laughter, nature, good wine and food, or safe sex. Although all of these and more are a part of life. We simply are celebrating life itself. The foremost concept to bear in mind at all times is "to be alive, only to be alive—may I never forget the privilege of that." Powys, at the age of 25, went into a sanitarium for tuberculosis.

I made the resolution that never again, would I suffer myself to be submerged by the commonplace. If only I was permitted to live one more year, two more years, how eagerly I would mark the passage of the sun each day across the sky, the recurring phases of the treacherous moon, and the naked beauty of each starlit night.

We are celebrating the commonplace: Clocks ticking, Mama's sunflowers, food and coffee, freshly ironed dresses and hot baths, sleeping and waking up! I can imagine someone visiting here for the first time laughing at us at the office tomorrow. "It was the craziest place since Big Sur. The minister who looked well into his sixties told them 'to make love to life' and the old fools were hugging and kissing each other during the coffee hour and repeating his words as they went to their cars "to be alive, only to be alive, may I never forget the privilege of that."

Delivered December 16, 1990, Third Unitarian Church of Chicago.

Soaring Without Wings

Two weeks ago, I quoted a man who was confined to an iron lung:

One evening lying there alone, feeling particularly hopeless and bored, I looked down the corridor wishing for, perhaps expecting, someone or something. But I saw only the darkened hallway with a few doors opening into it. There was no activity and there were no people to be seen. My despair mounted and I felt as though I could no longer stand it. Then slowly, I began to look at the corridor differently, and I began to see variations, shades of gray and darkness, shadows and light. The doorways opening onto the corridor formed subtle geometric patterns according to the different ways the doors were ajar. I began to look carefully and wonder at this scene that only a few moments before had depressed me so. It now seemed startling beautiful. My perception had shifted, my eyes miraculously refreshed. This experience was full and whole. I looked down the hallway for a long time. I think I probably fell asleep, but I am not sure. I do not know how that perception arrived, or why it left, but from then on I understood that what I sought was possible. My task now was to discover how to change this one state to the other.

These are the words of Arnie Beisser, who lived in an iron lung for a year and a half. Only a few months before this experience, Arnie graduated from medical school and had been playing tennis in a national tournament. At the age of 10 he had written down his life plan, "Win a national tennis championship by the age of 23." He actually won it at age 24. Item two was "to graduate from medical school at the age of 27," which he accomplished four years early.

The year was 1950. U.S. troops were in Korea and President Truman called up young doctors. Dr. Arnold Beisser had passed his physical and was given orders for duty. On his way to the hospital where he was assigned, he was transformed from a doctor to a patient and from an athlete to a cripple. Polio so ravaged his body that he could not move, stand, walk, sit, eat, drink, or even breathe by himself. "The person I had known myself to be was quite suddenly trapped in an alien body, one which did not perform automatically on command or indeed even perform at all." He spent a year and a half in the iron lung and three years in a hospital ward with 30 other polio patients.

> I had been thrust backward in the developmental scale, and my dependence was now as profound as that of a newborn. Once again I had to deal with all of the overwhelming, degrading conditions of dependency that belong with infancy and childhood at the same time that I considered myself a mature adult.

His bladder and bowel functions were no longer automatic, his most private and personal functions rested in the hands of others. When he said he was cold and asked for a blanket, he sometimes was told that he was not cold.

> Those who attended my body did things according to how they believed they should be done, and I seemed to have little or no part in this except to feel the effect of what they did. They were not unkind but they were more the owners of what lay inside the tank, than I.

He was not even acknowledged as a separate person. Those caring for him knew how he felt better than he himself. He was always at the mercy of the feelings of those attending to him.

> Everything that affected their lives affected me. If I were cared for willingly and without reluctance, I felt good and the world was sunny. If my care was given grudgingly or irritably, in a callous way, powerful feelings of degradation swept over me.

His polio struck in the era before electric wheelchairs. Being wheeled by an attendant off the hospital grounds for the first time was a historic step. He did not know what the outside world held for a quadriplegic. A woman crossed the street to reach out and rub his back. When he questioned her, she seemed surprised that he did not understand. "It's good luck if you touch a cripple," she said.

This sermon is not about quadriplegics. The message this morning deals with that first paragraph about the horrible loneliness of looking out into an empty corridor. Suddenly, Arnie's perception changed and what he saw was miraculously beautiful. The task before him—and us—is how to change states from seeing emptiness to seeing beauty.

If you know someone who is not in occasional need of this skill, then he or she should address us next week. *Suzanne Black*, a previous member of this congregation, once spoke here about the California hiking accident that put her on crutches the rest of her life. She chided us that her limitations where obvious, while ours were hidden. We all have limitations and need to discover how to find satisfaction in life despite our handicaps (which tend to increase over time). Tennis champion Arnie Beisser had to find satisfaction as a spectator rather than a contestant. A friend wrote, "Arnie worked hard at medical school but sports were his first love. It was beautiful to watch him play tennis, with his sense of single-minded concentration, strength, fair play, and a grace that I had never witnessed before." Arnie, who had been bored by the performances of others, began to savor his role as a spectator. And he also began to look upon his disability as a competitive sport—one in which he himself was the opponent. "What I loved about sports was that they called into play all of my capabilities: power and guile, skill and discipline, force and subtlety." He would now marshal these qualities to confront and cope with the limitations of paralysis.

Arnie decided that psychiatry was a medical discipline that he could handle from his wheelchair. It required three more years of school—with a 24-hour attendant. During this period, electrical wheelchairs became available. "My freedom was largely illusionary, since somebody still had to be with me to recline me. But it felt wonderful, like soaring! I do not imagine that an astronaut's lift-off at Cape Canaveral would have been more exciting." After completing psychiatry he became director of the Outpatient Clinic at the hospital. He later became Education and Research director, overseeing all the residents. Today, Arnie Beisser is a clinical professor of psychiatry at UCLA.

During Arnie's first year in the iron lung, he fell in love with a nurse named Rita. She admits that she prayed, "Oh God, don't let me fall in love with him." Rita was Boston, Italian, Catholic. Arnie was California, beach, tennis, Jew. It took Arnie a long time to understand that Rita didn't see in him what he saw in himself. He still could not accept himself as he was, not as a young physician, a star athlete, a part of a Pepsi Generation commercial. He assumed that his limitations were like a great wall between them; she saw them as "inconveniences." She was not oblivious to their significance, but they were less important than other things. (David Mamet wrote a play about a couple who obtain physical intimacy almost instantaneously but are never able to share any other part of their lives.) Arnie had to be convinced that there is more to him than the body that housed a national tennis champ.

After their marriage, Rita developed rheumatoid arthritis. The couple now depends upon shifts of helpers to look after both of them. This book testifies to the fact that they both are living their lives with a sense of well-being. The World Health Organization defines health as the absence of illness and a positive sense of well-being. Yet these two qualities do not always go together. Many people who do not suffer from an illness lack the sense of well-being exuded by people such as Arnie and Rita.

A wide range of limitations affects those congregated here. They include: handicaps that are as obvious as Arnie's; deaths of loved ones; retirement and loss of status; loss of hearing or sight; or the loss of such special gifts as singing or athleticism. There is the loss of independence, financial limitations, or giving up one's car or home. There is the loss of sex appeal, when heads no longer turn.

Arnie felt that the person he had known himself to be was trapped in an alien body. My former secretary, now 75, wrote me at Christmas saying almost the same thing, "I feel just the same and then I look in the mirror and see an old lady." Now, you will not like Arnie's solution—and you may be shocked that it is being advocated from the Thomas Paine pulpit. Arnie says that the solution is surrender.

In the beginning, he approached his illness as though it had a solution— some way out. He looked upon his disability as a problem to be solved. Arnie, like most of us, had grown up believing that if you wanted something bad enough, and worked hard enough, you could obtain it. In the ward, Arnie was told that his degree of improvement would be equal to how hard he tried. Yet, beyond a certain point, exertion just inflicted more damage. There were health providers who implied that if you're not improving, then you don't want it enough. Surrendering to paralysis seemed like cowardice—a cop out. At some point, a friend shared with Arnie the Alcoholic's prayer, "Give us the grace to accept with serenity the things that cannot be changed, courage to change the things that should be, and the wisdom to distinguish one from the other."

This morning we focus on surrendering with serenity to aspects of your life that you cannot change. Arnie believes that the four stages of accepting death, which psychiatrist Elisabeth Kübler-Ross once shared with us here in this room, can be applied to any loss. First comes denial: My legs are not really paralyzed. A friend of mine told me that he has not played racquetball in 10 years but still keeps his equipment in his YMCA locker. He is in denial that his racquetball days are over and have been replaced by his new sport—swimming. Remember the book *Is There Life After High School?* Former athletes fill neighborhood bar stools, trying to find meaning in their lives long after their fans stop cheering. We may deny that our children are independent and no longer need us because we can't relinquish our identities of being nurturing parents.

After denying that we have lost what we valued, we then seek to blame our loss on something or someone. If we had just had another doctor or went to another hospital . . . If the government had prevented cigarette advertising . . . If we had taken a different job 20 years ago, we would not have been forced out in this merger.

Next we bargain. If the kids will only move back to Chicago, we won't be demanding. If I can just pass this driver's test, I'll volunteer to drive those who can't drive. If I can just die in my own home, I'll will it to church. The final step is acceptance or surrender to that which cannot be changed. And it is not just accepting what is impaired or gone, it's also accepting what is new (e.g. the athlete who becomes a spectator or now sees life like an artist—appreciating how shadows and light form geometric patterns). Perception does not shift from something to nothing; it shifts from old perceptions to new ones.

It sounds un-American and un-Unitarian to speak of surrender and acceptance. But Dr. Beisser writes,

> At some point in our lives we all must come to terms with declining energy, health, and ultimately death. Inevitably we are both winners and losers, and we must find ways of valuing each aspect of ourselves in order to use our full potential.

Losing and disabilities are part of life. Dr. Beisser writes,

> No winner is ever permanent, no athlete is perpetually strong and healthy. Success is only momentary and in the next competition he may be beaten. And even if he wins frequently, ultimately he will be beaten by others. The person who can find no place in his life for the loser must

deny aspects of his own humanity and the humanity of others. We are all winners at times. We are all cripples at times, and ultimately we all lose to death.

Pre-polio, Arnie viewed life as a ladder. one simply climbed it, one rung after another. It seemed endless. After his paralysis, he viewed life as more of a roller coaster, with giant sweeps that take you up, followed by a long plunges into the depths, and then back up again.

Life is not always what we want it to be. There are times of surrender, when your only option is to let that which you have not chosen give you new knowledge and experiences. Let's face it, Arnie Beisser did not have much of an inner life before. He simply had not needed it. He was fortunate to come out of his iron lung with a whole new perspective on life. Many of those on his ward failed to do so, living out meager lives as invalids. It was horrendous to emerge from the iron lung and have to leave behind his image of himself as an athlete and as a particular kind of lover. For the first time he understood that life imposes limitations. He says it taught him about the hazards of pride and vanity. He believes that these lessons are valuable and that there are more of them to come.

Dr. Beisser now is in his early sixties.

> My energy and physical strength have, as to be expected, slowly but inexorably declined. My workday has shortened consistent with reduced breathing capacity and sitting tolerance. Each functional loss is painful, and I am never prepared for it, although I anticipate it. Sooner or later, I know that I will face something again that seems horrible to me. Will I once again find a way to accept what seems now unacceptable?
>
> To accept gracefully something that is awful seems impossible and a contradiction in terms. But once you get the hang of experiencing things from inside, anything becomes possible. Surrender and acceptance are talents which must be learned.

Dr. Beisser asked himself in the polio ward, "Are peace, happiness and joy possible if one is severely disabled?" A sense of well-being is something that comes from within. "Health" comes from the same root word as "holy." Arnie's life and his book testify to the fact that he feels that he has been blessed, that something has been lost and that something also has been gained. When he thinks about the things that he cannot do he feels disabled. When he thinks of those things that he can do, he feels well-being.

Satori in Zen Buddhism is a state of enlightenment that approximates a burst of laughter, a state of wonder. It is what a child must feel when surrounded by playthings, unencumbered and free. Dr. Beisser and those who know him say that he experienced satori—a state accessible to homecoming queens, tennis champions and quadriplegics. Dr. Beisser says, "There are times for activity in the world; and times for activity within." Not long ago a woman in our congregation was moving away and I suggested, "Wouldn't it be better to find an apartment where you can walk to whatever your need when you no longer have a car?" I could see that she did not understand my question and hadn't come to grips with the fact that she would someday be without a car. Many of us seem to believe that we will drive to the crematorium or to the University of Illinois Hospital to donate our bodies for research. We see television commercials for adult diapers without grasping the immense size of the incontinence market. We are proud and assured of our independence. Yet I could count on one hand all the people I have buried in 30 years who have escaped this world without becoming dependent.

Initially, the only satisfactions that Arnie could comprehend were those that he had known before polio struck. Before 90 percent of the people in this room die, we are going to have to learn new satisfactions that we cannot now imagine. I do not mean this as a threat. The whole point of Arnie's life has been to make of it a challenge. Isn't the first rule of reasonable living to recognize the unalterable and to submit to it without tears? William Schulz, the president of our national Unitarian Association, writes that the moment of truth comes when one recognizes that happiness is sometimes too much to ask. But we can always ask—against all odds—for nobility instead. There are former athletes and ex-prom queens on the streets today who are enduring impotence, carrying mastectomy scars, bearing radiation burns, or wearing hearing aids, diapers or colostomy bags. The best of them have learned how to surrender, to exude well-being, and to carry themselves with a semblance of dignity.

March 5, 1989, Third Unitarian Church of Chicago.

Foxes and Hedgehogs

don't know at what point in my life I was converted. Several years ago I was at one of those meetings where you had to go around and give your name and say something about yourself. I said that I was a Unitarian-Socialist. Perhaps today I would say I am a Socialist-Unitarian. Jesus instructed John the Baptist, "Go and tell John what you have seen and heard; the blind receive their sight, the lame walk, lepers are cleansed, and the deaf hear, the dead are raised up, and the poor have good news preached to them." This seems to be a list of ascending miracles, and the climax is not the miracle of raising the dead but preaching good news to the poor.

The top one percent of our citizens possess more net wealth than the bottom 90 percent. If there is going to be good news for the poor it probably will take not a revolution but some new legislation. George Bernard Shaw wrote, "It was believed that you could not make men good by an act of Parliament, we now know that you cannot make them good in any other way." I recall reading that President Roosevelt considered limiting how much income anyone in the United States could earn. Plato thought that the richest citizens ought to be no more than four times as wealthy as the poorest. In U.S. Civil Service there was a principle that the ratio between the highest and the lowest salaries should be no more than 10 to one. We must not haggle over the exact ratio but another FDR could lead us in this kind of legislation. There will be no change so long as we think of inequality as an economic, social or political phenomenon. It will change—as everything has—when we make poverty a moral issue. Bertrand Russell said in 1917 that,

> If a majority in every civilized country so desired, we could within 20 years abolish all abject poverty. . . . It is only because men are apathetic that this is not achieved— only because imagination is sluggish, and that what always has been is regarded as what always must be.

"The poor we shall always have with us."

The 90 percent of Americans who possess one percent of the net wealth obviously are the majority that Lord Russell believed have the power to turn things around. Robert Heilbroner wrote,

> The time will soon be at hand when the have-not peoples of the world will become so aware of what they do not have, and accessibility to weapons of modern war will make them so able to threaten those who do have, that we will either distribute the world's wealth or be destroyed.

No revolutionary, Heilbroner is an economics professor at the New School of Social Research.

Those of you contemplating leaving because you walked into a political diatribe will be relieved to know that I am going to switch gears. I am indebted to the British historian Isaiah Berlin for the concept of Hedgehogs and Foxes. He said that a fox knows many things but the hedgehog knows one big thing. He divided people into these two categories. I hope that we are composed primarily of hedgehogs—who know the one big thing. That one big thing is consistent with the teachings of Jesus, who talked of the pearl of great price and all the lesser pearls that are sold in order to obtain it. He said that the way is broad that leads to destruction and the way is narrow that leads to life. He said that you can gain the whole world and lose your soul. To save our souls we must know the big picture.

Last week I quoted a new book by Julius Lester, the black militant of the 1960s who recently converted to Judaism. Lester says of his son, "I live with the terror that my son will believe that what he has is more important than who he is." What worthy parent has not wrestled with that dilemma? Erich Fromm explores this dichotomy in a book titled *To Have or To Be?* No man can serve two masters. One cannot pursue both having and being!

It takes a lot of time and energy to develop "beingness." I won't have enough time or energy for it if I work overtime to make money for car payments or a kitchen remodel. There are many people whose identity is centered around what they own. Whether they verbalize it or not, their children get the message. There are those who find their happiness through possessing, collecting, gathering, accumulating. Some learned early that if you don't have much, then you aren't much. Capitalism is addictive. It is not good for your health. It breeds egotism, greed, and selfishness. It can only survive in a populous that believes that, "The more I have the more I am." William Wordsworth warned, "Getting and spending, we lay waste our powers."

Some people take the gambler's approach. They invest in having until they are 65, planning to devote the last years of their lives to nature, music, theater, friends, family, physical exercise, gardening, citizenship, volunteering, reading, travel, meditation, and developing a philosophy of life. Combatting this tact, Ernest Callenbach wrote in his book *Living Poor With Style*,

> If coveting is your trip, you should at least get through it as quickly as possible. Work your ass off, put your money into all the goodies you can manage, spend your time in stores, read *Consumers Reports*, talk to the experts, really sink yourself in it for a while. Then kick it, and get back to figuring out what you really want to do with your life.

Bertrand Russell says that we must judge political and social institutions on the basis of whether they cultivate creativeness or possessiveness. He said that the aims of an economy should include:

1. The greatest possible production of goods and facilitating technical progress;
2. Securing distributive justice;
3. Security against destitution; and
4. Liberating creative impulses and diminishing possessive impulses.

In Sir Thomas More's *Utopia* written in 1516 there were to be just six hours of work a day. "The chief aim of its institutions and government, above all else, was to give citizens as much time as public needs permit for reading and developing their minds. In this they suppose the felicity of man's life is to consist."

We gather here today in that great Jewish tradition of the Sabbath that guards against getting caught up in getting and spending—and laying waste our powers. The Jews set aside a day simply for being. A day on which nothing was to be bought or sold, no cooking or shopping was to be done, a day for thinking, for studying, for praying, for singing. The Jewish philosopher Baruch Spinoza thought that the way of happiness is through optimal personal growth devoted to developing our artistic and intellectual powers. Happiness does not come through a Rolex watch or Mercedes-Benz. The transcendentalist Margaret Fuller taught that,

> A house is no home unless it contains food and fire for the mind as well as for the body. For human beings are not so constituted that they can

live without expansion. If they do not get it one way, they must in another, or perish.

I have two true stories to tell about this and I don't know which I love best. A friend of mine invited her sister to the Art Institute of Chicago. Her sister replied that she had no interest since "none of the paintings are for sale." One sister lived for being while the other lived for having! My other story is of a dear woman in my first parish in rural Indiana. She once told me that she would listen to her radio for a while in the morning and then turn it off so that others could listen for a while. Maureen never comprehended that the radio, like a great many things, can be enjoyed by large numbers of people—without diminishing the quantity or the quality available to everyone.

Another lady in my first church, Lila Maines, feared that she might lose her sight and started memorizing poetry. *Goodman Mottelson* in this congregation traveled light and carried much, including the poetry that he also loved to memorize. Writer Paul Zweig recalled that, "Poetry was part of my father's self-respect." Poetry, like listening to the radio, does not diminish the supply available for others to enjoy. It is unlimited. The more people who possess it, the richer we all are. A good percentage of us will spend our last days in nursing homes—some of us with failing eyes and ears. *If* our minds last, what we have memorized is about all that we will have left.

Mental and spiritual goods do not belong to one person to the exclusion of another. If one man is a great writer or one woman a great painter, that does not prevent others from pursuing these arts. Instead, it creates an atmosphere in which others will express their creativity. In science, one person's discovery enriches the scientific community worldwide. Lord Russell wrote of such riches, "Any increase anywhere tends to produce an increase everywhere." In mental and spiritual goods, the gain of each is the gain of all. These are the things that moth and rust do not consume, that thieves cannot steal. A person filled with the joy of life does not diminish the amount or joy in the world but increases it. I think I have made the point; to continue would undo it.

Bill Moyers recently interviewed five leading intellectuals. The theme seemed to be that everyone wants to be clever, to be successful and to win— and that they are willing to do whatever is necessary to achieve this. We have corrupted the whole idea of individualism. Being an individual once meant to develop your own potential, your own resources to let your intellectual, creative, artistic and spiritual powers blossom. But we have corrupted the term to mean, "I'll get mine—and the devil take the hindmost."

I do not believe this statistic but I will quote it. Sociologist Herbert Gans did a study that found that privatism and a near incorrigible avoidance of political participation characterize 40 percent of our population. Forty percent of Americans have pretty well opted out to pursue their own private interests. Their private desire to get ahead adds up to a kind of moral indifference about the rest of the world. They are not bad people. But their lives are preoccupied with getting by, getting through, getting on, and getting ahead.

This sermon ends like all the rest—like those by Reverends Billy Sunday, Billy Graham and Bill Schulz: "Choose ye this day." Jean-Paul Sartre says that we are condemned to be free—condemned to make our choices. We can center our lives on being or on having. How ironic that many people believe that "standard of living" is measured through material consumption—and not by human life at its best. I hope someday your children will say of you, "There never were people who traveled so light and who carried so much." E. F. Schumacher's classic book, *Small Is Beautiful*, describes the journeys that people like our own *Goodman* and *Georgia Mottelson* took from having to being.

> Many of them had a better time than they ever had in their lives because they were discovering a new freedom. The less you need, the freer you become. They discovered and kept discovering that they were carrying far too much baggage and so they dropped pieces right and left all along the way. And the more they dropped, the happier they became.

I never thought of it before, but the murals in this church depict those who traveled light and carried much: Gandhi and Harriet Tubman, Jesus and Socrates, Buddha, Dr. King and Thoreau.

During the Vietnam War LBJ let it slip that the Vietnamese "want what we have." Material possessions can be taken by force and enjoyed by robbers or invaders. Our orientation to life can be possessive or creative. Material possessiveness is defensive or aggressive. It seeks to possess something to the exclusion of others or to keep something that others may covet. But if you embrace creativity instead, LBJ's comment stops making sense. The Vietnamese are welcome to our poetry, our library card, our friendships, our family rapport, our enjoyment of nature and our scientific understanding!

The fox knows many things, while the hedgehog knows the one thing that is important. For us and for our species, that is the concept that life is being and not having. Sinclair Lewis' character George Babbitt confessed, "I have never done a single thing that I wanted to in all my life." A man awaiting a train on the El platform near here pointed toward the Chicago Loop and told me, "I die a little bit down there every day." Choose ye this day! "I call heaven and earth to witness against you this day; that I have set before you the ways of life and death, blessing and curse. Therefore choose life that you and your descendants may live."

Delivered September 18, 1988, Third Unitarian Church of Chicago.

Condemned to Gaiety and Hope

was here last November. If you ask me back again, make it at another time. Thanksgiving is my favorite season and you will conclude that I have but one sermon. Thanksgiving is better than Christmas or birthdays because there are no gifts, no commercializing, just a good meal in the presence of friends, family, and, hopefully, "strangers in the land of Egypt," whom you invited to join your table. I hope some of you are acquainted with the novelist Romain Gary, who has written 26 novels. I am concerned this morning with the one called *Promise at Dawn*.

Romain Gary was born in 1914 in Vilna, a town that has been a possession of Lithuania, Poland and the Soviet Union. Gary did not know who his father was. He did know that his mother once had had a great love and that she loved Romain not only for himself but because he reminded her of his father. Romain and his mother were refugees following World War I and one of his mother's two great dreams was that they must make it to Paris.

Gary says just two people spoke of France with the same tone of voice: General Charles de Gaulle and his mother. She spoke of France as other mothers speak to their children of Snow White or Robin Hood. "I have never entirely succeeded in ridding myself of that image of France—seen as a never-never land of shining heroes and exemplary virtues. I am probably one of the few men alive who have remained completely loyal to a nursery tale." When he was 8 years old she began telling him, "You are going to be a French ambassador." She repeated this mantra with great conviction. Hence the title of his biography, *Promise at Dawn*. It is in the promises whispered at birth or dawn of future triumphs and greatness—the values of justice and love—it is in these whispery prayers that Romain Gary believes more than anything else.

They started their pilgrimage from Vilna to Paris with 24 pieces of silver heirlooms, which they gradually sold off to finance their journey. The one exception was the silver samovar. They could not sell it since Romain would need it when he became ambassador. No sacrifice was too great for this mother of a future ambassador. She read palms in restaurants. She made hats when they were in Poland and sewed for an exclusive French millinery shop. She worked as a hairdresser and performed the same services for dogs at a kennel. She hawked jewelry from the lobbies of one hotel to another. She took in roomers and boarded cats, birds, and dogs in their small apartment.

When they first arrived in Paris, they slept in the waiting room of a relative who was a dentist. They had to remain on the streets until office hours were over. Gary's mother was diabetic and not in the best of health. Yet he writes, "She was always waiting for the intrusion of the magical and marvelous into her life." Even as a young boy he felt, "I longed to see my mother holding the arm of someone who had better manners, less cruelty or indifference than life itself." As a young boy he understood something of their struggles for existence yet never questioned the fact that each day when he came home from school for lunch there was a beefsteak, which she declined to eat because she was a vegetarian. The steak symbolized to his mother her victorious struggle against adversity. One day, by chance, he found her in the kitchen with a chunk of bread, sopping up the steak fat. "When she saw me, she quickly tried to hide the pan with the napkin, but it was too late; the true reason for her vegetarian diet was now obvious to me."

Whenever he had problems at school, his mother said, "Your teachers don't understand you. The time will come when your name will be inscribed in gold on the wall of their wretched school. I'll go and tell them so tomorrow." Money was scarce but it was always found for French, Latin, and German lessons, for elocution and dance, for fencing, riding school, and pistol shooting. His mother was not religious in the traditional sense but they were more or less Jewish. In a crisis, his mother might speak the name of God in a way that showed a certain bourgeois respect for somebody who had made good. She had always shown a high degree of consideration for the Creator, but with the verbal and impersonal deference that she kept for persons occupying high positions.

Once, when his mother was ill, he entered Notre-Dame Cathedral. He kept it a secret, fearing that she would see his appeal to outside help as a sign,

> that I had lost my confidence and faith in her, and also an indication of the gravity of her condition. I thought she might suddenly imagine that I had felt I could no longer rely on her and was looking for support elsewhere and that in turning to another, I was abandoning her.

His mother taught him that there are four gods who control the world: the god of stupidity, the god of absolute truth (for all true believers and bigots), the god of mediocrity, and the god of acceptance and servility. Her mission for her future ambassador was to defeat these gods and to establish a reign of dignity and justice among men.

In Gary's novel *Roots of Heaven*, the character Morel doesn't know how to give in to despair and give up. Gary identifies with this quality. Near the end of his life he writes,

> The greatest effort of my life has always been the effort to give up, to attain despair, and to know peace at last. But it's no good. Something of her courage had passed into me and it has remained with me ever since. Her courage and her will continue to burn in me even now and make life very difficult when it would be so easy to give up, to give in. She condemned me to gaiety and to hope. My mother had told me too many beautiful tales, and with too great a talent in those whispering hours at the dawn of life when a child's every fiber takes an indelible imprint. We had exchanged too many promises and I found myself bound by all of them.

She had condemned her son to a life of gaiety and hope. He was destined to defeat the gods of stupidity, absolute truth, mediocrity and servility, and to establish a reign of dignity and justice. He wrote, "My life did not belong to me. It was an instrument of justice. I had a promise to keep." Gary left home to enter law school. His mother sent him frequent letters couched in lapidary terms exhorting him to show courage and tenacity. They resembled the proclamations issued by generals to their troops on the eve of defeat, pulsating with promises of victory and honor. She was his commander in chief. "Courage my son, you will return home crowned with laurels." Once when she was ill and unable to work, he suggested dropping out of school. "She looked at me reproachfully, and began to cry. I never returned to the subject."

The legend of his future kept the old woman alive. Her son was in a race against time to keep a promise, to give an absurd, fond dream at least some kernel of reality. Later in life he could say: "I lived until the age of 22 on the sweat and toil of a sick and exhausted old woman and I still feel mad at her sometimes." At college he entered into numerous love affairs and always his mother's concern was whether she was suitable to be the wife of an ambassador, capable of the kind of social training and intellectual discussions that would be required of her. She admonished him to explain to his girlfriend's family, "This is what we have; this is what we are giving: a writer, a diplomat, a hero. And what are you prepared to give to the union?"

In 1938 he completed his law school requirements and entered military service on the eve of World War II. Many families stood at the station as their sons left but only one mother carried a flag and shouted *"Vive La France!"* long after the train passed from sight. France fell in 21 days because men submitted to the gods of stupidity, mediocrity and servility.

General de Gaulle issued a call from London in June 1940, asking for volunteers to fight for a free France. Romain Gary writes,

> My mother's rally was sounded on the 15th or 16th at the Buffa market from Mr. Pantaleoni's vegetable stand and numerous witnesses can bear me out on this point. Twenty persons were later to describe to me this frightening scene. The sight of which, thank heaven, I was mercifully spared: my mother standing on a chair among carrots, beet roots and lettuces, brandishing her cane and calling on all good men to reject the shameful armistice and continue to fight.

When Gary went to England to join de Gaulle's fight, the neighbors were to look after his mother. "They knew perfectly well that what mattered was not her or me, but our old human companionship, our shoulder to shoulder struggle and progress in pursuit of justice and reason."

Gary writes of trying to get himself a plane at the air force base in England.

> My mother's vitality and her will power drove me forward. Indeed it was not I who was wandering from plane to plane but an old lady dressed in grey, stick in hand, and a Gauloises between her lips, who had made up her mind that she would go to England to continue the fight and that nothing was going to stop her.

He called her to say goodbye and she assured him that nothing was going to happen to him. She had always felt that he was to be her victory, her happy ending, that she had exchanged her botched life with fate, so that he could be triumphant. With a ridiculous, sobbing voice she cried, "We'll get them."

The last elementary, the most naive form of human courage, sank deep into my heart and remains there forever. I know that it will live long after I am dead and that someday or other, mankind will know a victory far greater than anything we can imagine.

When the BBC would announce that the French Air Force bombed Germany from British bases, an old woman paraded around the Buffa Market, waving her cane with a radiant face. She spread the good news that her son, the future ambassador, had taken matters into his own hands. He was gone for over three years. Having heard of the letters that she wrote to him in law school, just imagine the ones he received flying bomber missions. For three and a half years the umbilical cord fed his blood with the fighting courage of a heart more gallant than his own.

Near the end of the war the letters got shorter, though still audaciously filled with hope. They always ended, "My glorious son, I am proud of you. *Vive La France!*" She had been writing other letters, too, for he received an official form to be filled out for an appointment in the French Diplomatic Service when the war was over. During the war, Romain Gary published a book in England and he was bringing that home to his mother along with the Legion of Honor, the Cross of Liberation, and the *Croix de Guerre*. But at her apartment he encountered new occupants, who knew nothing of her whereabouts. Romain Gary—soon to be named the French Consul General to the United States—learned that his mother had died a few weeks after he left for England. But remembering the promises that she had made at dawn, she wrote nearly 250 undated letters, which a friend mailed at regular intervals.

It was only after my fortieth winter that I began to understand. It is wrong to have been loved so much, so young, so early, at the dawn of your life. You thus acquire a bad habit, the worst habit there is. You can't get rid of it. You believe that you have it in you to be loved, that it is your due, that it will always be around for you, that it can always be found again, that the world owes it to you, and you keep looking, thirsting, summoning. In your mother's love, life makes you a promise at the dawn of life that it will never keep. You have known something that you will never know again. You will go hungry to the end of your days, leftovers, cold tidbits, that's what you will find in front of you at each new feast.

Good Lord Almighty! Do you know what it means to be condemned to a life of gaiety and hope? Do you know what it means to know whispers and promises at dawn?

This sermon may or may not be about mothers. But it most definitely is about thanksgiving. And thanksgiving is most assuredly not about the home in which we dwell, for the days will come when that house will be sold. Thanksgiving is not about good health, for that, too, shall go. Nor is it about family, for one of us will be the last leaf on the family tree "and friends shall go and every fire burn low."

But as long as the brainwaves function, we shall give thanks that someone touched us. Someone laid a finger on us. Someone called us out of the crowd. Someone planted a hunger in us for righteousness, a taste for beauty, a thirst for reason. Someone took us up onto the mountaintop and exposed the false gods of stupidity, absolute truth, mediocrity, and servility. That's why we are here today, not pushing a shopping cart at Water Tower Place, eating at the House of Pancakes or the Drake Hotel, or watching television. Someone showed a great light and all the darkness has not overcome it. Someone gave you a book. Someone introduced you to the *Nation* or *Mother Jones* magazine. Someone took you to hear Eugene Debs, to demand justice for the Scottsboro Boys, or to march in Selma. An old lady paid your bus fare to Washington to protest the Vietnam War. Somebody gave you a ticket to the symphony, a play, a ballet, or an art museum. Someone said you'd make a good counsellor, organizer, or teacher. Someone wrote you the letter you needed. Someone made "the call" that changed you. Someone held out the hand that saved you. And that is why you keep on keeping on. You also were made promises at dawn that prevent you from surrendering to the gods of mediocrity, stupidity, servility, and absolute truth.

Is it any wonder that you feel chosen, special, singled out? Is it any wonder that you feel lonely in this materialistic, selfish culture? Its ways are not your ways. Its thoughts are not your thoughts. You have been condemned to gaiety and hope. What a cause for thanksgiving!

Delivered November 15, 1987, Third Unitarian Church of Chicago.

Part Five

Humanism

The unexamined life
is not worth living.

SOCRATES

Snake Oil Religion

spoke here 30 years ago and it is nice to be invited back. I shall try to be less controversial this time. This congregation and Third Unitarian Church share a piece of unique trivia: We are the only congregations with pulpits named for Tom Paine. That is rather like Ken Kesey and the Merry Pranksters selecting "Further" as the destination of their bus. A Tom Paine pulpit is destined to go "Further" because there are no limits to the freedom of a pulpit so named.

Recently I have been reading the daily papers through Tom Paine's eyes. Last weekend a headline read, "Most Americans believe in Angels." Seventy-two percent of the population believe angels exist; a fifth of Americans say they have seen an angel or know someone who has. These angels are not related to Christianity (for those of you looking for a whipping boy). Many angel believers have no religious affiliation; they identify simply and perhaps self-righteously as "spiritual."

I love the *New York Times* article each Sunday featuring somebody's wedding. Last Sunday they ran a photo of an affluent WASP couple who spent their wedding day in a sweat lodge and were married by Chief Phillip Crazy Bull—a Lakota medicine man. Using sage, cedar and tobacco as offerings, Chief Crazy Bull asked for blessings from their ancestors, whose spirits were brought to the lodge in the form of heated rocks. The chief, whose body was covered in scars from ritual piercings, gave the bride and groom the bowl and stem of a pipe, whose union would symbolize their own. At any time they could separate them and their union would be dissolved.

Picture old Tom Paine reading that the Pope is elevating Juan Diego to sainthood. The Pope will go to Mexico in July for the canonization. Juan Diego saw an olive-skinned Virgin Mary on the site of an Aztec shrine in 1531. He then performed a miracle for another mother by saving the life of her son, who had jumped from a building and cracked his skull.

Liberal Congresswoman Maxine Waters and Republican Senator Jim Inhofe made strange bedfellows when they lobbied together for Philippe Sauvage, a faith healer in Brittany. He was deported to France for entering the United States on a false passport. Sauvage is said to have saved people from cancer, cystic fibrosis and third-degree burns. At a United Nations conference on AIDS, 150 traditional healers issued a statement calling on all countries to put in place legal measures allowing them to participate in the search for an AIDS cure.

That same day a *New York Times* headline read, "Study rebuts belief that support groups can extend life." The article reported that, "The study disputes a belief that has been stated so often it is almost considered a truism that the mind influences the course of advanced cancer so powerfully that a patient can hold off death by getting emotional support in a group. That same paper ran an article about an Argentine shrine visited by 600,000 people a year. It has 17 chapels filled with the wedding gowns of women whose wish for marriage was fulfilled after a visit and trophies from soccer, tennis and bowling champions who prayed there for victory. The Unitarian Universalist *World Magazine* had an ad for a service that will pray for you every day. I wrote to discover the cost, which I am happy to share with those who are interested. I could go on, but there would be few left to listen. G. K. Chesterton said that it is because people don't have anything to believe in that they will believe in anything at all. William James said, "Our task is not to believe too little or too much." I would wager that most of us are trying to strike a balance.

The biologist E. O. Wilson maintains that there is a biological basis for religiosity, though one cannot locate it in a specific gene. He believes that humans have to believe in something. Wilson's colleague, Richard Dawkins, dared to say in the *Guardian* that the September 11th attack would not have happened without religion. "The after-life-obsessed suicidal brain really is a weapon of immense power and danger," he said. "If it had not been for religion, the very concept of a Jewish state would have had no meaning in the first place. Nor would the concept of an Islamic land, as something to be invaded and desecrated." Picture a world without sky-God religions, the crusades, the inquisition, pogroms, or the religious wars today in Ireland, India, Pakistan, Afghanistan, the Philippines, and Bosnia.

The French mathematician Blaise Pascal said, "Men never do evil so completely and cheerfully as when they do it from religious conviction." Hitler asked, "Who said that I am not under the special protection of God?" Let us assume that there is a religious gene and everyone must find some kind of religion, some worldview, some way of making sense of their place in the world. John Dietrich, the Unitarian father of religious humanism, said that religion is almost wholly a matter of temperament and there are those who need a sky-God, which nobody can reason them out of.

I think that we all have had the experience of waking up one day and thinking, "Why did it take me so long?" We are simply not ready to entertain some ideas when we first hear them. We have to embrace them on our schedule. We criticize some old couple in their 80s who waited too long to sell the big house, or someone who spends their whole life oblivious to the blatant wrongs of capitalism. I was 50 before I joined the Democratic Socialists. I rationally know all the advantages of a computer, but typed this sermon on a portable Royal typewriter that I had in college. Friends and relatives cling to the fairy tales of the Bible and believe that they are under the care of a sky God, despite all the evidence to the contrary. I learned of humanism when I was 19 and it took me 15 years before I changed my religious affiliation. Or take Martha Burton. She was the prettiest girl in high school. When I went to my 50th class reunion this summer, Martha announced that—after 48 years—she was getting a divorce. "It never was right," she said. I am sure that her mother, her kids, and her therapist must have suggested divorce long ago. Like all of us, she had to act out of her own temperament. She had to face reality when the time was right for her.

John Dietrich is credited with preaching the first humanist sermon in America in Minneapolis on December 18, 1925. A holy day to many of us. Your own Kendyl Gibbons has become minister of Dietrich's church. What Dietrich said in that sermon 78 years ago is that we are not at the mercy of a just or an unjust god, but live in an indifferent universe to which we must accommodate ourselves. Why would anyone abandon a cozy belief in a loving heavenly father who looks after you to embrace an indifferent universe? The only reasons I can suggest are moral integrity and mental honesty. Otherwise, why not just keep pretending? Ralph Waldo Emerson said, "Nothing is at last sacred but the integrity of your own mind." William Bennett, Reagan's Secretary of Education, countered that, "Hypocrisy is better than no standards at all!"

My favorite minister, Dr. Duncan Littlefair up in Grand Rapids, says that theism is a symbol that means everything is in order, that no matter what happens you may rest assured that it is within the will of God (September 11, 2001). There is nothing unplanned, there is nothing evil that will not somehow be used by God for the emergence of good. Contrast that with the definition of humanism that Sir Julian Huxley gave when speaking from Third Unitarian Church's Tom Paine Pulpit on the centennial of Darwin's *Origin of the Species* in 1959:

> I use the word Humanism to mean someone who believes that humans are just as much a natural phenomenon as an animal or a plant, that our bodies, minds and souls, were not supernaturally created, but are the production of evolution, and that we are not under the control or the guidance of any supernatural being or beings, but have to rely on ourselves and our powers.

Again, what would possess anyone who was safe in the loving arms of a heavenly father to embrace this humanist philosophy? Any Meadville Seminary student can quote Huxley or Dietrich (oh, that they would!) but I feel that I must quote my distinguished predecessor at Third Church, Dr. Wakefield Slaten:

> When you become a humanist, you cut loose from the old mooring and set out on what seems a dark and dangerous voyage. The old comforting infallibilities disappear. You are on an open sea with no hand on the tiller but your own, no chart to guide you but your own reason and conscience; no bright harbor to steer to but one of your own choosing.

Imagine printing that on a pamphlet to recruit new members! Yet Dr. Wakefield Slaten makes it even bleaker:

> You have stood perhaps upon the point of some great rock that jutted out over the roaring sea. You have crouched upon some dizzy mountain height and clung fast, and gazed in fascination into the abyss below. But now you are asked to look out upon the Universe, to place yourself, as it were, upon some projecting spar and look into the frightful depths of infinite space. You see vast worlds rolling in restless precision. You realize that you are in the grip of cosmic forces. You sense your isolation, that you are physically alone in a terrifying, and uncaring universe and that when your little span of life is done you sink down to extinction, the blackness of darkness forever!

You would think that humanist congregations would attract more mountain climbers, skydivers, snow boarders, gamblers and other people seeking excitement and adventure. It's an open universe. The dice are not loaded. The cards are not stacked. The game is not rigged. No one has any idea how it is going to turn out. Just think how different religions would be if we read our holy books as religious adventure stories. Dr. Slaten writes that the Bible is like *The Arabian Nights*. Its pages open a door into an Oriental fairyland.

> While we read, we join ourselves to nomadic caravans as they wander across the Tigris-Euphrates valley, we see miracles: the sick rise up before our eyes, graves open, dead men walk about the streets, angels appear dressed in dazzling white, and God himself speaks to us from the sky.

Picture that beside a humanist sermon, manifesto, or tract.

Nonetheless, men and women in Hinsdale with PhDs will still quote the Bible and say that we should be fruitful and multiply although we are adding one New York City to our population each week, and one Mexico each year. They still believe that the Bible says that God gave the holy land to the Israelites. They still believe that nature is here for our misuse; that we can do with it whatever we please. The more radical branches of the Israeli settler movement are fired up by the eschatological belief that reclaiming the land will hasten the coming of the Messiah.

It is hard to believe that evolution is still the central conflict in America's culture wars today. Whoever wins that battle wins the war. We need to keep scoreboards in our churches. Last year Kansas restored evolution to the science curriculum and the Board of Education in Hawaii said no to teaching Creationism. I believe that your board of trustees should require all of your members to read the two articles on evolution in the *New York Times Book Review* last October. One opens with these stirring words:

> It is no secret that science and religion, once allied in homage to divinely crafted harmonies, have long been growing apart. As the scientific worldview has become more authoritative and self-sufficient, it has loosed a cascade of appalling fears that the human soul, insofar as it can be said to exist, may be a mortal and broadly comprehensible product of

material forces; that the imminent caring God of the Western monotheisms may never have been more than a fiction devised by members of a species that self-indulgently denies its continuity with the rest of nature; and that our universe may lack any discernible purpose, moral character, or special relation to ourselves. But as the intimations have spread, the retrenchment known as creationism has also gained in strength and has widened its appeal, acquiring recruits and sympathizers among intellectual sophisticates, hard-headed pragmatists, and even some scientists. And so formidable a political influence is this wave of resistance that some Darwinian thinkers who stand quite apart from it nevertheless feel obliged to placate it with tactful sophistries, lest the cause of evolutionism itself be swept away.

As everyone knows, it was the publication of the *Origin of Species* in 1859 that set off the counter-revolution that eventually congealed into creationism . . .

The theists have decided not to fight evolution as the Fundamentalists did at the Scopes trial in 1925, but to adapt it to their use. The facts are too overwhelming to fight so they have modified it with the theory of Intelligent Design. Not only has the Pope said that at "some point in evolution there was a divine infusion of the soul," but his church also teaches that intelligent causes are responsible for the origins of life in the universe and for all of its diversity. Proponents of Intelligent Design say that this can be proven scientifically. Your Minister Emeritus, Gene Kreves, said the Unitarian movement "needs to get back to the basic insight of Charles Darwin, whose work recognized the fact that evolutionary life is a happenstance without any inherent meaning or purpose."

Proponents of Intelligent Design say correctly that this view of life is too harsh, too terrifying, too depressing. Evolution yes, but we must give it a theist buffer—which goes in the face of all that evolution means. Nature alone is the driving force and natural selection is clumsy, wasteful, blundering, and cruel, and many evolutionary changes are due to nothing other than random chance. Not too many can live in a world of random chance. I was raised to believe that his eye was on the sparrow, that the very hairs on our heads were numbered, that under us were his everlasting arms. I grew up singing "He's Got the Whole World in His Hands" and "My God and I Walk Though the Fields Together."

The culture war is not simply about evolution but also these questions: Is the universe friendly? Is there any direction? Is anyone in control? In philosopher Max Otto's words, "Is there a power at the heart of things which will not let us suffer ultimate defeat?" How can we make the humanist worldview more cozy, more inviting, more beautiful? John Dietrich says that the answer is "Mystical Ecstasy" (his words, not mine.) Perhaps Eustace Haydon does a better job of describing this than Dietrich. He said the humanist,

> is conscious of himself as an earth child. There is a mystic glow in his sense of belonging. Memories of his long ancestry still linger in muscle and nerve, in brain and germ cell. On moonlit nights, in the renewal of life in the springtime, before the glory of a sunset, in moments of swift insight, people feel the community of their own physical being with the body of mother earth.

Is there any way that we can bring that into humanist services? Is there any way that we can prevent services from being a Sunday morning version of the Gong Show? What would it entail to make Mystical Ecstasy the heart of humanism? Could we include Paul Tillich's definition of prayer, "A great deep sigh"? Could we return to Matthew Arnold's definition of religion as "morality touched with emotion"? Could we one Sunday a month direct our thoughts from the moral law within to the starry heavens above? The great rationalist John Dewey wrote,

> Something seems to be left out which is more profoundly characteristic of the religious mood than any kind of special knowledge, or devotion, or service. This is a response to the awesome and mysterious in life and the world. A positive response to the awesome and the mysterious has had a central place in the most varied religions throughout history.

But where can we find that? How can we help people experience that here we are on this little planet that is almost lost in our solar system with its thousands of millions of miles of space; and that this solar system is merely a point of light in the vast depths of stars that form our universe; and that beyond our universe are others, universe beyond universe, on to unimaginable depths of space. Aren't we, with our scientific orientation, better equipped to provide that experience than anyone else? I have cautioned you about believing too little or too much. Is it too much to believe in the mystery, to approach it with awe and wonder? Julian Huxley said, "accepting the universe is accepting the basic and universal mystery, the mystery of existence in general and the mind in particular."

I am going to leave a blank check everywhere I speak this year. It is the amount of my monthly Social Security check. I will sign it when someone tells me that they have walked into a humanist service and found a congregation that spontaneously fell silent because they felt that they were in the presence of more than they can ever know or imagine.

Albert Einstein said, "The most beautiful experience we can have is the mysterious. It is the fundamental emotion which stands at the cradle of true art and true science. Whoever does not know it and can no longer wonder, no longer marvel, is as good as dead."

Delivered January 13, 2002, Naperville Unitarian Universalist Church.

Was Gandhi More Spiritual Than Jesus?

On December 8th—a day that will live in infamy—the *New York Times* devoted a half page to Unitarianism. It was the accompanying photo that incensed me. It showed the minister of our church in Cambridge, Massachusetts, decked out in robes that would have made the Holy Father envious. He waved a tambourine that he was using in a healing service! Beside him was an even-more-bedecked woman, who made Pentecostal Foursquare Church founder Aimee Semple McPherson look like a frumpy house frau. The minister told the *Times* that Unitarians had been daring in embracing humanism in the 1930s, but now need to daringly embrace spiritual alternatives. This minister with degrees from the University of Chicago and Harvard showed the reporter his books on the soul, on angels, and on testimonies of near-death experiences. Some Unitarians compete today over "who is more spiritual than whom?" The tone of the article was that those who had embraced supernaturalism were more spiritual than the plain old humanists. The article suggested that Unitarians—known for decades for no-nonsense, rational humanism—are entering "the New Age."

There are more than 1,500 different religions in the United States. I rejoice in the variety, even as I believe that we are a unique haven for those seeking a rational religious experience. We have entered a period of postmodernism following 300 years of reason, science, and progress. Postmodernism asserts that all things are relative. There is no objective truth, because everything is subjective. This postmodernism comes at a time when the president has focused his second term on preparing children to enter a job market dominated by the need for science and technology.

Friday's *Chicago Tribune* featured an article on the astronomer Carl Sagan—who was chosen as our Humanist of the Year. Sagan said, "I worry that pseudo-science and superstition will seem year by year more tempting, the siren song of unreason more sonorous and attractive. The candle flame sputters. Its little pool of light trembles. Darkness gathers. The demons begin to stir."

When Sagan grew up, kids had chemistry sets. Now they have TV sets. The first set of tubes is far more instructive than its successor. Opinion polls report that most Americans think we have been invaded by UFOs, and almost half the population believes in psychic healing. The CIA spends tax dollars to see if clairvoyants can locate submarines on the ocean floor. Twelve percent of American Psychological Association members reported that they had treated patients who had been abused during satanic-cult rituals, although the FBI has not been able to find a single case of satanic abuse. Astrologers far outnumber astronomers in the U.S. today.

There are one billion humanists in the world. They are as prevalent in Holland and Norway as traditional religious groups. Walter Lippmann said of us, "When men can no longer be theists, they must, if they are civilized, become humanists." Those who cannot believe in God must believe in man, or nihilism is the result. We didn't ask to become humanists. Many of us paid a great price when we left the tender care of our heavenly father. Humanism is not for sissies. We face the fact that life is solitary, poor, nasty, and brutish. We became humanists when confronted with the choice of giving up our minds or our theism. It was not an easy choice, for as children we had been reared to love God with our hearts and minds. At some point, we found it impossible to love God with our minds. As I have said many times, I am a Christian from the neck down. I gave my life to Jesus when I was a 12-year-old boy. So far as my heart is concerned, I never took it back.

My first congregation as a young graduate of the University of Chicago Divinity School was a Christian Church in a small town in Indiana. That congregation's conservatives and liberals fought over whether just some parts of the Bible were inspired, or if it was inspired from cover to cover. With the wisdom of Solomon, I said, "If the Bible inspires you, then it is inspired. If Shakespeare inspires you, then he is inspired. If Paul Tillich, Dorothy Day, or Cornel West inspire you, then they are inspired." And that is my position on my topic today, "Is Gandhi more spiritual than Jesus?" Each is spiritual to the extent that he inspires you.

Someone tried to corner Emily Dickinson on what particular combination of words constitute poetry. She replied, "All I know is that if a particular writing makes my whole body so cold that no fire can warm me, if I physically act as if the top of my head had been taken off, these are the only ways I know." In that vein, A. E. Housman said he recognized poetry "by a shiver down the spine, a constriction of the throat, a precipitation of water to the eyes, and a sensation in the pit of the stomach." We have no conflict with the church at Cambridge. These are good guidelines for identifying "the spiritual." And humanists and theists can respond accordingly.

Dr. King said that two kinds of churches have failed:

> The one burns with emotionalism and the other freezes with classical scholarship. The former, reducing worship to entertainment, places more emphasis on volume than on content, and confuses spirituality with muscularity. The danger with such a church is that they may have more religion in the hands and feet than in their hearts and heads. The other type of church that has failed has a worship service that is cold and meaningless, with music dull and uninspiring, and the sermon little more than a homily on current events.

I would hope that we would steer clear of both of these extremes, and that this little "house of reason" would be as warm, cozy, and as inviting as your grandmother's kitchen.

It is interesting that proponents of New Age Unitarianism make the audacious assumption that women are less rational than men. Since most of our seminary students today are women, they argue that the church must be feminized, by which they seem to mean that our rational approach to religion cannot be maintained. I cannot read such statements without hearing the voices of women in my congregation—*Peg Sering, Kel Shoup*, or *Rose Oplatka*—saying, "Over my dead body."

Many of us had truly believed that questions about the mental differences between men and women had been settled once and for all in a darkened theater in Copenhagen in 1879. That's when Nora Helmer in Ibsen's *Doll House* told her dazed husband, "I believe before all else I am a reasonable human being as much as you are." If we burn incense, wear psychedelic robes, if members get up in the service and spill their guts, then some assume that feminists like Gloria Steinem, Jane Addams, Susan B. Anthony, Virginia Woolf, Mother Jones, Sandra Day O'Connor, Ruth Bader Ginsburg, Iris Murdoch, and Lorraine Hansberry will stream into the church. I do not doubt that New Age Unitarianism will appeal to the needs of some women, just as humanism appeals to the needs of others.

Similarly, there are those who say that we must embrace New-Age Unitarianism to attract African Americans. Again, the implication seems to be that the way to their minds is with a bongo drum or a tambourine. Show me a picture of Dr. King in a multi-colored robe, banging on a tambourine, and inviting people to come down and be faith healed. The West Side of Chicago has no shortage of what Dr. King called "religion for the hands and feet." And I really doubt if clapping our hands and singing "Kumbaya" will attract the likes of W. E. B. Du Bois, Julian Bond, Paul Robeson, Whitney Young, Ralph Bunche, Bayard Rustin, Judge Evelyn Clay, *Howell Triplett*, and *Cyd Carpenter.*

Did you see in the paper last month that hundreds have flocked to a Nashville coffee shop to see the likeness of Mother Teresa that appeared on a cinnamon bun? Bakery owner Bob Bernstein said that crowds line up daily to behold the miracle. A couple of years ago, an orthodox church on Harlem Avenue had an icon that shed tears. Traffic backed up worse than the Eisenhower Expressway at rush hour. Citizens in Blanco, Texas, gathered this summer not to dance— but to pray— for rain. Not to be outdone, San Antonio's Catholic bishop sent a letter instructing the 74 churches in his diocese to pray for rain. Assembly of God Pastor Gene Benningfield said, "It was time to bombard heaven with our prayers." Rev. Benningfield said that he would settle for nothing less than four inches of rain. I do not know if the six pastors involved in the Texas rain prayers included a New-Age Unitarian.

> How many turn back toward dreams and magic, how many children
> Run home to Mother Church, Father State,
> To find in their arms the delicious warmth and folding of souls.
> The age weakens and settles home toward old ways.
> An age of renascent faith: Christ said, Marx wrote, Hitler says.
> And though it seems absurd, we believe.
> Sad children, yes. It is lonely to be an adult, you need a father.
> With a little practice you'd believe anything.
> "THEBAID" BY ROBINSON JEFFERS

What any congregation does in its service determines the kind of people it attracts. With the right format, I do not doubt that we could fill this place with astrologers, witches, wizards, sorcerers, warlocks, snake handlers, speakers in tongues, peyote smokers, or satanic cultists. We tried voodoo economics, why not voodoo Unitarianism?

Surveys show that most Unitarians would be Quakers if they had to choose another faith. Of all the religions, I have always regarded the Quakers to be "the most spiritual," with their silent worship and their plain speech, dress, meeting houses and wooden caskets. Quakers refuse to take oaths. They believe with the book of Matthew, "Let what you say be simply 'yes' or 'no,' anything more than that comes from evil."

Though not a Quaker, Hemingway wrote clean, uncluttered speech. He wrote, "I have always believed that the person who begins to live more seriously within, begins to live more simply without." Oh, let this little house of reason always reek with Quaker simplicity. Let it be a place where our music, our preaching, our rituals are conducive to rational thought. If I had it to do over, I would ask you to call me "rabbi." We have gotten away from the Jewish tradition in which a religious leader is primarily a teacher.

St. Paul defined "the fruits of the spirit" as: love, joy, peace, patience, kindness, goodness, faithfulness, gentleness, and self-control. I hope that New Age Unitarianism's spiritual quest will yield such spiritual fruits. A. E. Housman believed that "the most important truth" which has ever been uttered and the greatest discovery ever made in the moral realm were the words of Jesus. His disciples had an argument over "who was the greatest" among them. Housman says that Jesus's response holds the key to life. "Whoever would be the greatest among you must become the servant of all."

After all these years there are passages that still trigger a shiver down the spine, a constriction in the throat, a precipitation of water in the eyes. "What greater love hath any man that this, that he lay down his life for his friends." The words from the cross, "Forgive them, for they know not what they do." "I was hungry and you gave me food, I was thirsty and you gave me drink, I was naked and you clothed me, I was a stranger and you welcomed me, I was sick and you visited me, I was in prison and you came to me." "As you did it unto the least of these my brethren, you did it unto me." The father said, "Bring quickly the best robe and put it on him, and put a ring on his hand, and shoes on his feet, and bring the fatted calf and kill it, and let us eat and drink and make merry, for this my son was dead and is alive again, he was lost and he is found." A traveler from Jericho to Jerusalem fell among thieves. But a Samaritan saw him, bound up his wounds, and took him to an inn, saying, "Take care of him, and whatever you spend, I will repay you when I come back." These stories are spiritual because they inspire and they show how Jesus spoke rationally to his disciples.

I suppose the real question is, "Do we want to be inspired?" The *New York Times* recently reported on Broadway theater. I quote,

The traditional audience for plays has been dwindling. The upper-middle class, upper age, Jewish Westsider is moving to Florida or dying out. That educated theater audience is getting harder to find. With serious theater a difficult sell to a spectacle-oriented public, producers have sought to add dazzle.

When *Death of a Salesman* opened on Broadway 48 years ago, people did not clap when the final curtain fell. They did not get out of their seats when the lights went on, for tears were running down their faces. Arthur Miller had accomplished what good theater—and good religion—should do. It made those present recognize themselves. The audience was weeping for their husbands, their fathers, themselves. Willie had given his life to the wrong dream, the dream of business success. His son weeps at his grave, "He never knew who he was." When we can reach the minds of men, the hands and feet will follow.

"Entertainment" is not only killing the theater, it is killing humanism. The *New York Times* reported that Chaucer, Shakespeare, and Milton are no longer required by most top colleges and universities in the United States. The students want pop culture. Hence, courses in "The Gangster Film," "Melodrama and the Soap Opera," and "Twentieth Century American Boxing Films." Robert Brustein, director of the American Repertory Theater, said, "Most English departments are now held so completely hostage to fashionable political and theoretical agendas that it is unlikely Shakespeare can qualify as an 'appropriate' author."

The most famous living Unitarian addressed our National Assembly 10 years ago. Kurt Vonnegut said,

If there were freethinker societies today, lonely rationalists, children of the Enlightenment, wouldn't have to consider throwing away their brains, as though their heads were nothing but jack-o-lanterns, in their desperate search for spiritual companionship.

Vonnegut's architect father practiced Occidental-style meditation, also known as reading books. Thank God most of us here have reading lists longer than our grocery lists. Vonnegut defined Unitarians as men and women who know nonsense when they hear it. He suggested that we adopt as our logo a sausage with a line slashed through it—international sign language for "no baloney." (Our trustees voted 5–4 against my recommendation to adopt Vonnegut's sausage logo.)

I wish that I could cut my conscience to fit this year's religious fashions and join the New Age Unitarians. But they do not inspire me. I will seek my inspiration elsewhere. Some of you can remember that night at Triton College when we heard Simon Wiesenthal and felt a shiver down our spine; the afternoon that we heard Margaret Mead at Harper College and felt a constriction in the throat; or when Noam Chomsky left a sensation in the pits of our stomachs at Northeastern Illinois University. We shall go on Tuesday night to hear Dick Gregory, and next month to hear Tom Wolfe. We need succor for our mind as regularly as food for our body.

It's déjà vu all over again. Do you remember the story of the prophet Elijah, who was seeking that which was spiritual in his day? And there was a great and strong wind that rent the mountain, and after the wind, an earthquake, and after the earthquake a fire. But the Lord was not in the mighty wind or the earthquake or the fire. Instead, the Lord spoke in a still, small voice. I would wager that that is the best place for us to seek the spiritual today—in the still, small voice. We, too, shall be struck with the starry heavens above, and the moral law within. Dr. Carl Sagan never found reason and wonder to be incompatible. Science, he said, was the ultimate playground.

> I feel a tingle of exhilaration. My heart races. . . .This 15-billion-year universe is so filled with mystery that each tentative step toward understanding reveals new mysteries. Nature is always more subtle, more intricate, and more elegant than we are able to imagine.

It's time, now, for politicians, preachers, and playwrights to "talk sense to the American people." I want to close with an invitation from the book of Isaiah. It is one of the most beautiful invitations the world has ever known. "Come, now, let us reason together."

Delivered February 16, 1997, Third Unitarian Church of Chicago.

As If . . .

O f all the sermons I preached (only the Lord knows how many), two stand out in my mind. While attending the University of Chicago, I spent a summer at a small country church in Fandon, Illinois. I intended to take some of its young people to summer camp but was informed that they were needed in the fields to pick strawberries. A theist at the time, I countered with a sermon titled, "To Hell with Strawberries!" I suggested that God could send a drought to dry up the berries, or he could produce a bumper crop that farmers wouldn't be able to give away. I suggested that even after they were picked and frozen, God could send a black-out and the freezers would give out. They relented and we took a busload of kids to summer camp!

The other memorable sermon—delivered from this pulpit—was about Christmas letters. I collected hundreds of them and quoted them in front of God and everyone. The point was that the letters revealed what people felt was important in their lives—which was pretty trivial. Like diaries, the letters testified as to how the authors spent their time, energy, money, and lives. Many people felt that I betrayed their confidences by giving their Christmas letters a religious interpretation that they never intended.

For many years I also have been collecting obituaries. Not even Christmas letters are as revealing about a person's life and what they wanted to be remembered for. When Joseph Kaplan died at 98, for example, his obit headline read, "Put Color in Shower." Pre-Kaplan, all shower curtains were made of white duck cloth. Kaplan introduced colored fabrics, which eventually were made of plastic. When Christian Nelson also died at age 98, his obituary eulogized the inventor of the Eskimo Pie. On that fateful day in 1919, a kid walked into Nelson's confectionery and couldn't decide whether to buy chocolate or vanilla ice cream. Right on the spot, Nelson combined the two flavors and eventually mounted them on a stick!

As you probably know, the great American inventor Victor Dorman discovered how to put paper—now plastic—between slices of cheese. Before Victor, or "BV" as it's known in the dairy industry, cheese was sold in bulk and sliced in grocery stores. Victor Dorman registered his invention with a snappy slogan. Are you ready? "The cheese with the paper between the slices." Before dying at the age of 90, Carlos Herrera concocted the world's first Margarita just south of Tijuana in 1935. His *Chicago Tribune* obituary is larger than anything that anyone from this congregation ever received from his or her hometown paper. It goes into great detail about how he mixed that historic jigger of tequila with lemon juice and a touch of salt. John Benson, the ad man who created "The Marlboro Man," deservedly received another lengthy obituary. There is no question that his work touched many lives—and accelerated many the obituary.

The *Chicago Tribune* ran this headline a few years ago, "David Goodman, 63, Cleaned Clothes of Stars." Goodman laundered for the likes of Bob Hope and Johnny Mathis when they came to Chicago's Lyric Opera. Raymondo Pietro Carlo was the hair-dresser who invented the "Teasie-Weasie." As *Ruth Dear* can tell you, this was the style that left a curl falling down the forehead. In 1982, Queen Elizabeth awarded Pietro Carlo the Order of the British Empire for service in hairdressing. I am simply going to call her "Ms. A," as some of you-might-know her. The obituary that her family wrote said, "Ms. A bowled in three leagues and her favorite hobby was knitting. She knitted many of her own dresses as well as outfits for her grandson." My personal favorite obit headline was, "Los Angeles Man Dies Mooning." A witness reported that his pants were down around his ankles and he was bent over with his back to the vehicle when he was struck on the southbound lane of the Pacific Coast Highway at 1 am. He never saw death coming!

Philosopher Immanuel Kant suggested that all of us should live our lives *as if* they could be universalized. We should live *as if* the life that we lived could be emulated by everyone. As existentialists, we have to make or create our own lives and offer them as a gift either to the creator or to the communities which sustain us. Harvard philosopher William James said that, "The great use of life is to spend it for something that outlasts us." Think colored shower curtains, Eskimo pies, Margaritas, the Marlboro Man, and the Teasie-Weasie.

African American Rev. Bennie Newton was watching TV when he saw a news flash about the riots that erupted after the acquittal of four L.A. policemen in the beating of Rodney King. Rev. Newton sped to the scene, where a mob had dragged Fidel Lopez from his truck and stripped, beat, kicked, and sprayed him with paint. Rev. Newton threw his own body over Lopez and eventually was able to take him to the hospital, where Lopez received 58 stitches just in his forehead. As a result of leukemia at age 60, Rev. Newton's obituary was unfortunately published just a few years later.

When Nanny Washburn died at 95 last month, her *Atlanta Constitution* obit called her "a crusader for civil rights." She began working at the age of eight as the daughter of a white sharecropper. She would become an active organizer of textile workers, and also organized against the poll tax, lynching, and nuclear weapons. The latter cause took her as a delegate to the World Peace Council in Stockholm. In 1965 Washburn watched on TV as marchers were beaten on the Selma bridge. She drove there that night with her two children, and they spent the next six months in Brown's Chapel cooking for the marchers, and nursing the injured protesters in Demopolis. The mayor of Atlanta proclaimed it Nanny Washburn Day because her life exemplified the noblest qualities of human beings: truth, courage, conviction, and compassion.

Imagine how this one jumped out at me: "He Died in the Class Struggle." This epitaph that Fred Siders chose for his tombstone was used as the headline for his obituary. I quote from his tombstone, "Workers were his brothers, exploiters were his foes. And he never stopped fighting until he died at 82." When Siders was leading one strike, they were ambushed by company thugs. But some of the miners were combat vets of World War I and they had come to the strike armed with hunting rifles. When the battle ended, seven miners and 13 thugs lay dead.

When she died at 77, she had written an epitaph to be sung at her funeral:

Celebrate my death for the good times I've had,
For the work that I've done and the friends that I've made.
Celebrate my death of whom it could be said.
"She was a working class woman and a Red."
My mate was the best, a comrade, and friend
Fighting on the good side, to the very end.
My child was a darling, merry, strong and fine,
And all the world's children were mine.

We knew her as Malvina Reynolds. She sang "Little Boxes" in this room a few years before her death.

As different as night from day was Millicent Fenwick, whom Garry Trudeau portrayed as Lacey Davenport in his *Doonesbury* comic. She was born into wealth and elected to Congress as a Republican. But she came from a family that believed that public service was an obligation. One of her congressional causes was providing bathrooms for migrant workers, earning her the nickname "Outhouse Millie."

The *New York Times*-had an unusual headline for a deceased physician: "Doctor Charged $5." Dr. Hector Perrone died in Greenwich Village at 77. He didn't charge all of his patients $5—the homeless and indigent he treated for nothing. His wife, who had been his receptionist, said he worked till 7:30 the night before he died. "He was an old fashioned man," Ms. Perrone noted.

A final example of a man who lived by Kant's categorical imperative was Fred Rosenstiel. One seldom sees an obituary with the heading "Devoted His Life to Planting Flowers." Fred arrived in New York City from Holland in 1951 and spent the next 45 years of his life planting flower gardens in the city. He founded a group called "Green Guerrillas." They planted flowers in parks, vacant lots, school yards, housing projects, hospitals, and homeless shelters. Never forgiving himself for surviving the Holocaust, he sought to atone and "pay back" by bringing beauty to the lives of others.

This is a longer introduction than I am accustomed to. As you also know, this sermon has nothing to do with *these* obituaries. It is concerned with yours and mine. I agree with Gandhi, "Almost anything you do will be insignificant, but you must do it." We are all replaceable. I have seen members die and the lives of their loved ones go on. I have seen children grow up without fathers or mothers, and husbands and wives take new spouses. Perhaps it seems that our individual lives do not matter, but we must choose to act *as if* our lives were of the utmost importance in the total scheme of things. Rev. Bennie Newton, Nanny Washburn, Fred Siders, Malvina Reynolds, Lacey Davenport, Dr. Perrone, Fred Rosenstiel, they were all living proofs that individual lives can make a difference.

Religion, if it is anything, is the affirmation that life is not vanity. The words of William James are the essence of what this congregation is about. "Be not afraid of life. Believe that life is worth living, and your belief will help you create the fact." Our beliefs prompt our actions. Our thoughts about ourselves determine our acts. Beliefs have consequences. The first act of free will is to believe in it. It *is* an open universe. The outcome is undetermined. The future depends upon men and women like us, who believe that our lives will make a difference. William James said that there is no way we can steer safely between believing too little or too much. I am only asking that you believe that one single, solitary life can change the world. Rev. Jessie Jackson knows that if a young kid in the projects believes that he is "somebody," he has turned the corner and is on the right track.

Act *as if* you can make a difference, and you will. Act *as if* you are good and you will be better. Act *as if* you are strong and competent, and you will become more so. Act *as if* this congregation needs you and depends upon you and you will find yourself a place in the hearts of our people. Act *as if* Austin or Oak Park or Elmhurst depends on what you do and say.

I don't know at what point I began to act *as if* this congregation were one of the major institutions of this city. Through the days when our congregation split, I began to believe in the domino theory—that if this institution fell, Chicago's whole West Side would fall. I have spoken to you about the Field Museum, the Art Institute, the University of Chicago, the Chicago Symphony, and Third Unitarian Church *as if* they are all of the same importance. I have acted *as if* we are a congregation so unique and special that the whole humanist movement—dating back to the Greeks—was being defended here. If we did not survive, then all was lost!

I believe that we have reached that point now that anyone of us would be ashamed to die without a bequest for this institution in their will. And we must so act, as a congregation, that what we do can be universalized by any of the 250,000 congregations in the United States. The point is not that we have a scholarship fund, a food pantry, a job bank, a day care center, or that we shelter illegal immigrants. The larger point is that these acts can be universalized.

Jan de Hartog wrote a novel about the Quakers in England called, *The Peaceable Kingdom*. It describes a period when Quakers were persecuted and imprisoned for their beliefs. A Quaker woman being tortured and starved to death is visited in prison by a friend who has an epiphany:

> Maybe it is the secret of my ultimate ineffectualness that at the core of
> my being there is the knowledge, the immutable conviction, that we are
> nothing. But as I sat there, that terrified hand in mine, listening to the
> wandering voice gibbering in the terror of death, I realized that unless
> I could grab hold of some hope, some belief, true or false, I would quite
> literally lose my mind. I could face the ultimate truth only for a few sec-
> onds: even I, indestructible in my self-centeredness, could not survive in
> the vacuum of nothingness. I had to find something I could hold on to,
> some delusion that would give me the notion that there was some sense

in my fighting to survive, other than the animal urge that made the little monster in my womb grow and flex its muscles and buck its knees,
driven toward its tormented half minute of consciousness called life.
Had I been a Muslim or a Buddhist, I would have grabbed hold of some
other notion. But as the accident of my birth had placed me in England,
where a delusion held sway called "Quakerism," all I could grab hold of
in that slide toward insanity were the words, "All He has is Thee."

Jan de Hartog knew it was a delusion. The woman speaking knows it is a
delusion. Yet it is all she has to hold on to. "All He has is Thee." She takes hold
of that idea and it gives her strength, courage. That's not a bad *as if.* You act *as
if* you're good and you'll be better. You act *as if* you are strong and competent,
and you'll be stronger and more competent. You act as *if* you could make a difference, and you'll make a difference. You act *as if* you could influence the future, and you'll influence the future.

Transposing that Quaker experience from the 16th century into our humanist experience at the end of the 20th century, it means "All We have is
Thee." You must act *as if* the future of this congregation and this community depends upon you. Lord Acton said, "There is nothing so fearsome as
one lone Calvinist in possession of the truth." You have a truth, not the whole
truth, but a portion of the truth. It is that if we act *as if* we can make a difference, then we will.

Delivered June 9, 1996, Third Unitarian Church of Chicago.

'Tis a Pity She's a Whore

ee Atwater was President George H.W. Bush's campaign manager in 1988, when they ran their racist Willie Horton ads against Michael Dukakis. Later dying from brain cancer, Atwater confessed:

> The 80s were about acquiring—acquiring wealth, power, prestige. I know. I acquired more wealth, power, and prestige than most. But you can acquire all you want and still feel empty. What power wouldn't I trade for a little more time with my family? What price wouldn't I pay for an evening with friends? It took a deadly illness to put me eye to eye with that truth, but it is a truth that the country, caught up in its ruthless ambitions and moral decay, can learn on my dime. I don't know who will lead us through the 90s, but they must be made to speak to this spiritual vacuum at the heart of American society, this tumor of the soul.

During the 30th anniversary of the Civil Rights march in Selma last March, former Governor George Wallace asked for permission to welcome the celebrants. The *New York Times* ran a photo of the 75-year-old, wheelchair-confined governor linking hands with African Americans singing, "We Shall Overcome." The article began with these words, "The marchers swarmed around the old man in the wheelchair, some to tell him he was forgiven; some to whisper that he could *never* be forgiven, not even a million years from now!" An aide read Governor Wallace's welcome, in which he said that we are all, in our own way, different people today. "We have learned hard and important lessons in the 30 years that have passed between us, since the days surrounding your first walk along Highway 80." Rev. Joseph Lowery, the national president of the Southern Christian Leadership Council, responded, "You are a different George Wallace today. We both serve a God who can make the desert bloom and the crooked places straight! We ask God's blessings upon you."

The 50th anniversary of the end of World War II has brought mixed responses from the leaders of Japan and Germany. Chinese diplomat Chen Jian expressed outrage when the Japanese minister of education said that the Japanese do not need to apologize for their wartime behavior.

The war launched by the Japanese militants brought about great sufferings to the people of China and other Asian countries. These are historic facts; the Japanese brutally colonized Korea from 1910 to 1945— and ruled portions of China before and during World War II. Because of the American bombing of Japan, many of them feel that they should think of themselves as 'victims.' Some compare themselves to the Jews of the Holocaust! They make no moral distinction between the Jews who were killed in death camps by the Nazis and the 100,000 civilians who were killed in Tokyo during a single night's bombings by B-29s in May of 1945.

The *New Yorker* reported that Germans have come to feel that Hitler seized Germany in 1933 and occupied it for 12 dark years—until Germany was "liberated" in 1945. In other words, they envision Germany as if it were Holland or one of the concentration camps. "They want to 'have suffered from themselves' the way that everybody else suffered from them."

Lee Atwater, George Wallace, the Germans, and the Japanese are but an introduction to Robert McNamara's book *In Retrospect: The Tragedy and Lessons of Vietnam*. McNamara served as Secretary of Defense for JFK and LBJ from 1961 to 1968. At the age of 80, he looks back over the longest war in U.S. history, which killed 58,000 Americans and 3 million Asians. Another 100,000 American Vietnam vets have committed suicide. Looking back, McNamara says, "The war was wrong, terribly wrong." To my knowledge, McNamara is the only leader of that war who has made this confession. Arthur Cyr of the Chicago Council on Foreign Relations writes, "He deserves our respect and credit—admitting error is always tough, and among our national leaders, extremely rare."

McNamara says that during the McCarthy period, we discredited and expelled those in the Foreign Service who could have given us the correcting perspective that we needed about Southeast Asia. He says that everyone at that time was captive to the Domino Theory. "We looked upon Ho Chi Minh as an associate of Stalin and a believer in Nikita Khrushchev, whereas now I think he was probably an Asian Tito." Even still, the information that McNamara possessed at the time was sufficient for him to know that the war was wrong. But to have stated this would have given aid and comfort to the enemy. Asked why he didn't resign, he said, "I believe that would have been a violation of my responsibility to the President and my oath to uphold the constitution." He says that even if he had spoken out *after* he left office in 1968, it would not have helped stop the war. "My voice would not have made any difference."

Interestingly, some of the papers that have criticized McNamara's belated confession did not speak up themselves. The *Boston Globe* was the first mainstream U.S. paper to editorialize against the war, and that was in 1969. Anthony Lewis did the same for The *New York Times* that same year. Some papers have said, "Why should we make Johnson or General William Westmoreland or McNamara our scapegoats when the war was the responsibility of *all* who failed to stop it."

One dividend of McNamara's book is that President Clinton can run for reelection next year as a non-war hero! If "the war was wrong, terribly wrong," then Clinton is absolved of his refusal to participate in it. Columnist Alexander Cockburn, however, chides him,

> It's a measure of Clinton that he should be muddying up *the* most visibly principled act of his life—namely, his opposition to the war in Vietnam. He hops about, telling one silly fib after another, 'til he's managed to convert principle into something devious. Why be apologetic for refusing to napalm peasants, shoot old women in paddy fields, or herd villagers into concentration camps, while dumping Agent Orange on their forests?

Should there be a Washington memorial to those young men who grasped 30 years ago what McNamara is admitting now? A controversial monument has been erected In Erfurt, Germany to the 20,000 young men who were executed as deserters during World War II.

My goal in this sermon is the same as always: to somehow relate public events to our private lives and vice versa. My sermon topic comes from the title of a play written in 1629. I have no idea what the play was about but its title aptly describes our minds! Reason is a whore. We can justify whatever we want.

Martin Luther spoke of "the whore reason," and in another passage said that "reason is an ass." A Congregationalist minister recently wrote in the

Christian Century, "The mind can defend itself against almost any rational argument that tries to scale the walls. Rationalizations, justifications, and counter attacks are called up at a moment's notice to join in the fierce defense of our actions." A book about the Vietnam War's U.S. leadership—including Harvard graduate Robert McNamara—is titled *The Best and the Brightest.* Three-quarters of the men in the Nazi SS held doctorates. For two bits, the whore reason will provide rationale for whatever we want to do. Columnist Ellen Goodman wrote, "We are reminded of 'the other lesson' of Vietnam. The sorry, infuriating, bewildering reality that the best and the brightest can still succeed brilliantly at analysis and fail utterly at understanding."

Our scripture this morning is an example of "the whore reason." When King David wanted Uriah's wife Bathsheba, he sent Uriah to the frontlines of battle. He could not see the evil of his deeds until the prophet Nathan told him a parable of a rich man who had taken the only lamb of a poor man. The righteously indignant King David thundered, "The man who has done this deserves to die." Nathan retorted, "Thou art the man."

The 10-day Rosh Hashanah begins a week from tomorrow in preparation for Yom Kippur, the Day of Atonement. Ten days for self-examination, reflection and self-judgment. Ten days for sorting out our lives, for acknowledging our weaknesses, blunders, and sins. The Unitarian Minister Ken Phifer writes,

> When will we be honest about the times we have surrendered to lust and called it love; honest about the times we have practiced petty selfishness and called it principles, honest about the times we have acted with smug bigotry and called it courage?

How many of us could make McNamara's words our own? "I have been wrong, terribly wrong." How many times have we prostituted our minds to justify wrongdoing? I hope that someday we will have the insight and hindsight to confess what Lord Byron wrote in his diary. "I fear one lies more to oneself than to anyone else."

Michael Werner, president of the American Humanist Association, writes,

> Unitarian Universalism consequently remains cognitively empty at its center. Our ministers, like any others, must try to hold on to the affections of their congregations. They must show membership growth if they want to remain in their positions or advance. The pecuniary and psy-

chological incentives of attracting the largest possible audience can sway the most prophetic voice.

How could I possibly preach a sermon like this without saying that "I have been wrong, terribly wrong," guilty of catering my truth to what this market will bear.

A friend of mine was at an anthropology conference where a speaker said that the American Indians had *never* fought among themselves until the white man came to their shores! He said that not a person in the audience believed this, yet nobody rose to that moment of truth. We are living at a time when "Indians are in" and "white Europeans" are out. The *New York Times* reported this year that "throughout history, both Indians and their conquerors have found that the struggle for day-to-day survival leaves little room for long-term environmental concerns." Many tribes stayed in one place no more than a generation. When the firewood had been burned, soil depleted and game eaten or frightened away, they would move again. Indians are people! Like the rest of us, they did not always make the best land-use decisions. There is no super race.

We recently had lunch with a woman on the faculty of a prominent law school, where another woman was proposed for tenure. Our guest spoke against it. She had to earn tenure 20 years before and believed that this other woman had published nothing of note and brought no other special gifts to her students or the faculty. After the meeting, all of the other women faculty castigated her and warned her not to ever speak against one of "the sisters" again!

Our nation survived the Salem witch trials and the McCarthy scourge. We shall survive this Third Wave that discards historical facts to "create" whatever truth is necessary. Friedrich Engels said that "ruling ideas are the ideas of the ruling class;" truth is merely an extension of power. Today, power groups are manufacturing truths almost faster than our whoring minds can absorb them! We do not simply interpret the past. We create it—just like the Japanese and the Germans. We postpone the day of reckoning as long as possible. When Lee Atwater was confronted with cancer, and when George Wallace and Robert McNamara reached their own end years, it seemed to give them incentive to see more clearly. Often that clarity accompanies the words, "I was wrong, terribly wrong."

I have heard parents say that they wish that they knew what they know

now and could raise their children again. I have heard divorced people say, "For years I was blind to his obvious faults. I was in a state of denial." I have seen people retire and start a new career and admit, only then, that they were never cut out for what they had been doing for 30 or 40 years. I have seen people at 60 or 80 discover a new religion and admit that they never believed in the old one. We have the ability to lie to ourselves more than we do to anyone else. We have the ability to justify and rationalize whatever we want. Most of us have no Nathan in our lives to confront our behavior—to enable us to strike out on a new path and become new people. We should *envy* George Wallace. Having learned hard and important lessons, "He is a different person," Rev. Lowery told him. How many of us here could have that said of us?

Some people believe that it is an either/or situation. We must choose a religion that is preoccupied with changing the individual or one that is preoccupied with changing the world. Why can't it be both? Where is the conflict? Czechoslovakian President Václav Havel said, "Seek the company of those who are looking for the truth, but run from those who have found it."

We must continually evaluate and reflect upon truths that we embraced years ago. There are people who believe that the ideas of the New Deal have been engraved in stone and that to move on is to betray our parents or nullify our own youth. There are people here who fought after World War I to ensure that the United States *never* armed itself again. Then came Hitler's domination of Europe and Pearl Harbor. The *Sun Times* and the *New York Times* had contradictory editorials this week on Congress underwriting a new missile defense system. The thing that I most admire about China is its government's policy of limiting its population, yet Hillary Clinton went there and chastised them for it. Are the GATT and NAFTA trade agreements right or wrong? On many of these controversies, only time will tell. Havel said that social engineering must be done but it,

> may never achieve more than partial improvements in particular areas, and we will always have to wait to see whether the change was the right thing to do, and we must always be prepared to rectify what life has shown to be wrong.

Philosopher Arthur Schopenhauer reminds us that all truth passes through three stages: first, it is ridiculed; second, it is violently opposed; third, it is accepted as self-evident. If we as individuals—and as a congregation—are in-

volved in the pursuit of truth, it means that some of our ideas are being ridiculed, some are being opposed, and some are being accepted as self-evident.

If McNamara continues his self-reflection, we might expect another con-
fessional book about his term leading the World Bank. Fifteen of the world's
most repressive governments received a third of all the loans on McNamara's
watch. The book *Fifty Years Is Enough* says,

> Despite all the rhetoric about development and alleviating poverty, the
> central function of these multilateral lending institutions has been to
> draw the rulers and governments of weaker states more tightly into a
> world economy dominated by large, transnational corporations.

Was World Banker Robert McNamara "Wrong again, terribly wrong?"

After the first atomic blast in New Mexico, J. Robert Oppenheimer said,
"We physicists have known sin." Lee Atwater, King David, George Wallace,
and Robert McNamara have known it. Soon we Unitarians and the Radical
Right will be the only ones left not to admit that we have been "wrong, terribly
wrong." Remember the parishioner who said she wanted to make a death-bed
confession—causing her poor Unitarian minister to drop dead from shock? It
is not politically correct to quote Soviet dissident Aleksandr Solzhenitsyn. But
he was the one who recognized that, "The line separating good and evil passes
not through states, nor between classes, nor between political parties either—
but right through every human heart."

I just received a pamphlet from the American Humanist Association
that says, "Join the champions of reason." Reason is the jewel in the humanist crown and to call it a whore seems unforgivable in a congregation that has
been humanist since 1907. *Nation* magazine theater critic Harold Clurman
closes his autobiography with a summary of his world view—and mine.

> I believe that life is essentially irrational, but I also believe that human
> beings must use their reason, with due recognition of its limitations. I
> believe that men and women may not be perfectible, but they must act
> as if they were. I believe that although we may not possess free will, we
> must behave as if we did. I believe life is terrible and glorious.

Delivered September 17, 1995, Third Unitarian Church of Chicago.

A Famine of the Worst Kind

was shocked to read that the prophet Amos had a public ministry of two or three months. It occurred 750 years before the birth of Jesus, when the nation of Israel was at the height of its prestige and prosperity. This shepherd from Tekoa saw moral decay eating away at the nation and didn't feel that it had long to live. Called by God, he journeyed to Samaria. He took on the politicians, merchants, priests and—I hesitate to say on International Women's Day—he also took on women.

> You cows of Bashan, who are in the mount of Samaria; who oppress the poor, who crush the needy, who say to your husbands, "bring more that we may drink," behold the days shall come upon you when you shall be dragged by the nose with hooks and by your buttocks with fish spears, even as dung you shall be dragged out one by one.

Merchants didn't fare much better, "You have sold the righteous for silver and the needy for a pair of shoes. You trample upon the heads of the poor, the meek are denied access to the courts." He preached that God really didn't have much interest in the priests' rituals nor offerings. "Take me away from the noise of your songs. The melody of your harps I refuse to hear. But let justice roll forth as a fountain of water and righteous as an ever flowing stream."

The Amos verse that most intrigues me this morning is,

> "Behold the days are coming," says the Lord God, "that I will send a famine on the land. Not a famine of bread, nor a thirst for water, but of hearing the words of the Lord. They shall wander from sea to sea, and from north to east; they shall run to and fro, seeking the word of the Lord, but shall not find it."

For our purposes this morning, "the word of the Lord" is whatever inspires you, whatever speaks to you, whatever gives you sustenance. Religious humanists find the word of God in the Bible, in literature, in great statesmen, and in editorials. Amos speaks to us, who have more food than our bodies can handle—fattened like the cows of Bashan. He warns not of a food famine but a drought of that that speaks to us and inspires us.

Amos, who pictures us running to and fro, would be amazed how we travel the world. Europe is nothing—China, Africa or Australia is where it's at. We run to the arts theater and then to the Candlelight Playhouse. We line up to see *Peggy Sue got Married* or hurry home to watch *Hannah and Her Sisters* on TV, taping it to watch again. Did you ever see so much running to and fro? Do you know anyone who isn't busy and proud of it? Do you know anyone who would dare admit, "I spent all day Saturday cuddled up with the best book?" Could all this frantic running be prompted by a famine of "the word"? I'm not starving yet. But I'm hungry. When *Chicago Magazine* arrives, the first thing I do is see what is going on this month. In page after page of movies, music, and theater, I am lucky if there are one or two offerings that speak to my hunger.

I remember some great nights in Orchestra Hall when we used to have the Sunday Evening Club. The greatest time for me was the night that Martin Luther King spoke. We were living in Indiana then and thought nothing about driving 100 miles to hear him. The Oak Park community lectures began as extension courses from the University of Chicago. Outstanding professors would come lecture. When the university stopped the program, a committee formed to bring in the likes of Will Durant, Lowell Thomas, and Norman Cousins. There were 10 lectures each season. The Oak Park Lecture series used to fill the high school auditorium. Then, after 60 years, they folded up, surrendering to such television shows as *Sanford and Son*, *Falcon Crest*, and *The Golden Girls*.

I am not limiting my definition of "the word of the Lord" to someone speaking, even though down through history that has been one of the ways that people have found meaning, purpose, and direction for living. Philosopher Eric Hoffer wrote,

> We know that words cannot move mountains but they can move the multitude; and we are more ready to fight and die for a word than anything else. Words can shape thought, stir feeling, and beget action. The priests, prophets, and intellectuals have played a more decisive role in history than military leaders, statesmen or businessmen.

They were mere words, but imagine what they meant to the British during World War II?

> We shall fight in France, we shall fight on the seas and oceans, we shall fight with growing confidence and growing strength in the air; we shall defend our island, whatever the cost may be. We shall fight on the beaches, we shall fight on the landing grounds, we shall fight in the fields, and in the streets, we shall fight in the hills; we shall never surrender. Let us therefore address ourselves to our duty and so bear ourselves that if the British Commonwealth and Empire last for a thousand years, men will still say "this was their finest hour." I have nothing to offer but blood, toil, and sweat.

Adlai Stevenson eulogized him as "the voice that led nations, raised armies, inspired victories and blew fresh courage into the hearts of men." Clement Attlee said of him, "Words at great moments of history are deeds."

There was no famine of the word on this continent when Thomas Paine was writing and speaking. George Trevelyan wrote in his history of the American Revolution that Paine's pamphlet "Common Sense" "turned thousands to independence who could not endure the thought. It worked nothing short of miracles and turned Tories into Whigs." There was no famine of the word when Lincoln, Adlai Stevenson, or John F. Kennedy spoke. Theodore Dreiser's novel *Sister Carrie* says,

> The world is always struggling to express itself. Most people are not capable of voicing their feelings. They depend upon others. That is what genius is for. One person expresses the desires for them in music, another in poetry, another in a play.

I was amazed to read that the only major Hollywood film made about Vietnam in the 1960s was *The Green Berets*. Television largely ignored the war until the late 1960s. Do you know what turned America around? Folk music. Those songs were anti-authoritarian, anti-militaristic, anti-nationalistic. They urged resistance to an immoral war and blew the whistle on the American leaders who were lying to the public. Songs by Pete Seeger, Bob Dylan, and Joan Baez helped crystalize the anti-war movement on college campuses. They helped convince the uncommitted. They served as vehicles to talk about social and political protest.

Imagine that nothing speaks to you. What if you find the evening news shallow and the newspapers superficial? What if the radio broadcasts banal and inane music? The Hebrew people experienced this in captivity in Babylon. "By the waters of Babylon, we sat down and wept, on the willows there, we hung up our lyres. How can we sing the Lord's song in a foreign land?" Do you feel like you are in a foreign land after switching channels, listening to the president or to challenger Gary Hart, or after spending an evening with people who don't share your values?

I just read Pulitzer-Prize-winning Chicago playwright David Mamet's essays *Writing in Restaurants*. He says films and plays need backers who want to make money. This is a system of self-censoring—not government thought police. He believes that the theater should be a place to hear the truth. It affords the opportunity for communication and inspiring ethical behavior. The theater, true to itself, teaches that it is possible to substitute action for inaction, courage for cowardice, humanity for selfishness. Let me quote Mamet,

> Who is going to speak for the American spirit? For the human spirit?
> Who is capable of being heard, of being accepted, of being believed?
> Only that person who speaks without ulterior motive, without hope of
> gain, without even the desire to change, with only the desire to create;
> the artist, the actor. The strong trained actor dedicated to the idea that
> the theater is the place we go to hear the truth, and equipped with the
> technical capacity to speak simply and clearly.

Tennessee Williams, Arthur Miller, and Eugene O'Neill knew this. You don't come out of one of their plays discussing if you liked it or not. Mamet wants you to ask, "Do I feel impelled? Do I start to move? Does it make me want to do something?"

The New Testament says, "The word of God is living and active, sharper than any two-edged sword." You know, in other words, when you encounter it. This also was true of those listening to Theodore Parker, John Haynes Holmes, Rabbi Abraham Heschel, or Malcolm X. In one of my favorite Easter plays, a soldier at the foot of the cross says, "Seems a bit awful for a man to come to this, just for using a few words." And the Roman soldier replies, "There is a great power in words. All the things that ever get done in the world, good or bad, are done by words." It is my thesis this morning that there is such a famine of "the word" in America today that we do not even realize how much we hunger for the word of God, for words of inspiration.

It is no secret that one of my wishes for Third Church is that we obtain the best, most articulate, most thought-provoking, guest speakers that we can find. I, for one, have not forgotten the influx, excitement, and creative interchange produced here by the visits of Jonathan Kozol, Rev. C. T. Vivian, Steve Fritz, Milton Rosenberg, Ashley Montagu, Eleanor McGovern, Dr. Benjamin Spock, Barry Commoner, Senator Mike Gravel, Congressman Ron Dellums, and David Dellinger. To enter this pulpit is to sense the excitement of knowing that they were here. But maybe we no longer hunger for that which is sharper than a two-edged sword, that which impels us to substitute action for inaction, courage for cowardice, or humanity for selfishness. William Sloane Coffin arguably is the greatest preacher in America today. For weeks I promoted his Evanston speech. The response was nil.

We cannot live on bread alone. The human body was not designed that way, and that's why it's all out of shape. Part of our nourishment, sustenance, and energy has to come from inspiration. I'm not a fundamentalist who will tell you what inspires you. You have to decide and then go out and get it—at the art museum, the concert hall or the Goodman Theater. It might be foreign films, poetry readings, or novelists. I like to think that some of it comes from conversation, and that we set aside times to discuss whatever speaks to us. I don't know how much of that kind of conversation you had this week. I love the story about when Jesus met a woman at the well and told her everything she'd ever done. There is a thirst for that kind of intimacy, that kind of sharing.

This is one of those sermons where I hope your minds have been wandering. For only you know what speaks to you—and what life will be like when nothing speaks to you. Imagine when the press, television, church, political commentators, and dinner conversation say nothing to you—when life is a wasteland. A friend of mine, who is a deacon in an Oak Park church, confessed, "My minister doesn't say much and I'm not sure I want him to."

Hosea predicted a time when "thorn and thistle shall grow up on the altar" and we shall say to mountains, "cover us," and to the hills, "fall upon us." Mamet described such conditions at a Harvard lecture last year. "Our civilization is convulsed and dying, but it has not yet sunk into complete barbarity, and I often think that nuclear war exists for no other reason than to spare us that indignity." Flora Lewis wrote in the *New York Times* about a massive failure of contemporary thought by modern intellectuals. There is a vacuum of spirit. It requires conscious effort to show the joys of learning and the marvel of the unknown—to educate and explain why doubt exists, so that hope can flourish. "Faith is necessary and irrepressible," Lewis wrote. "But without a message of wisdom and humility in human affairs, it can turn vicious." The prophet Amos, 750 years before the beginning of this era, prophesized that the worst fate that can befall us is a famine of the word. He said that we shall wander to and fro, switching from this channel to that, from this cult to another one, from this bed to that bed, from this therapist to that, seeking out something that will make sense, something that will speak to us, something that will inspire, impel, quicken.

I have been speaking of something within the experience of each one of you. I doubt there is a person here who does not carry a quote in his billfold or her purse, who does not have some words pasted on their desk top or refrigerator door. No one needs to tell us about the necessity of food for thought. We know the power of words, and there is not one of us who could not relate an experience when someone spoke to us the words we needed to hear at that time in our life. We can remember when a presidential candidate campaigned with the motto that he would talk sense to the American people and when campaign speeches could be read by college students as literary essays.

I want to close with a picture of an old woman in a nursing home two blocks from here. *Jean Devaud* has come to visit her this morning, as he has many mornings before. As she eats the homemade soup that he has brought, he reads to her from the Psalms. Both of them are out of place in this secular, sterile institution. And something speaks to the old lady that hasn't spoken to her in a long time. He has brought the word and it is as warming, energizing, and sustaining as the soup. Let us be carriers of the word that speaks to the needs and condition of others. And let us hope—no, let us pray—that someone shall bring us that word in our hour of need.

Delivered March 8, 1987, Third Unitarian Church of Chicago.

Sensitized or Anaesthetized?

At age 26, Pat Moore disguised herself as a woman of 85 to experience aging in America. She recorded her findings in her book *Disguised*. An interviewer asked Moore, "What was the worst thing that happened to you?" She described how six 12- and 13-year-old boys beat her up for sport. "I still have nightmares about it and the same thing happens in Lincoln, Nebraska, Clearwater, Florida, and Boise, Idaho."

Here is a transcript of a psychologist's interview with a 14-year-old boy who murdered a woman by setting her on fire:

> Q. Did you have a good night's sleep?
> A. Yeah.
> Q. In the morning, what happened then? Did you feel upset at all, after you had poured gasoline on the woman and she burned to a crisp?
> A. No. She didn't burn to a crisp.
> Q. She didn't burn to a crisp?
> A. No. She lived a week before she died. The next morning was just like on every other morning.
> Q. Did you cry afterwards?
> A. No. To tell you the truth, I had no feeling after I did it.
> Q. No feelings at all?
> A. No, I forgot all about it until they caught me.

I read a *New York Times* article about a woman who was attacked on a train platform during daylight. She was up there with her baby in a stroller. Her hostility and hurt are not just at the boys who attacked her but at the people who watched and did nothing. Playwright David Mamet, commenting on his character Edmond, explains, "Edmond is the rock bottom man, the man who is dead inside, who can't be either happy or unhappy, one enraged at his own emptiness." Another person comments on the growing number of these rock-bottom "Edmonds,"

> These people are not dead in the conventional sense, nor indeed are they likely to kill themselves in acts of release from a dreadful boredom. However they might form corps of living corpses, legions of zombies, who, because of their defection from living, prey upon those who have not yet fallen into the cavern of contemporary despair.

Social psychologist Erich Fromm wrote of these dead men years ago,

> A somewhat less identifiable trait of the necrophilous person is the particular kind of lifelessness in his conversation. This is not a matter of what the conversation is about. A very intelligent, erudite necrophilous person may talk about things that would be very interesting were it not for the way in which he presents his ideas. He remains still, cold, aloof; his presentation of the subject is pedantic and lifeless.

It is as though the mechanization of life has culminated in the mechanization of man. We have created machines that act like men and it has reciprocated into men who act like machines. I want to throw out maybe 10 ideas of what may have brought about these dead, empty, hollow men, devoid of feelings.

There is an old Chinese saying, "One may judge a king by the state of dancing during his reign." In what year did the de-socialization of the dance take place? Someone making a study of American dance halls said that the problem stems from the modern city, with its dominant characteristics of mobility, impersonality, and anonymity. Sex has become depersonalized, as well. Anthropologist Ashley Montagu writing of Alfred Kinsey and Hugh Hefner said, "If they helped to remove the dark shrouds of guilt and shame from the dominion of sexual expression, they also helped to dissipate its atmosphere of tenderness, caring, and concern."

What shall we say of the joy of sports that consume so much of our time—the competitive sporting life that builds character, instills discipline, teaches teamwork, and produces loyalty? Sports were almost synonymous with such values as integrity, fair play, decency, friendship, honor, patience and fortitude. Then Woody Hayes said, "I'd rather die a winner than live a loser." Vince

Lombardi echoed, "Winning isn't everything, it's the only thing." And Leo Durocher added, "Show me a sportsman and I'll show you a player I'm looking to trade." President Ford—who played football without a helmet—said,

> We have been asked to swallow a lot of home-cooked psychology in recent years that winning isn't all that important any more, whether on the athletic field or in any other field, national or international. I don't buy that for a minute. It is not enough just to compete. Winning is very important. Maybe more important than ever.

After giving Lynn Swann a concussion, George Atkinson of the Oakland Raiders said, "I treat a pass receiver the same way you would treat a burglar in your home." The all-pro guard Conrad Dobler said, "If you can get Lawrence McCutcheon or James Harris 'out of there' when you play the Rams, then you've got a hell of a chance to win." The new name of the game is to put your opponent out of commission. Lineman Alex Karras said,

> I hated everyone on the football field, and my personality would change drastically when I got out there. I had a license to kill for 60 minutes a week. My opponents were all fair game, and when I got off the field, I had no regrets. It was like going totally insane.

An estimated 32 college and high school football players are converted into paraplegics every year, while 28 are killed outright.

If you don't follow sports, there are always television and movies. When I was a kid we had horror movies and we had comedies. Today you can see a horror comedy. The 1982 film "Student Bodies" presented violent assault, rape, and murder as if they were amusing, acceptable, and worthy of applause. Filmmaker Roger Corman disavowed responsibility, saying "We have the most murders and assaults. We have been called the rape capital of the world. I think the function of the artist is to reflect the times."

Stanley Kubrick said,

> I'm interested in the brutal and violent nature of man because it's a true picture of him. Man isn't a noble savage, he's an ignoble savage. He is irrational, brutal, and weak. Any attempt to create social institutions on a false view of the nature of man is doomed to failure.

"People are basically bad, corrupt," the star of Kubrick's *A Clockwork Orange*, Malcolm McDowell, wrote in the *New York Times*. "Liberals, they hate *Clockwork Orange* because they're dreamers, and it shows them the realities; it shows 'em not tomorrow, but now. Cringe, don't they, when faced with the bloody truth?"

No wonder that reviewer Pauline Kael writes that she often comes out of a movie feeling desolate. "Often it's a movie that the audience around me has reacted too noisily, as if it were having a high, great time, and I think I feel that way because of the nihilism in the atmosphere." She says of Roman Polanski's *Chinatown*,

> He seals the picture with his gargoyle grin, now evil runs rampant. The picture is compelling, but coldly suffocating . . . you don't care who is hurt, since everything is blighted. Life is a blood-red maze. He shoves the rot at you and large numbers of people seem to find it juicy . . . the nihilistic, coarse-grained movies are telling us that nothing matters to us, that we're all a bad joke.

Brian Garfield wrote the novel *Death Wish* about the dangers of the vigilante mentality. The hero begins by killing muggers and ends with killing children. When the novel was made into a film, the director portrayed vigilantism as noble and heroic. Garfield was aghast when he saw the film in Times Square and the audience cheered "kill that mother!" He later made a failed attempt to stop the film from being shown on television.

Rock songs? Chicago resident Alice Cooper acquired great notoriety with songs like "Love It to Death," "Killer," and "Dead Babies." When singing the latter he would hack a doll to pieces on stage with an ax, drawing a shower of simulated blood, then hurl the limbs to a howling audience. A group called Adolescence sang "I Hate Children;" the Dead Kennedys band has a song, "I Kill Children." Trying to one-up Alice Cooper, Patti Smith spits on fans. Johnny Rotten vomits on them. Dead Kennedys lyrics describe their favorite ways of doing children in: feeding them poisoned Halloween candy, lethal drugs, shooting out the tires of their school bus or handing them live electrical wires. The punk group T.S.O.L has a song titled "Fuck the Dead," prompted by their inability to get along with girls in school. Some of you may recall the Ink Spots, who solved the same predicament with the song, "I'm going to get myself a paper doll to call my own."

Philosopher José Ortega y Gasset spoke 40 years ago of the dehumanization of art by rejecting the recognizable human. "The question is not to paint something altogether different from a woman, a mountain, or house, but to paint a woman who resembles a woman as little as possible." Ashley Montagu says that the modern art museum is the last place to go for tranquility. "On the testimony of our artists, then, contemporary civilization lacks heart; for the main body of their work displays no element of compassion, no look of love, not even an awareness of the still sad music of humanity."

Luther Emmett Holt of Cornell Medical School published a leading child-rearing manual, *The Care and Feeding of Children*, in 1894 that was widely used well into this century. It advised mothers not to pick up their children when they cried, to abolish the cradle, to feed them by the clock and not to pamper them with too much handling. Some cures are worse than the disease. An estimated 50,000 lobotomies were performed in this country during the decade after they were discovered—so-called icepick lobotomies, where a sharp-pointed instrument was inserted through the skull into the prefrontal lobes. An estimated 200,000 Americans received more than one million electric-shock treatments.

I have described the desensitization of music, art, sports, medicine, films, and dance that helped bring us to this point. It's a point where Lt. William Calley can say of the My Lai massacre,

> I did not sit down and think in terms of men, women and children. I felt then, and I still do, that I acted as I was directed, and I carried out the order that I was given and I do not feel wrong in doing so.

Watergate plumber G. Gordon Liddy writes of killing a squirrel as a boy. "I was furious with myself not because I'd caused the pain, but because I had not been able to kill without emotion. I had to do something to free myself from this disabling emotionalism." Do we want our feelings and consciences anesthetized or sensitized? Where we spend our time and with whom shapes that outcome. I cannot generalize and say what will make someone else more sensitive. But we need to be aware of our feelings and ask ourselves, "What is this art exhibit, rock concert, or television show doing to me as a person?"

Katherine Anderson tells the story of asking her husband to pick up a hitchhiker along the highway but he drove on by. When she quietly began to cry, *Bill* said, "Oh all right, I'll go back." I'm trying to discover what creates that kind of sensitivity to the feelings of another human being. Is it any wonder that—consciously or unconsciously—we find life easier if we're anesthetized? The Unitarian divine Kurt Vonnegut asks,

> What happens if you credit a bum with human dignity, a drunken bum
> with his pants full of shit and snot dangling from his nose? If you give
> to that sort of stranger the uncritical respect that you give to friends and
> relatives, you will also want to help and understand him. There is no way
> to avoid that. Be warned, if you allow yourself to see dignity in some-
> one, you have doomed yourself to wanting to understand and help who-
> ever it is.

Isn't the secret to keep these people out of sight—so that we can ride into the Chicago Loop without seeing anything that would test our humanity? The protagonist of Camus's wonderful story *The Fall* is Jean-Baptiste Clamence. He is the kind of man whom you would want for a neighbor, a member of your church, or to marry your daughter. Walking home one night, he hears the terror-stricken cry of a woman drowning in the river. Instead of attempting a rescue, he chooses to ignore her cries and walks faster. His discovery of who he really is marks Jean's fall from the Garden of Eden, confronting him with his own cowardice and inhumanity.

Jean not only experiences guilt but now feels hypocritical about the difference between how others perceive him and what he now knows about himself. After that night on the bridge, this lawyer becomes a judge. He concludes that we all are guilty and stand in need of each other's forgiveness. He doesn't want another chance, for he feels that he would do the same thing again and that few of us will risk ourselves for another. How easy it is for us to become anesthetized to the cries of others; how few of us even achieve Jean's self-realization. The way that modern life is organized, it becomes ever harder to hear the cries of others. In a society so economically segregated, we can live out our lives without hearing the cry from the bridge that reveals our true natures.

In Aldous Huxley's *Brave New World*, the "Director of the Hatcheries and Conditioning" pronounces, "They'll grow up with an instinctive hatred of books and flowers. Reflexes unalterably conditioned. They'll be safe from books and botany all their lives." Again, I can't prescribe what books, flowers, poets, artists, composers, vocalists, friends, or social institutions will sensitize you. You know the experiences, relationships, and organizations that shape you for the good. You must seek out whatever it is that assists you in becoming the person you want to become.

I'd like to close with another thought from Kurt Vonnegut about the kind of people whom we should become. Vonnegut's human ideal is the volunteer firefighter. I have lived in a small town where the siren goes off and the butcher rushes from his shop with his apron on and the John Deere mechanic lays down his tools. They drop everything when the alarm is heard. Vonnegut cites them as perfect examples of enthusiastic unselfishness—the essence of humanism. These firemen aid, rescue, and comfort any person, regardless of his or her wealth, esteem, or worth. The question "Are they deserving?" never enters the equation.

The play is over. It's almost midnight as you cross the Wacker Drive bridge over the Chicago River. There is no one in sight when you hear the cry of distress. Only you ever will have to know what kind of person you really are . . .

Delivered February 16, 1986, Third Unitarian Church of Chicago.

From Disobedience to Obedience

Social psychologist Erich Fromm writes that history began with an act of disobedience and is likely to end with an act of obedience. In both Hebrew and Greek mythology, human history began with disobedient acts. Adam and Eve disobeyed God in the Garden of Eden by eating the fruit of knowledge—severing the umbilical cord to live as free agents. In disobediently stealing fire from the Gods, Prometheus similarly laid the foundation for man's evolution. Fromm says that man has continued to evolve spiritually and intellectually by disobeying "authorities who tried to muzzle new thoughts and to the authority of long-established opinions which declared a change to be nonsense."

Antigone is the classic example of the dichotomy that we face when we must choose between religious convictions and individual conscience. In deciding to bury her brother, Antigone defied King Creon and the unqualified majesty of his law. She defends herself before Creon, arguing that she was loyal to the eternal, unwritten laws that transcend human laws. "Nor did I think your orders were so strong that you, a mortal man, could overrun the gods' unwritten and unfailing laws. And if you think my acts are foolishness, the foolishness may be in a fool's eye." A man who can only obey is but a slave. Human history is the record of these who felt compelled to go beyond the laws of their time: Moses, Jesus, Socrates, Thoreau, Gandhi, King, Tubman, Robert Mapplethorpe, Thomas Parker, Susan B. Anthony. The murals on these walls depict history's great law breakers.

We are always tempted to obey the power of the state, the church, and public opinion. So long as we do, we feel safe and protected. Despite all the progress made by law breakers, obedience continues to be identified with virtue and disobedience with sin. "The minority rules over the majority," Erich Fromm explains. "This is made necessary by the fact that there are only enough of the good things of life for the few. If the few want to enjoy the good things and to maintain them, the many had to learn obedience." The minorities who monopolized wealth, also had a monopoly on the civil, military, and religious power, and harnessed educational systems to teach the majority obedience.

Obedience often need not be imposed by force. Early on, children learn to fear being different—to stand out from the herd. Today, most men and women need or want to obey. They are not even aware of the fact that they obey. The ability to doubt, criticize, and disobey are characteristics that we only admire in our forefathers: the revolutionary soldiers, the abolitionists, the suffragettes, the trade unionists. We seem to believe that such disobedient behavior is no longer needed. That is why Fromm argues that human history began with disobedience but will end with obedience. Calculations that half the population could be wiped out in a thermonuclear war strike many as quite acceptable.

I am dealing with one of history's oldest questions. "What are the limits that we owe to Caesar?" William Ellery Channing, whose mural hangs to my left, wrote, "Is the city of Washington the most virtuous spot in this republic? Is it the school of incorruptible men? Is it the oracle from which the responses of justice come forth?" Channing wrote these satirical words long before the Reagan administration brought us Ed Meese, Raymond Donovan, John Fedders, and William Rehnquist. He continues,

> Has the duty of obeying government no bounds? Is the human sovereign a God? Is his sovereignty absolute? Have you no right to judge his acts? Is the government in Washington to be trusted with our consciences? I say we must put our confidence in the common sense of men and suppose them capable of distinguishing between reasonable laws and those which require them to commit manifest crimes.

Fortunate are the theists who believe that they know God's law and can determine what it is that they owe to Caesar. We humanists must rely upon something as fragile—and perhaps as fickle—as private judgment, the intuition of conscience, or what Channing called "common sense." Sir Isaiah Berlin wrote, "Every person carries some image or notion more or less clear of what human beings are, and therefore what actions will diminish or destroy the minimum degree of humanity without which human beings cannot live as human beings." There is no more precious history than reading the records of these who used common sense to judge Caesar, who believe that the actions of any government are as subject to moral judgment as those of any citizen.

There is almost no crime that was not legal at some time. It was legal to buy and sell human flesh. The Massachusetts Puritans outlawed being a Quaker or opposing state-mandated baptisms for infants. In 1658 four persons were hanged and others were beaten, branded or had their ears cropped. The goods of Quakers and Baptists were seized and sold to raise the money that they refused to pay in taxes to support orthodox ministers. What did Hitler do that is not legal in South Africa today? Racism is the law of that land. To be a law-abiding citizen there means to be a racist.

Brown University President Francis Wayland, who opposed the Mexican war, wrote,

> I see in all the array of civil magistrates, nothing but men, fallible men, of like passions with myself. Every page of history of time past has shown that men placed in such positions have been exceedingly prone to error and to do wickedly. I cannot therefore worship men in power. I have a right to inquire whether his actions in office conform to the principles of justice. He must claim for himself no immunity from scrutiny on account of the dignity of his station. The magistrate may not only be wrong, but he may command me to do wrong. I will regard it as I do any other command to do wrong, I will not do it.

Wayland then says,

> If we expect moral independence of our representatives, we must show them that we possess it ourselves. If we ask them to peril their political influence for right, we must at least show them that the moral principle of their constituents will sustain them in well-doing.

There was no question in Francis Wayland's mind of what he should render unto Caesar. He believed that there are legal and constitutional limits and that the individual must set these limits, saying, "Thus far and no farther." Wayland believed that he owed his highest respect to the concept of justice, and not to magistrates or the laws of men. All the freedoms that we hold dear were won by men and women who had the courage to disobey the law. These include freedom from poverty and ignorance, from slavery and imperialism, from the tyranny of kings and oligarchies. In every case, one or more individuals said, "I will render you this much and not one bit more."

Was there ever a more gentle man than Henry David Thoreau, another opponent of the Mexican War? He writes, "Who can be serene in a country where both the rulers and the ruled are without principle? The remembrance of my country spoils my walks. My thoughts are murder to the state and involuntarily go plotting against her." Before Thoreau famously refused to pay a poll tax he refused to pay a tax supporting an established church of which he did not consider himself a member. He would have been imprisoned if someone else had not paid the tax on his behalf. In 1838 Thoreau's neighbor, Universalist minister Abner Kneeland, was sentenced to 60 days in jail for blasphemy. The Supreme Court upheld the decision against Rev. Kneeland, who had likened the biblical account of Jesus's life to Greek myths.

Theodore Parker, whose mural hangs to my left, denounced the fugitive slave law, which required even those who lived in Northern free states to return a slave to his master in the South. "I will do all in my power to rescue any fugitive slave from the hands of any officer who attempts to return him to bondage," Parker said.

> I will do it as readily as I would lift a man out of the water, or pluck him from the teeth of a wolf, or snatch him from the hands of a murderer. What is a fine of $5,000, and jailing for six months, to the liberty of a man? My money perish with me if it stand between me and the eternal law of God. What grasshoppers we are before the law of men; what goliaths before the law of God. When a man's liberty is concerned, must we keep the law, must we betray the wanderer and expose the outcast. Justice, the law paramount of the universe, extends over armies and nations.

Margaret Sanger went to jail because she believed in the right to family planning. Some people knowingly broke the law that forbid teaching slaves to read. I suspect that the National Guardsmen who lethally fired upon four Kent State students for protesting the Vietnam War believed that they were upholding the law. Susan B. Anthony was criminally indicted and fined for attempting to register to vote. She refused to pay her bail or fine. Like Antigone of old, she believed she was adhering to principles that transcended men's laws. Sisters Abby and Julia Smith of Glastonbury, Connecticut refused to pay their property tax because they were not allowed to vote in the town meeting. When the collector agreed that women of property should perhaps be able to vote, Abby Smith retorted that women without property needed the vote more.

An amazing thing about the human mind is that we can acknowledge the necessity of breaking past laws—and honor those who did it—yet we believe that the need for disobedience is behind us. One hundred years from now, coming generations will look back upon our blindness and celebrate our dissidents. Blessed is the person who knows the prophets of his or her own time.

Timing is crucial. If George Washington had mistaken 1765 for 1775, he would have ended on the gibbet. The resistance in Nazi Germany came too late. Ordinary German citizens could have made a difference when the Nazis were just seizing power, when their evil was incipient. Once Auschwitz was in operation, the time of effective internal resistance had passed. I cannot understand the mentality in America today that the time for resistance and disobedience has not yet come. Meanwhile, 50,000 Americans have pledged their resistance, saying that if our government invades Central America that they will engage in acts of civil disobedience as their consciences instruct. I do not know if this is the first time that citizens have pledged preemptive civil disobedience.

With the defeat of Nazism, the Nuremburg trials officially turned traditional ideas about obedience and disobedience on their heads. Nuremburg established that a citizen cannot exonerate himself by arguing that he acted on the orders of a superior. Moral decisions are an individual responsibility. Obeying evil, unethical laws or orders is a crime, one that demands individual civil disobedience. The best citizens never cease to be skeptical, critical, responsible, and intelligent. They cherish dissent.

I want to tell you two of my favorite dissent stories. In the fall of 1940 a group of Union Seminary students, including Dave Dellinger and Don Benedict, issued this statement,

On registration day, some of us will register in support of the Selective Service Act. Some will register as conscientious objectors. Some will present to the government officials a statement of their inability conscientiously to register at all. Regardless of our disagreements, we will hold in respect and reverence those who in sincerity and humility remain loyal to their conscience.

The other is the story of Dr. John Haynes Holmes, who remained a pacifist through both world wars. He speaks of the young men in his parish who chose to fight,

He will have obeyed his conscience and thus performed his whole duty as a man. And if necessary, I shall bury him with all the honors not of war, but of religion. But I also have a conscience and that conscience I also must obey. False to my own soul, I will not be.

I think both cases illustrate the kind of community that we want here. We want to nurture each other's conscience as members of the church. We do not want to make our decisions in isolation. We come here willing to expose our views to others and to enter into dialogue so our consciences can be taught and corrected in fellowship. We must attribute the same respect to others that we want for ourselves.

I opened by saying that human history began with disobedience and will probably end with obedience. The great danger before us is that those who have led us to the abyss will destroy forever the joy and the beauty of this planet. Two great world powers each want to dominate the world, with each demanding obedience from its citizens. There are laws above the laws of both of these states. There is the higher loyalty that Daniel knew in the lion's den when he disobeyed the laws of Persia. Meshach, Shadrach and Abednego heeded it when they faced the fiery furnace. Antigone summoned it before King Creon. Socrates told the civil authorities of Athens,

Many thanks indeed for kindness, gentleman, but I will obey the gods rather than you, either let me go free or do not let me go free, but I will never cease from being a philosopher, even if I am to die many deaths.

Thousands of courageous individuals throughout history somehow managed to put the powers of the state in proper perspective. Thoreau said,

I could not help being struck with the foolishness of that institution, which treated me as if I were flesh and blood and bones to be locked up. I saw that the state was half witted, that it was timid as a lone woman with her silver spoons, and that it didn't know its friends from its foes, and I lost all my remaining respect for it and pitied it.

My feelings toward the government also are much more pity than awe. The best citizens are those who only render unto Caesar his due, with each citizen deciding for himself or herself what that might be. When I joined Third

Church in 1969 it was a much different time. The congregation had passed a resolution against the Vietnam War and underwent a kind of self-purging, as more conservative members resigned and sought "greener pastures."

Perhaps I have been at fault and each member who joins here should receive a copy of the letters that our youth director *Henry Hulseberg* sent to the draft board, my son sent to President Carter resisting conscription, and the letter that *Marvin Wolberg* wrote to the IRS opposing war taxes. These are our holy writings, for they are inspired. If because of empty church coffers I have lead anyone to believe that we urgently need new members or that we were just another church conducting business as usual, then I apologize. For this is a special place, surrounded by "great lawbreakers." We have never sought to be large or prestigious.

Delivered March 17, 1985, Third Unitarian Church of Chicago.

Robinson Jeffers

They had one of the unique marriages in the annals of literature. His bride of 40 years wrote,

> He never goes to bed without going outdoors about midnight and walking around the place, watching the stars in their courses, marking the rising or setting of the constellations, and feeling the direction of the wind and noticing the tides at ebb or flow. He observes the barometer closely in winter (one hangs by his bed) and is exhilarated by storms.

The quote is from Una Jeffers, wife of poet Robinson Jeffers, describing their oceanfront home near Carmel, California. He built the house from stone, and spent his mornings writing in its tower overlooking the Pacific Ocean. Afternoons were spent working with stone or caring for the hundreds of trees surrounding the house. At least one complete day a fortnight was spent with his wife and two sons in the nearby hills and canyons, closely examining rock formations, trees and flowers, water courses, and animals. He and his wife usually took a brisk 2–3 mile walk along the shore just before sunrise each day. He believed that man was the one smear on the face of nature that deserves little praise. Man is the only creature who commits cruelty willfully.

Robinson Jeffers is fitting material for Unitarians. He did not write for the masses but for individuals who possessed "the cold passion for truth which hunts in no pack." He was America's most philosophical and scientific poet. He once wrote that, "The "happiest and freest man is the scientist investigating nature or the artist admiring it; the person who is interested in things not human." He believed that the most important verb is "to understand" and that in order to understand we need to have some detachment from life. Far from attempting to escape from the world in his rock tower by the sea, he sought to live on the closest terms with life and to select as friends those who were most integrated and whole. He regarded the urban dweller as the true escapist, who insulates himself from the earth, surrounding himself with baubles and noise. Jeffers wrote, "The human race is bound to defile. I've often noticed it. Whatever they can reach or name. They'd shit on the morning star if they could reach."

Jeffers was born in Pittsburgh in 1887 and died at Carmel in 1962. His father was an Old Testament scholar. He had one brother who became an astronomer, which the poet called "the most noble science." At the age of 12, he knew German, French, and English and had a thorough knowledge or Latin and Greek. He spent much of his youth in Europe and in private boarding schools. He spent three years in medical school before transferring into forestry at the University of Washington.

He met his future wife in college but it was to be eight years before they were married. When they met, Una was married to an attorney. For the son of a turn-of-the-century Christian minister to come between a husband and wife was to undermine the very foundations of society. Interestingly, there is a biography of Una Jeffers written by her first husband's second wife, who became Una's life-long friend. Robinson said of his wife, "She gave me eyes, gave me ears, and arranged my life." Upon her death 40 years later, he wrote, "I am mutilated; for you were part of me."

Robinson Jeffers was ranked with T. S. Eliot as America's foremost poet between 1925 and 1935, when he was considered second only to Eugene O'Neill as a writer of tragedy. His popularity declined with the Depression and with the outbreak of World War Two. He believed America's entry into the war marked her transition from a nation to an empire. Jeffers believed that this sealed her doom—that the American dream could no longer be fulfilled. As the war began, Jeffers wrote, "Clearly it is time to become disillusioned, each person to enter his own soul's desert and look for God—having seen man." Random House felt compelled to state in the preface to one book that the poet's opinions conflicted with those of the publisher.

Jeffers believed that the role of the poet was to become immersed in—and express—that which is permanent in life. The poet should focus on those things that will interest readers a thousand years from now, as well as the things that concerned sober minds a thousand years ago. "Poetry must concern itself with permanent things," he said. "These have poetic value; the ephemeral has only news value." He saw permanence in rocks, water, air, mountains, and trees. He hoped that by writing of these "permanent things" we could discover the substance to live our lives. He invited readers to:

Turn outward, love things, not men, turn right away from humanity,
Let that doll lie. Consider if you like how the lilies grow,
Lean on the silent rock until you feel its divinity
Make your veins cold; look at the silent stars, let your eyes
Climb the great ladder out of the pit of yourself and man.

The closing line of that poem reads:

Be born of the rock and the air, not of a woman.

In poem after poem, he comes back to the view that man separated from nature is ugly. He uses the analogy of severance, "A severed hand is an ugly thing and man dissevered from the earth and stars and his history . . . for contemplation or in fact . . . often appears atrociously ugly."

George Santayana visited California and addressed a California audience about the time that Robinson Jeffers was writing. "When you escape, as you often do, to your forests and your sierras, I am sure that you do not feel you made them, or they were made for you," he said. "In their non-human beauty and peace they stir the sub-human depths and the super-human possibilities of your own human spirit."

I confess that I am coming to an appreciation of nature late in life. I remember when my wife, Ann, read the Unitarian religious educator Sophia Fahs's advice to teach our children a love of nature because it will never fail them. I thought at the time, "What has that got to do with religion?"

Robinson Jeffers says that we must be born again, "born of the rock and the air, not of a woman." He writes,

when the cities lie at the monster's feet there are left the mountains. And boys, be in nothing so moderate as in love of man, a clever servant, insufferable master. There is the trap that catches noblest spirits, that caught—they say—God, when he walked on earth.

Jeffers was suspicious of people, especially people who felt the need to travel in packs. He was trying to shock us I think when he wrote that he would "sooner, except the penalties, kill a man than a hawk."

He believed that to live well you have to understand. And you only can achieve understanding through detachment. His own life was as solitary as Poe, Melville, Thoreau or Dickinson. He wrote:

> Soon, perhaps, whoever wants to live harmlessly
> Must find a cave in the mountain or build a cell
> Of the red desert rock under dry junipers,
> And avoid men, live with more kindly wolves
> And luckier ravens, waiting for the end of the age.

He felt sorry for those who were always changing allegiance from Freud to Jesus or from Marx to Roosevelt. He felt pity for those who were lost without a leader or without dogma.

The proletariat for your Messiah, the poor and the many are to seize power and make the world new. They cannot even conduct a strike without cunning leaders: if they make a revolution their leaders must take power. The first duty of men in power: to defend their power.

A Jeffers biographer writes, "He had no complaint with the conditions of life: of birth, growth, decay, death and change." This was his quarrel with Christianity. He believed that it grew out of an attempt to deny death and to abolish it forever. He held to a cyclic view of history. He did not believe that mankind was moving upward and onward, nor that every day, in every way, we are getting better and better. The universe was not created for man; it is indifferent to his needs. Jeffers could not understand the existentialists who called this an absurd universe. Jeffers considered it childishly egocentric to whine that the universe was not created to our specifications. Such naturalism has never been as popular as supernaturalism. Naturalism explains much and promises little, while supernaturalism explains little and promises much.

His was a religion of endurance. The nature of life is straight and constant change. Those who learn to live best are those who learn to endure pain.

> Though joy is better than sorrow joy is not great;
> Peace is great, strength is great.
> Not for joy the stars burn, not for joy the vulture
> Spreads her gray sails on the air
> Over the mountain; not for joy the worn mountain
> Stands, while years like water
> Trench his long sides. "I am neither mountain nor bird
> Nor star; and I seek joy."
> The weakness of your breed: yet at length quietness
> Will cover those wistful eyes.

I have yet to mention what Jeffers's philosophy is called. It is upsetting to we humanists, who transfer our allegiance from a faith in God to faith in man. Rejecting that, Jeffers's philosophy is called "inhumanism." It is defined as "a shifting of emphasis and significance from man to not man." I believe that this serves as a corrective balance to humanism. Protagoras taught that "man is the measure of all things." Jeffers counters that nature is the ultimate measure.

In inhumanist philosophy, the human is not the ultimate, the permanent, nor the goal of creation. The human will be wiped utterly away. We will go down like countless other species in history. Jeffers's poetry asks us to look beyond humanity, to break out of the narcissism that narrows our perspective. Explaining one of his poems, he wrote,

> It seems to me that the whole human race spends too much emotion on itself. Certainly humanity has claims on all of us; we can best fulfill them by keeping our emotional sanity; and this by seeing beyond and around the human race.

"Look beyond humanity to become truly human" is his message. The poetry of Robinson Jeffers is an antidote to humanism and narcissism. We must "be born of the rock and the air, not of a woman." We must see ourselves as a part of nature and we must not lose perspective on the smallness of man in the vastness of the universe.

He writes:

> I believe that man too is beautiful,
> But it is hard to see, and wrapped up in falsehoods. Michael Angelo and
>   the Greek sculptors—
> How they flattered the race! Homer and Shakespeare—
> How they flattered the race! . . .
> One light is left us: the beauty of things, not men;
> The immense beauty of the world, not the human world.

In another poem he writes,

> Men suffer want and become
> Curiously ignoble; as prosperity
> Made them curiously vile.
> But look how noble the world is,

The lonely-flowing waters, the secret-
Keeping stones, the flowing sky.

Jeffers vowed not to tell any lies in his poetry, promising,

Not to feign any emotion that I did not feel, not to pretend to believe in
optimism or pessimism, or irreversible progress; not to say anything because it was popular, or generally accepted, or fashionable in intellectual
circles, unless I myself believed it; and not to believe easily.

Jeffers summed up his philosophy in a couple of points. First, we have
learned within the past century or so that humanity is only a temporary and
infinitesimal phenomenon in a large universe. This knowledge involves a re-
adjustment of values that can only be managed by seeking to look at humanity objectively, from the outside. Second, he found it wasteful that almost the
whole of human energy is expended inward, on itself, in loving, hating, gov-
erning, cajoling, and amusing its own members. It is like a new born babe,
conscious almost exclusively of its own processes and where its food comes
from. As the child grows, its attention must be drawn from itself to the more
important world outside it. We must look beyond humanity to become human, we must be born again of rocks and water and air, lean on the silent rock
until we feel its divinity.

The coast hills at Soberanes Creek
No trees, but dark scant pasture drawn thin
Over rock shaped like flame;
The old ocean at the land's foot, the vast
Gray extension beyond the long white violence:
A herd of cows and the bull
Far distant, hardly apparent upon the dark slope;
And the gray air haunted with hawks:
This place is the noblest thing I have ever seen.
No imaginable human presence here could do anything
But dilute the lonely self-watchful passion.

Nietzsche said that which doesn't kill you makes you stronger. Jeffers is
the poet of human endurance. He believes that we can endure tragedy and

move beyond it. The very hallmark of maturity is the ability to love life without demanding that it meet our terms. In the words of Job, "even though He slay me, yet will I love Him." Robinson Jeffers's poetry invites us as individuals and as a species to look at life from the perspective that we are only here temporarily, that we are not the center of creation. We need understanding to live and we only obtain understanding through detachment. To get perspective on our personal and planetary problems, we need to appreciate how life prizes all that is not human. Jeffers tells us to "lean on the silent rock until you feel its divinity." He invites us to "Be born of the rock and the air, not of a woman."

Delivered November 16, 1980, Beacon Unitarian Church, Oak Park, Illinois.

Emancipator George Burman Foster

Most of us know that an earthquake shook San Francisco in 1906. Fewer of us know about the earthquake that shook Chicago that year. It was triggered by a book published by Dr. George Burman Foster titled *The Finality of the Christian Religion*. *Chicago Tribune* headlines about the book read, "Learned Critic Rips Theology. Startling Book Written by Professor in University Divinity School Assails Cannon of Bible. Declares Miracles Incredible. Says Proof of Resurrection is Lacking." Foster was a Baptist minister on the faculty of the University of Chicago Divinity School. His colleagues were not pleased with his attack on Christian faith, voting 48–22 that his subversive views ran contrary to scripture.

Foster wrote in a world expanded by Copernicus and Darwin. Difficult and painful as it might be, man had to wean himself from the thought that the universe revolves around his friendly and familiar dwelling place. He had to dismiss the beautiful idea that occurrences transpiring on earth are fraught with cosmic destinies. He called the earth "this grain of sand on the shore of the infinite sea," questioning how centrality and supremacy still could be accorded to it. "How can Christianity maintain itself as a world power when it represents only the special experience of this small grain of sand on the shore of an infinite sea?"

He spoke of the limitations of Jesus, who lived in a world with no sense of natural order, expected the end of the world, and believed in demons and angels. There is no way that we can imitate him without spelling "the downfall of modern culture." As the old man was saved by faith, the new man will be saved by doubt. And there may be more faith in the new doubt than in the old belief. "Criticism is better than dogmatism, as manhood is better than childhood." We should have the courage to follow our convictions—as Jesus followed his. You can imagine how that Baptist hierarchy sputtered over this.

In 1907, a year after Foster published his controversial book, Third Unitarian Church invited him to be its minister, even as he maintained his University of Chicago teaching duties. Foster published his second book, *The Function of Religion in Man's Struggle for Existence*, while minister of our congregation, then located at Monroe and Kedzie Avenue. Foster's second book says that God is a symbol for our ideals. "To say that we are so made that we must make gods is tantamount to saying that we are so made that we must make ideals." God is like Uncle Sam, rather than George Washington. "The supernatural is man's self-projection of that which he wants to prevail." He said of conservatives that in "sticking to the truths, they had lost their truthfulness." He accused the Baptists of out-Pope-ing the Pope himself in their dedication to the authority of the Bible. He invited people to write their own additions to the Bible, "some line, some poor letter, must we write with life's blood. That line will be the worth of our lives to the world. Then, too, shall we have labored on the world's Bible."

In the introduction to this second book, he wrote, "I would rather have a minimum that was sure, than a maximum that was not." He added that he would not hurt the feelings of anyone nor incite them to a change that they did not need. He hoped that his book would not fall into the hands of those who were "happy in their present religious state." Still, the Baptist Ministers Association summoned him. When he refused to submit to an inquisition, the group expelled him on a vote of 39–9. When the Baptist-founded University of Chicago refused to punish Foster, conservative Baptists founded the rival Northern Baptist Theological Seminary.

Who was this man who dared to take on Billy Sunday in his own hometown? This man who debated celebrated attorney Clarence Darrow and whom Darrow called "the most intelligent man I ever knew"? This best friend of Abraham Lincoln Centre founder Jenkin Lloyd Jones? This man whose disciples included Eustace Haydon, Curtis Reese, John Dietrich, and whose intimate friends included Jane Addams, Rabbi Emil Hirsch, William Wallace Fenn, Edward Scribner Ames, and Margaret Anderson?

Foster was born of West Virginia pioneer mountain stock in 1858. He attended Rochester Theological School with Walter Rauschenbusch, the founder of the Social Gospel in America. He also studied at the Universities of Berlin and Göttingen; Ohio's Denison University awarded him an honorary doctorate. The University of Chicago's first president, William Rainey Harper, hired him to teach at that Divinity School. He taught there from age 39 until his death at the age of 60 in 1918. He was described as "a hulking Lincolnesque figure, with sad eyes, an enormous hooked nose with a shock of brown hair. . . .His face was melancholy and brooding, beckoning to dark places of the soul."

Two of Foster's five children died before maturity. Another was killed in World War I. He described one of the two surviving children, who was mentally disabled, as "living in the shadows." Around the time of his Third Church ministry several other events caused him to doubt conventional Christian wisdom. They were: Chicago's 1903 Iroquois Theater fire that killed more than 600 people; the 1906 San Francisco earthquake; and the Titanic's demise in 1912. After the Iroquois Theater fire he suggested that, "The God who would change water into wine but would not suspend the nature of fire to save little children from being burned to death, is not a moral God."

Foster initially taught that God symbolized our best human ideals or values and that the universe promoted them. He wrote in his second book, "Religion is the conviction that cosmic existence is such, that man is an ideal-achieving being, and that the achievement of his ideals is possible. Or, religion is the conviction of the achievability of universally valid satisfactions of the human will." In the last year of his life in 1918, Foster reviewed a book by Dr. Edward Scribner Ames, writing, "I myself think that we are witnessing the passing of theistic supernaturalism. Mankind is outgrowing theism in a gentle and steady way." He said this with sorrow and regret. He would like to have believed that there was cosmic support for man's deepest values and longings. But then he begins to accept this aloneness in an alien or neutral universe as perhaps the best of all possible worlds. He asks, "Is the world in which the dice are loaded in man's favor the kind of world that will make him the best kind of man? Or is it the condition of nobility in man, that the All should be against him? If there were a foregone assurance of victory, what kind of man would that develop?" In other words, isn't man nobler when he stands and struggles for justice in a world where justice is not assured?

He told his students that Jesus would see the world much differently if he were alive today and they should not feel guilty to move beyond his worldview. "We can never be satisfied with this Jesus religion as a finality," he said. He even predicted that the word "Christianity" could pass from the scene—yet the world might become more Christian and have more faith and hope and love. He cared less about what faith his students held than about the imperative that their faith not be second-hand. "While no man has any right to be Pope for any other man, he must be his own Pope." "It is in religious doubt that a new kind of joy celebrates its entry into the life of modern man—the joy of investigating and working with one's own powers and gifts. Whoever insists on a violent halt being called to this spirit of inquiry, or resigns himself to the dictation of others, foregoes the highest, innermost pleasure of the soul—the pleasure of one's own growth and free development."

Unitarian Jenkin Lloyd Jones was a prohibitionist but Baptist George Burman Foster was not. Foster said of divorce, "Is it a sin, or a mismatchedness in marriage?" Concerning morals in general he said "Let us not legislate for other people with reference to dancing, the theater, and the playing of games. Asceticism must be an individual matter entirely." He dared to ask students 75 years ago: Is the church's conception of rewards and punishment ethical? He said that the "reward of morality is moral strength for further moral conduct. "Do good because it is good and not for any other reason."

Although expelled from the Baptist Ministers Association, Foster remained a member of the Hyde Park Baptist church until his death. This classmate of social-activist theologian Walter Rauschenbusch remained a thinker and teacher, rather than an activist. He was not above poking fun at the churches of his day that desperately tried to be "relevant" by making bread, instructing the mayor, passing temperance resolutions, and sponsoring psychotherapeutic classes.

Foster believed that it is imperative that ethics not try to make it on their own without a cultus. "Would not the patriotic life suffer abbreviation without the flag, and holidays, and national songs, and public buildings?" He quotes St. Paul writing to the brethren, "I long to see you, in order that I may impart to you some spiritual gift, and so give you fresh strength—or rather, that both you and I may find encouragement in each other's hopes and dreams and ideals." He compares religious people getting together to artists who do the same. "Artistic genius forms a community in which it is understood, in which it is fructified ever anew, by mutual intelligence—in which the artistic sentiment is expressed and enjoyed and enriched. The artistic sentiment grows by expression."

I have mentioned two books written by George Burman Foster in 1906 and 1909. A third book was published two years after his death by some of his students and a fourth book, was published by Curtis Reese and Eustace Haydon in 1931. The last aspect of his thought that I will deal with comes from a series of articles that he wrote about Friedrich Nietzsche for Margaret Anderson's *Little Review*—the foremost literary magazine of the time. Nietzsche's name and philosophy is not accepted today and was even less popular when

Dr. Foster wrote amidst the anti-German feeling surrounding World War I. Nietzsche and Foster both believed that we are saved more by doubt than by faith (Foster defined doubt as the flower dropping its petals that the fruit may grow). Both men believed that if we could doubt religion, why not science? They protested against a totally rational explanation of the world. They emphasized mystery—not the mysteries of the trinity, the incarnation, and resurrection—but the fundamental mystery of life itself. They valued art, music, poetry and those forms of religion that treasured fundamental mystery.

George Burman Foster was a magnificent preacher and a fearless critic of unintelligent dogmatism. He shook the very foundations of orthodoxy. There cannot be a three-year span of any American congregation that surpasses ours between 1907 and 1910. What Dr. Foster would say to us today is: Beware the orthodoxy of Liberalism! Don't idealize Foster's religion. We ourselves must be on the cutting edge today, as he was in his. He wrote, "O admit that what is truth to us now, may be error bye and bye—that is not always an exhilarating confession to make."

The highlight of the Unitarian General Assembly in Boston last week was a lecture by Conrad Wright of Harvard Divinity, our foremost Unitarian historian. He named four or five religions like the Shakers, that came into being for a specific purpose, only to die out because they failed to change with the times—losing their ability to inspire and attract new adherents. Wistfully, as though thinking out loud, he reminded us how our national membership continues to decline. In a time of diminishing resources and expanding population, he asked if our Unitarian ethic of individualism is the message that will serve us in the future. Or will it take a religion with a more corporate and social nature that stresses global responsibilities more than individual rights? I am saying that you should doubt what this church has stood for and rethink its message and its mission. Be your own Pope! But before moving into the future, let us take one last, nostalgic look back to when George Burman Foster served this congregation so courageously and creatively.

Delivered June 25, 1978, Third Unitarian Church of Chicago.